D0992377

JUDGE MEDINA

From a recent portrait of Judge Medina by Maurice L. Bower. Courtesy of Mrs. Standish F. Medina

JUDGE MEDINA

A

BIOGRAPHY

BY

HAWTHORNE DANIEL

WILFRED FUNK, INC.

NEW YORK

Printed in the United States of America
by H. Wolff, New York

Library of Congress Catalog Card Number: 52-9783

TO

THOSE WHO BELIEVE

IN AMERICA

CONTENTS

JUDGE MEDINA

1

BROOKLYN BOYHOOD

AMONG THE SKYSCRAPERS THAT RISE ABOVE LOWER MANhattan's maze of irregular streets is one whose tall central tower is topped by a gilded pyramid. It is the United States Court House on Foley Square, two or three minutes walk from the Manhattan end of Brooklyn Bridge; and in it sit the six circuit judges of the United States Court of Appeals for the Second Circuit and the sixteen United States district judges for the Southern District of New York.

These judges, whose chambers occupy half a dozen floors of the building's central tower, preside over eighteen courtrooms in its broad and heavily columned base. They handle far more litigation than ever arises in any other judicial district; and because trials of national significance often come before them, they have played their parts in many important chapters of the story of justice in America.

A world-wide struggle between two contradictory governmental concepts is taking place today, and one phase of this contest was brought sharply into focus in this Court House during 1949. Eleven American Communists were on trial before Judge Harold R. Medina, who was sixty-one at the time and a newly appointed United States district judge for the Southern District of New York.

Judge Medina, as I write, is a judge of the United States Court of Appeals, but when the Communist trial opened he had not yet attained that position and had been on the District Court bench only about eighteen months. He is deep chested, square shouldered, and sturdy. His black hair and neatly clipped mustache show signs of gray but his face is almost devoid of lines, and his obvious maturity still has about it something of the atmosphere of youth. He is a man of extraordinary energy, with a spring in his walk and a suggestion of vigor in his actions which make him appear taller than his five feet ten inches. He is erect, physically fit and, weighing 175, is hardly ten pounds heavier than when he graduated from Princeton in 1909.

He is genial—full of life and vigor—lusty and intense beyond most men his age. He is gregarious and spirited—impatient of the commonplace and doubly impatient of inefficiency. Studious and observing, he is also physically active, and, during the thirty-five years between his graduation from the Columbia University Law School and his appointment to the Federal bench, his ability and ceaseless energy brought him such success as we like to believe is typically American.

Admittedly, a biography of a man who still has so much active life before him must be incomplete, but Judge Medina (the name rhymes with *arena*) has played an important part in so dramatic a chapter in the history of America that his story is certain to serve a useful purpose in these difficult—these dangerous—days.

Judge Medina believes that those characteristics which have come to be recognized as "American" are the result of the fusing of the racial and national strains that make up our people. In Medina himself there is an innate determination and even a degree of stubbornness that may have come to him by way of his mother's Dutch and American Revolutionary ancestry—a quick, high-spirited self-confidence that may have reached him from Spain and Yucatan by way of his father's family. Other hereditary influences have been at work, of course, but some of these are hardly to be traced.

Judge Medina's father, Joaquin Adolfo Medina, was born in Merida, Yucatan, Mexico, on November 27, 1858. The son of Manuel Medina, a plantation owner, Joaquin was far more fortunate than most of his Mexican contemporaries. Mexico had won its independence from Spain thirty-seven years earlier, but independence had not brought peace. Warfare had been almost continuous, and remained so for another generation. Rival generals, the church, the army, and the privileged classes were constantly at cross-purposes, and the nation's instability was intensified by the extreme poverty of the peasantry and the almost utter absence of any middle class.

The State of Yucatan, however, occupying most of the northern portion of the peninsula of Yucatan, was far removed from the areas most affected by the political difficulties of the times. Devoid of railroads and even of highways, it was readily approachable only by sea, and it existed in a kind of separate world of its own. In fact, the region actually seceded from Mexico in 1839 and for four years maintained its independence. Later another revolution—this time in 1847—gave most of the peninsula a kind of semifreedom from outside influences that continued until Porfirio Diaz began to establish his power over all of Mexico in 1877.

Just when the Medina plantation first came into existence is not known, but by 1858, when his son Joaquin was born, Manuel Medina had added substantially to the acres he controlled. Locally important and economically secure, he had strengthened his position by marrying Maria Luisa Saenz de Santa Maria, daughter of a distinguished Yucatan family, which traced its ancestry in Spain back to the year 872 when a forebear fought in the battle of Clavijo. As further evidence of its aristocratic connections this family bore a quartered coat of arms with the motto *Beatificamus eos qui sustinuerunt* (We bless those who carried on).

The soil of most of the interior of Yucatan is thin and dry, barely covering the porous limestone that forms the backbone of the peninsula. There are few streams, and the limited rainfall quickly permeates the soil and disappears into the limestone below. Nevertheless, this inhospitable land is almost ideal for the production of henequen, from which binder twine is made, and the Medina plantation, which was concerned exclusively with that crop, spread extensively across the countryside in the vicinity of Merida. It was in Merida itself that the Medina family lived.

The city lies some twenty-three miles inland from the Gulf of Mexico, and from the time of its founding in 1542 has been the region's political and religious center. An imposing sixteenth-century cathedral overlooks the principal plaza; the government "palace" stands nearby; and the giant walls of a huge convent, which was permitted gradually to fall into ruins after the expulsion of thc Franciscan order in 1820, were still an impressive part of Merida in the days of Joaquin Medina's youth.

The community was essentially a simple one. Most of its inhabitants were pitifully poor Maya Indians. No middle class existed, and an almost immeasurable gulf lay between the mass of the population and those few who, because of the extent of their acres or because of their positions in the church or the government, dominated and controlled the community. Even for the most fortunate, however, life was simple. Lighting was by candle or by torch. Travel was on horseback. Entertainment, as we know it, did not exist, but servants were plentiful for those who could afford them, and amid the essential simplicity of their surroundings, the dominant few lived in a kind of splendor that was accentuated by Spanish architecture, Spanish customs, and Spanish styles.

Judge Medina never saw his Mexican grandfather, but, from what he was told, he visualizes him as having been tall and straight, black-haired, brown-eyed, and swarthy, with a high forehead that may have gained a little in apparent height from a moderate tendency toward baldness. He was a positive man, who insisted that his orders be carried out with no discussion, and he ruled his family with typical Spanish firmness, though with some consideration and wisdom as well. Definitely Spanish in type, though possibly with a little Maya blood to accentuate his swarthiness, he was a fine figure of a man, representative of the best of the old families of Yucatan. But typical though he may have been in this regard, he must surely have been something less than typical in his mental outlook.

His first wife, the mother of Joaquin and Joaquin's sister Sara, died while both children were small. A stepmother followed, and was ultimately succeeded by a second stepmother when the first, having borne several children, followed the mother of Joaquin and Sara to the Merida cemetery. Thus the recollections of the eldest two had to do not only with two stepmothers, but with a number of half-brothers and half-sisters as well. But clearest of all were memories of their father—of his solemnity when they attended mass at the cathedral—of his firm but tempered justice, and especially of his unique method of punishment when youthful high spirits resulted in broken rules or in disregard of the amenities.

At a time when corporal punishment was held to be essential to the training of the young, Joaquin Medina was rarely whipped. Instead, the punishment most commonly meted out was to be sent to his room to read, and the book he was most commonly ordered to read was a Spanish translation of the *Autobiography of Benjamin Franklin.* This was a surprising choice, for the war between Mexico and the United States had ended only ten years before Joaquin's birth, and Mexico, as a result of that war and of the war with Texas which had preceded it, had lost fully half of all its national territory to the United States. Americans, consequently, were far from popular below the Rio Grande.

It is not unlikely, of course, that the people of Yucatan, detached as they were from Mexico and independent in a sort of half-recognized way, were little concerned with the international troubles and injustices that were prominent in the minds of other Mexicans. Manuel Medina, at least, seems to have been anything but anti-American, and perhaps by design the "punishment" he inflicted on his son developed in the boy a great and permanent admiration for Benjamin Franklin and his philosophy.

When Joaquin was nearly fourteen his father decided to send him, not to Europe for further schooling, as was reasonably common among the wealthy Mexicans at that time, but to the United States. And so it was that the autumn of the year 1872 saw the boy at Seton Hall, a school in South Orange, New Jersey, homesick, no doubt, and ill at ease among surroundings so different from those he had theretofore known.

Until now Joaquin had been a somewhat typical son of a privileged family of Merida. He had been an altar boy in the cathedral. He had learned to play the flute and for a time played regularly in church. He had frequently been on horseback, riding with his father or dashing about the countryside with younger companions. But now, at Seton Hall in northern New Jersey, his horizons were broadening, and a whole new world was opening up before him.

Any reasonably normal boy in his early teens is apt to be

pliable almost beyond belief, and that proved true of Joaquin Adolfo Medina. Merida, Yucatan, and South Orange, New Jersey, of course, may not exactly have typified the opposite poles of community existence in 1872, but their differences were certainly extreme. Almost every detail of life in South Orange differed sharply from what Joaquin had previously known. The language, the people, the amenities, the houses—even the food, the clothing, and the pastimes—were new to the boy. But youth is a period of quick adjustments, of quick friendships that often prove enduring, of rapid growth, of changing concepts, of sudden development. Joaquin Medina, too, must have had characteristics of his own that gave him more than ordinary understanding and that caused him to respond eagerly to the friendships, the ideas, and the ideals he came upon. Throughout the remainder of his life, friendships that began at Seton Hall maintained their hold.

There is no record that tells in any detail of the doings of the Mexican boy at Seton Hall. He proved to be more than ordinarily bright in his classes. He had a quick mind and, for a boy, sound judgment. Unacquainted with the game of baseball when he arrived, he soon learned to play it and become a good second baseman. But, most important, his loyal and affectionate nature, evolving during those formative years in surroundings that were so different from those he had known, served not merely to fit him for life in the land to which he had come, but to *un*fit him for a permanent return to the land of his birth. Nevertheless, he returned to Yucatan after three years at Seton Hall.

By that time he was well acquainted with the United States. He liked the country. He liked the people. He liked their institutions, their freedom, their burgeoning progress, and their opportunities. And it may very well be that these advantages appeared even more desirable when they were viewed from the heat and dust and insularity of Merida. Certainly Joaquin discussed all this with his father, though his comments apparently had little effect. Manuel, though far from being anti-American, was obviously uninterested in his son's enthusiasm for life in the United States. With his normal disregard for opinions that were contrary to his own, he pushed the boy into a dry-as-dust mercantile job and told him to go to work. The fact that Joaquin did not like what he was supposed to do made no impression on his father. The work was there and needed to be done. "Do it!" was his father's order.

Joaquin stayed for a while on that uninteresting job and then he took French leave. Knowing that his father opposed the idea of his return to the United States, he told no one of his plans, but he made his way to New York. What funds he obtained or how he obtained them, no one can now tell, but he seems to have arrived with little enough cash in his pocket, though that proved to be no handicap. Almost immediately he got a job as office boy with the firm of R. H. Allen & Company, manufacturers of agricultural implements.

There is a record which gives the date of Joaquin's return to the United States as "about the year 1875." He would have been no more than seventeen at that time. Starting then as office boy, he advanced in the firm's employ until he became its export manager by the spring of 1880, and about the same time he conceived the idea of starting an export business of his own as a side line. In fact, he made a small beginning with the approval and encouragement of his employer, and actually executed his first order on May 1, 1880. He operated this little business in his spare time for the next three years. Then he resigned from R. H. Allen & Company to devote all his time to his own enterprise.

Joaquin Medina, now twenty-five, but only five feet two inches tall, had spent more than a third of his life in the

United States. His progress up to then, if not phenomenal, had been highly commendable, and in the years ahead he was to make more progress still. From the first, of course, he had labored under certain handicaps. Unlike most young immigrants, who in those days were entering the United States in such great numbers, Joaquin could turn for help and friendship to no established group of fellow countrymen. Few other Mexicans existed in the vicinity of New York, and Yucatecans must have been fewer still. Thus Joaquin was forced to find his friends and associates elsewhere. Some of his closest friends had been schoolmates at Seton Hall, but he made others, and one—a certain George Fash—was greatly to influence the young Mexican's future.

George Fash was a young man whose family had been in America since colonial days. Among his forebears at least one had fought in the American Revolution, and there were family connections that led back by way of the Bergen family even to the time when the Dutch were established in New Amsterdam. Bergen Street in Brooklyn, and Bergen County across the Hudson in New Jersey are even yet reminders of some of George Fash's progenitors and colonial connections.

This young man, not long after he and Joaquin became acquainted, invited the Mexican to his home in Richmond Hill, an unpretentious suburb of Brooklyn. That first visit was followed by others, for George's brown-haired, gray-eyed sister, Elizabeth, attracted Joaquin from the first. The two were almost exactly the same age, Elizabeth having been born on November 1, 1858, and Joaquin on the 27th of the very same month. Elizabeth was prepossessing. She was musical—at the time she was both organist and choir leader at the Episcopal Church of the Resurrection in Richmond Hill—and Joaquin's business was developing to the point that permitted him to think of assuming responsibilities of his own. They were married on September 15, 1886, and established their first home at 20 Monroe Street, in Brooklyn, where their first child, Harold Raymond, was born on February 16, 1888.

Harold Medina lived throughout his youth and early manhood in "the Bedford section" of Brooklyn, and was little more than an infant when his father bought a three story "brownstone front" on Jefferson Avenue, half a dozen blocks or so from that first Monroe Street house.

Time was when a brownstone front was a sign of more than average success—even of wealth—to the people of New York and Brooklyn. Nowadays, familiar though we are with standardized products of a thousand kinds, it almost appears to have been a marvel that so many miles of so many streets could have been lined with so many houses that were all but identical in size and style, in construction and arrangement. Block after block—even mile after mile—was literally filled with these narrow, repetitious structures crowded elbow to elbow. And nowhere, perhaps, did they dominate an area more completely than in the several square miles that make up the level and somewhat monotonous Bedford section of Brooklyn.

No newcomer to that portion of the city today will find it easy to recreate the atmosphere of sixty years ago. Those were the days of horses and carriages, of gas lights and home-baked bread, of haircloth furniture and Victorian manners, all of which have gone, but the neighborhood has changed in other ways as well. The Bedford section of those days was comfortable and secure and proper. It was never a fashionable neighborhood, and its social life was unpretentious, but when Harold Medina was a boy, that portion of Brooklyn which lay in the vicinity of 273 Jefferson Avenue was comfortable, wholesome, and respectable—even admirable in an unimaginative way.

The Medina house was a three-story-and-basement affair, twenty feet or so in width, and was sandwiched in between two other houses that were in every major respect identical. It had a front and it had a back. It even had a back yard of very limited dimensions, but it had no sides that it could claim as exclusively its own. Its side walls, in fact, were merely sturdy curtains of masonry that separated it from its next door neighbors.

A flight of brownstone steps led up from the sidewalk to the "parlor floor," and there the long, narrow front parlor opened to the left from the equally long front hall; and the back parlor, a broader and more comfortable room, looked out upon the narrow, colorless back yard, which was tightly surrounded by a high board fence beside which, in its shade, grew a little bed of lilies of the valley.

In common with many other parlors of that day, those of the Medina home were rarely used except on special occasions. They were adequately furnished—almost crowded—in the somewhat ornate but heterogeneous fashion of the day. The pictures, or some of them at least, had heavy, highly ornamented gilded frames. There was a piano. The floors were covered with tightly tacked Brussels carpets that spread from wall to wall. But except on the rarest of occasions, the shades were kept tightly drawn, and the rooms were so unused that the air that filled them seemed lifeless, and ever so slightly musty.

The dining-room and kitchen occupied the basement, the floor of which lay no more than a couple of feet below the level of the street. The dining-room window, guarded by a heavy grating of iron, looked out upon a narrow areaway to which the basement door opened beneath the high front steps.

The front room on the second floor—above the front parlor —was the household "sitting-room," the gathering place of the family, and behind it lay "the master bedroom" and a bath. The third floor contained two somewhat restricted family bedrooms and two very small maids' rooms, both of which were usually occupied, for the head of the house had established a business which consistently made possible the employment of both a cook and a maid. The principal difficulty in this connection arose because the natural shortcomings of cooks and maids, combined with the innate impatience of a somewhat particular housewife, made firings, resignations, and replacements too common for comfort.

It was in this house, in the very midst of a section of the city that was completely filled with similar houses, that Harold Medina gained his earliest impressions of the world. Ultimately an extension was built at the back of the house. A laundry was added in the basement. The back parlor became the dining room and had its own service stairs leading from the kitchen below. A "den" designed primarily for the senior Medina's use was added back of the bedroom on the second floor; but fundamentally the house remained the same, just as the neighborhood did for so many quiet years.

By comparison with more recent times, the world of that day was wonderfully peaceful. The American Civil War had ended twenty-three years before Harold Medina was born. The Franco-Prussian War had been fought seventeen years before. Nowhere was the peace of the world seriously threatened. Troubles and difficulties of many kinds were to be found on every continent, of course, but for most Americans—and certainly for the Medina family—it was a period of comfort, opportunity, and promise.

For almost five years Harold was the family's only child, and even after his brother Richard was born on September 3, 1892, the span that separated the two kept them from becoming the closest of playmates. Nevertheless, they were always good friends, and the family was always closely integrated; but from the first, this difference of age between the two boys, and probably other unnoticed influences, were at work in the creation of the independence of spirit and the self-reliance that later came to be so definite a part of Harold Medina's character.

Beginning in 1893, Harold attended Public School 44 on Throop Avenue near Putnam Avenue, no more than a couple of blocks from home. It was here, when the Spanish-American War broke out in the spring of 1898, that the lad, at the age of ten, had his first experience with a kind of unreasoning and ignorant prejudice which makes for much unhappiness in the world.

The name Medina was known by Harold's schoolmates to be Spanish, and Spain had suddenly come to be a hated enemy. It did not matter that Harold's father had never seen Spain, that the land of his origin had rebelled and had long ago gained its independence from the nation that now was an enemy of the United States. And apparently no one stopped to think that on his mother's side, Harold's family had been established in America since long before the American Revolution. Medina was a Spanish name, and Harold himself, therefore, was a "greaser." Insults, innuendoes, and fights came to be the order of the day, as Harold was called upon to battle in defense of his individual dignity and his Americanism.

"I never resented it," he has since explained. "Perhaps I even accepted it as natural under the circumstances, and therefore unavoidable."

He was an alert boy who always stood well in his classes, and already had developed an individuality all his own. It must have been about this time that he was told, on one occasion, to take his six-year-old brother to the barbershop for a haircut, a bit of mild torture and restraint which Richard, like other boys his age, rather heartily disliked. Harold, possibly fearing that his brother might prove difficult if he were told too plainly what was in store for him, did not mention the term "barber shop." Instead he explained that he would lead the way to a tonsorial parlor, which so intrigued Richard that he readily assented, and thus found himself unexpectedly trapped in a barber's chair.

Throughout these youthful years, Harold had no contact with his father's relatives, but his mother's family, which had moved to Brooklyn, was well known to him. Grandfather Fash had been born to some wealth, though it had all been dissipated long before his grandson's birth. There was occasional mention of "the skulduggery of the executors," and the inference was that such wealth as had once existed had disappeared because of trickery over which Grandfather Fash had had no control. It was reasonably apparent, however, that plain improvidence had played some part, for not only Grandfather Fash himself, but his sons, as well, were talkers rather than doers. All of them held firmly to their well-developed pride, and many great plans were advanced for recouping the family's finances, but day-by-day efforts in that direction and constructive economies with that end in view interested them not at all.

Grandfather Fash had a position with a bank, and was usually said to be "cashier," but the work he did was probably little more than that of a paying teller, and his salary was none too big. His sons, who to young Harold were Uncle George, Uncle Hobart, and Uncle Charles, were in many ways counterparts of their father—talkative, proud, and full of great plans, but little interested in the daily round or the basic responsibilities of life.

Harold's mother, on the other hand, was an industrious person. She was an unusually good housekeeper, and in matters relating to household affairs, she was not easy to please. That characteristic, combined with her natural determination, was probably the principal cause for the frequent hirings and firings of her cooks and maids, though otherwise it made for a comfortable, well-kept household. The social life of the family, however, was unusually limited.

Joaquin Medina, short, deep-chested, and heavily mustached, had been born and raised a Roman Catholic, and seems to have been somewhat mildly inclined to remain one. But in matters of religion Elizabeth Fash Medina brooked no opposition. She herself was an Episcopalian, and it was in the Episcopalian faith that her sons were reared. Even her husband went occasionally to the Episcopal Church along with his wife, though it may be that he occasionally but quietly attended Catholic services as well.

It was Joaquin's inclination to look upon Sunday as a pleasant, friendly, comfortable sort of day made to be enjoyed in almost any reasonably innocent way whatever. His wife had other ideas, and it was she who prevailed. Sunday, as a result, was most strictly observed. Everyone dressed stiffly in his Sunday best. Sunday school and church were attended regularly. Pastimes were forbidden, and, so far as Harold and his brother Richard were concerned, the day had little to recommend it. Their father had no real sympathy with so rigid a point of view, but being gentle and amenable he accepted it. "He never really had a chance," Judge Medina has admitted in discussing the restrictions that marked the Sundays of his youth.

Beginning when Harold was little more than an infant, the family spent each summer at the seashore far out on Long Island. These sojourns were not mere short excursions. They usually began in June and lasted until September, with the father attending to his business in the city during the week and spending the week-ends with his wife and children.

The first summer resort to which Mrs. Medina took her elder son, and one to which they returned for several years, was the Apaucuck Point House which stands even yet on Apaucuck Point and overlooks Moriches Bay, from a spot only a few hundred yards from where Judge Medina's own pleasant Long Island home now stands.

Apaucuck Point is on the south shore of Long Island at Westhampton, some seventy-five miles from Brooklyn. In addition to the hotel, a large frame building, the establishment formerly consisted of two cottages and that essential of those days, a large barn. A certain Charley Raynor and his wife ran the hotel in Harold Medina's childhood, and though there was nothing luxurious about the place, the food was good and the rooms were comfortable. It was not an exciting establishment, but it could hardly have been improved upon as a place for children to spend their summers.

Organized entertainment, such as is common at resort hotels today, never occurred to Charley Raynor, and even if he had had the idea, it probably would never have occurred to him to include the children in his plans. They were supposed to entertain themselves, and the younger ones were naturally eager to imitate those who were a little older. Furthermore, the more energetic ones among them, of whom Harold Medina was certainly one, sometimes evolved ideas of entertainment to which a number of the mothers took hearty exception.

A windmill is a structure that is certain to appeal to any energetic boy, and Harold Medina did not rest until he had climbed the one that stood behind the hotel at Apaucuck Point. Other children followed, of course, or threatened to follow, and frightened mothers were forced to issue stringent edicts in restraint of so dangerous a pastime. The windmill having been declared out of bounds, Harold climbed to the roof of the hotel which, being more difficult to reach, was all the more fascinating to those youngsters whose ambition it was to follow. Harold had naturally been engaged in other activities in the meantime, and may actually have been guilty of a few transgressions. At any rate, several mothers who had already come to be critical of Harold now decided not to let their children play with him at all. In fact, this climbing about on windmills and on roofs resulted in such unanimity of disapproval that a move on the part of the Medinas appeared advisable. Harold's mother, consequently, along with his young brother and himself, left the Apaucuck Point House for the Oneck House several miles away. Other seasons saw them at other places still.

When Harold and his brother were somewhat older the family spent a few summers at Orient, Long Island, where they kept a small motorboat, and here, near their cottage, a fisherman had set up his nets which ran out from shore for a considerable distance to a "pound" where the fish were caught.

One afternoon, in Harold's temporary absence, the fisherman hurried up to the Medina cottage in much excitement, explaining that there was a commotion going on in his fish pound and asking if one of the boys could help him with the Medina motorboat. Richard, and a friend who was present, gladly responded. Having reached the pound, they soon found that the fish that was making the trouble in the restricted area of the pound was a small shark. It was not difficult for the fisherman to get a rope around its tail and, once it had been towed ashore, it was executed for the crime of being a shark.

This, of course, was an adventure, as Richard and his

friend well knew—an adventure which obviously should be reported in all its exciting detail to the *Brooklyn Eagle*, a paper to which all good Long Islanders were subscribers. They wrote out the story, and promptly put it in the mail. They even embellished it slightly, the shark having grown in their account until it was eighteen feet in length and had frightened all the bathers in the summer colony. Naturally, too, the boys who had slain the monster were featured in a somewhat heroic role.

But now Harold appeared on the scene and, being told of the adventure, himself decided that a report should be sent to the *Eagle*—an idea to which Richard and his friend gave their approval without mentioning the story that they had already put in the mail. Harold wrote a meticulously accurate account, in no way departing from the truth, save to bring himself into it as a somewhat prominent participant.

It was two days later, when the copy of the *Eagle* arrived, and Harold, confident that his story would have been given nothing more than a little space in the second section, tossed the first section to Richard, and searched vainly for what he himself had written. But it wasn't there. Instead, and greatly to Richard's delight, there was a headline on Page One, reading: SHARK HUNT AT ORIENT and, under it, was that first carefully concocted story, eighteen-foot shark and all, proving to the delighted boys how flawlessly accurate such newspaper accounts can sometimes be.

With the return of the family to Brooklyn each autumn, life fell into a very different pattern. The demands of school and church regulated each week's activities to a considerable degree, though there was time for other things. Because the neighborhood was so solidly built up, playtime activities were somewhat handicapped. Still, there was hardly a high board fence about any of the narrow, nearby backyards that Harold did not scale. Except for vacant lots, open places were far from numerous, and real playgrounds were rare. Tompkins Park—a limited place—lay eight blocks or so away. Fort Greene Park and Prospect Park were each the better part of two miles distant, and the Navy Yard—no playground, of course, but nevertheless fascinating to most boys—was more distant still and consequently outside the Medina orbit. Still, the streets were broad, and in the utter absence of automobiles were reasonably satisfactory as playgrounds.

Not infrequently Harold and his brother were taken by their parents to Hyde and Beaman's Vaudeville Theatre on Fulton Street, and often, after the show, they went to Dennett's nearby white-tiled restaurant for butter cakes and coffee. Sometimes, too, they purchased and took home some of the fried oysters for which the restaurant was locally celebrated. Occasionally they stopped at a favorite delicatessen for Leon sausage, a firmly packed meat product with its full share of peppercorns and other spices, for cheese and crackers, and other appealing items.

Life was pleasant, even if not exciting. The Medina home contained few books, but the boys were not infrequently told stories of life in Yucatan. Spanish, however, was never spoken. Perhaps it would have been had Mrs. Medina not objected to the idea, but as it was, neither Harold nor Richard were ever given the opportunity to learn the language at home.

The elder Medina went daily to his office in New York, but the others rarely went so far, and when they did, they almost always crossed the East River by ferry. Brooklyn Bridge had been opened for traffic in 1883, but ferries continued for many years to serve the people of Brooklyn even within the very shadow of the bridge itself.

The Medina boys had few responsibilities, but from their very earliest childhood, their father consistently impressed upon them the utter inviolability of a promise. From the first, they were most firmly taught that every promise was to be kept. No change of circumstance could be accepted as affecting it. A due date meant *that* date, and not some later one. Business principles were invariably ethical to a degree, and of the strictest integrity.

Throughout the eight grades that Harold attended at Public School 44 he stood well in his classes. He liked school. Except for the interval during which, as the school's only "greaser," he was compelled to defend himself against attack, he readily made friends among his schoolmates, and he got along well with his teachers. When he reached the eighth grade, however, he began to find himself—at first, perhaps, by accident—in more or less constant scholastic competition with a boy named Schoonmaker. There was no enmity between them, but as first one and then the other gained some advantage in their classwork, a very definite competition developed, and the two vied quite consciously for the honor of holding first place in the class. The contest, too, remained in doubt until the diplomas were about to be presented. Then it appeared that these two—Schoonmaker and Medina—had attained the two highest marks, but Judge Medina remembers even yet that, when the final marks were ultimately made known, it was he who stood second.

Harold's father had long before decided to send his son to some preparatory school instead of to a public high school in Brooklyn, and now inquired about entering the boy at Hotchkiss, though no actual application was ever made. For some reason not entirely clear—possibly because of difficulties the school may have experienced in connection with students from Latin America—Mr. Medina turned elsewhere, and Harold consequently entered the much smaller and less-well-known Holbrook Military Academy at Ossining, New York. Even here, however, he came close to being rejected.

A number of letters of reference were required in connection with each application for entrance, and among those that were written about Harold Medina was one from the principal of Public School 44 in Brooklyn. To the concern of the authorities at Holbrook Academy, this letter somewhat bluntly said that the writer "could hardly recommend" the applicant.

Such a statement, of course, might have been accepted at its face value, but the Holbrook Military Academy decided to inquire further. Upon doing so, the fact came to light that the comment in question was a stenographic error, and should have read, as the writer had intended, that he "could *heartily* recommend" the boy.

In February, 1902, Harold entered Holbrook, and promptly encountered a difficulty. The school was small, and too few students entered at mid-year to permit the organization of special classes for them. Harold, consequently, was thrust into classes which, for the most part, had begun their studies the preceding September. This even happened in Latin, and the new student was faced with the task not merely of keeping up with the daily work of the class but also of making up the work he had missed. To this day, and despite the fact that he has come to be a Latin scholar of unusual attainments, he recalls that, because of this handicap, the foundation upon which his knowledge of that subject was originally built was especially and unfortunately weak.

The Holbrook Military Academy was a pleasant school, though it was never large and now has disappeared. It accommodated only about two hundred students in 1902, and though among its teachers there were several of real ability, others left something to be desired.

In view of the many evidences of Judge Medina's widespread reading—evidences that are frequently apparent in his judicial opinions as well as in his remarks from the bench—it is interesting to note that as a boy he read comparatively little.

"We had few books at home," he has said, "and as a boy, I was not exposed to them to any great degree."

Perhaps even at Holbrook he was not exposed to them excessively, and only two of his instructors made much impression on him. He remembers them as teachers of real ability—Mr. Bartow, who taught mathematics, and Professor Nagle, a genial, bearded Alsatian who taught both German and French.

Great changes have taken place in pedagogy in the years since Harold Medina wore the uniform of the Holbrook Military Academy, and the simplicity of life in the Ossining school contrasts more than a little with life in such schools today. It was a happy place, however, and Judge Medina recalls it pleasantly. At no time was he guilty of more than minor infractions of the rules, and being reasonably good natured, he experienced no difficulties of consequence. His comparative immaturity, however, kept him from reaching, or even from seriously attempting to reach, any position of leadership. Though he liked the military atmosphere of the place, and enjoyed the drills and exercises in which the small cadet body engaged, the only military promotion he earned was from private to corporal.

In his classes his marks were consistently good. In a few instances they were even somewhat remarkable. At the end of his junior year, for instance, he took not only the junior examination in mathematics, but also the senior one, and he passed both. He admits today that that experience was more harmful than helpful, for his success in passing the senior examination apparently gave him an unwarranted idea of his own ability, and an equally incorrect idea of what he assumed to be the simplicity of the mathematics that lay ahead of him. At any rate, it is his belief now that that momentary success did him no good.

It was customary at each Holbrook commencement to have a contest in which six selected students engaged. "Declamation" was an important subject at the school, and this was a contest in declamation—a contest in which each contestant was assigned to learn "by heart" a "piece" that was selected for him, and to speak it before the students of the school and their assembled friends and relatives.

Usually all six of those who were to speak were chosen from the school's sixth form, but at the end of Harold's fifth-form year, only five reasonably competent sixth form students appeared to be available. The sixth contestant, therefore, had to be chosen from the fifth form, though less, perhaps, with the idea that he would prove to be a serious contender than because custom demanded that six be entered.

It was Harold who was chosen for this sixth place, and the subject assigned to him was "Culture in Emergencies." The selection which bore that title was given to him to memorize, and he went to work. Over and over again he recited it aloud, with gestures in the proper places and with emphasis at appropriate points, and all the time he clearly understood that he was not really a contestant at all, but merely a filler-in, whose task was to occupy a place that otherwise would be completely blank. When the time to speak finally came, however, and he rose before that audience, Harold found that far from being frightened, as he had half expected to be, he was actually encouraged to do his best, and he proceeded, apparently, to do just that.

Normally the decision of the judges came promptly enough in these matters, but this time it was delayed. They had retired to a nearby room, and some of those who sat near the closed door now and then heard what they took to be somewhat angry voices. Even when the judges reappeared it was without a clearcut decision. It had been impossible, they announced, for them to decide between two of the speakers. The name of one of the boys selected is not a matter of record, and Judge Medina recalls only that he was a member of the sixth form and that his name was Ernest. But to his astonishment, and more than a little to his delight, Harold Medina was the other.

Long before he graduated from Holbrook Academy, Harold Medina had decided to study law. He does not recollect the origin of the idea, and knows only that it was clearly in his mind even while he was in grade school. Realizing now, as he did not realize in his youth, the methods his father used in guiding his brother and himself, he is certain that they were used here, though always so subtly and indirectly as not to be apparent. Perhaps this very thoughtful father made his points by speaking to others while his sons were present. Perhaps he now and again used effective illustrations drawn from the lives and experiences of others. He rarely issued orders. It was not in his nature to be demanding. Nevertheless, his influence was frequently a controlling factor in Harold's decisions, though it usually appeared most faintly, or did not seem to appear at all. There is little doubt that Harold's decision to study law was influenced by his father, and that is also apparently true of the boy's choice of Princeton as the university he wished to attend.

Throughout his final year at Holbrook Academy, Harold

found himself competing scholastically for first place with a boy named Robert Underhill—competing in much the same way he had with the Schoonmaker boy in eighth grade. Robert Underhill, it may be noted, later taught philosophy at Harvard, but that, of course, lay far in the future during those Holbrook days. Time and again each of the two gained and lost advantage after advantage, and as the term reached its conclusion and commencement came, these two were certain of the two leading positions. Who was actually to be first, however, did not appear until the final moment, but then again—as had happened in eighth grade—the final marks ultimately established that Harold Medina stood second.

He had taken part of his entrance examination for Princeton at the end of his fifth-form year at Holbrook, and he took the rest when he graduated. He was seventeen—would not be eighteen until the following February. He was socially inexperienced and more than a little immature, and because of this, was to find himself handicapped in the years immediately ahead. But Harold was conscious of no such problems as he left Holbrook. He was on the verge of young manhood and Princeton lay before him. After that, he knew, he would study law.

2

PRINCETON

IN JUDGE MEDINA'S OWN WORDS, THE CLASS THAT ENTERED Princeton in September, 1905, was "a motley crowd of something short of 383 boys. I say something short of 383 because that was the total number of members of our class and a few are included who joined up after freshman year. There were rich boys and poor boys, some prominent in society, some whose circumstances were such that they could hardly dig up the amount necessary to pay a meager weekly laundry bill. There was a spread of eleven years between the youngest member of the class and the oldest; the youngest was born in 1889 and the oldest in 1878. Many came from the great preparatory schools where their friendships had already matured and where everything was done to give them a foretaste of the freedom of university life. Some, like myself, came in groups of twos and threes from the small preparatory schools, and quite a number from the high schools. We were dumped into Princeton in the days of 'horsing' at its very worst and we found our respective ways, mostly by sheer force of circumstance, into the various freshmen eating clubs." *

A major attribute of almost every freshman is inexperience,

* From *The Princeton Class—a Study in Democracy*, an address given by Judge Medina, on November 10, 1950, before The Graduate Council of Princeton University.

but there are degrees of inexperience here as elsewhere. Harold Medina, only seventeen that autumn and one of the younger members of the class, had certain advantages. But he labored under certain handicaps as well. For one thing, his was a Spanish name, and even to many who never gave the matter a conscious thought, it no doubt seemed at least a little alien. There were only two other former Holbrook students in that class: Norman B. McWilliams, who is now a physician of Williamstown, Massachusetts, and Myles Standish Slocum, a great-nephew of Mrs. Russell Sage and now a resident of Pasadena, California. Young Medina, who from the time of his arrival at Princeton saw these two only occasionally, at first had no other acquaintances whatever in the class. He was forced to make new friends and to find new associates.

This is a common problem among freshmen, but those members of the class who had attended the larger and better-known preparatory schools—Lawrenceville, Hill School, Exeter, and others—arrived at Princeton with classmates whom they knew, and had the advantage not only of this kind of intimate and established acquaintance but also of the social experience and assurance that went with it.

It was, perhaps, in this field that Harold Medina was most handicapped. From his earliest days in school he had never found his studies difficult, and this continued to be true at Princeton; but his social inexperience now began to bring about a lack of confidence and a feeling of inferiority that was new to him. He had no inclination to withdraw into his shell or to shun the normal contacts of college life. The contrary was true. He was full of life and determination—stood five feet ten and weighed 165 pounds—and in subconscious self-defense, perhaps, he grew loud and bumptious, and under the "horsing" of the sophomores became noisy, full of fight, and something less than popular.

"One expression which will always stick in my memory," he pointed out some forty-five years after his class entered Princeton, "was the expression 'sad birds.' That phrase seemed to be on the lips of everyone, always with reference to someone else, of course. I never quite knew whether or not I was one of these 'sad birds,' but it troubled me much to think that perhaps I was. It was an expression of contempt which anyone might take to himself, and I rather suspect that it had a good deal to do with keeping us apart."

"Horsing", as it was called at Princeton, was an almost immemorial privilege of sophomores, and this form of hazing, though never carried to such lengths as it sometimes reached in other colleges, was probably close to its worst during Harold Medina's freshman year. Some of the more unfortunate freshmen—of whom Harold Medina was certainly one—were better "horsing material" than others, and they suffered accordingly.

The campus of Princeton University is unusually beautiful, and is reasonably extensive as well. In fact, its three adjoining tracts covered the better part of a square mile in 1905, and the main campus alone, lying along the south side of Nassau Street, totaled about 225 acres. Upper classmen, for the most part, lived in college dormitories, but these were not available for freshmen, and the members of each entering class, as a result, had to find accommodations "off campus."

It was in a little house on Edwards Place that Harold Medina found a room. Operated by a man named Goldie, the house was called "New Goldie's," and it stood just off University Place near the campus and in a part of the town where most of the freshmen lived, and where, as a result, the sophomores indulged in most of their horsing. And promptly, because he was loud and self assertive, young Medina—swarthy, curly haired, and oval faced—became the especial butt for sophomoric attention, so much so, and so unpleasantly, that it is now his impression that it went on "from morning to night."

The Judge has one recollection in particular that has to do with David McAlpin Pyle, a sophomore who made something of a habit of coming to New Goldie's "nearly every night" and shouting, "Bring out Medina!" When Medina appeared, Pyle would whack him once—hard, but not *too* hard—upon the head with a "club." This, apparently, was an almost invariable part of sophomore Pyle's horsing. Now and again, he brought with him "a little guy" with whom he tried to get Medina to box. The freshman, however, always refused. He knew nothing of boxing, despite his deep-chested sturdiness, and seems to have understood that "the little guy" was a "ringer" who was unusually good with his fists.

"I was quite innocent—even ignorant—of everything," Judge Medina has explained. "I was obnoxious and noisy, so instead of falling in with those who would otherwise have been my natural friends, I antagonized them. I didn't get off on the right foot."

There were no fraternities at the university, each entering student having pledged himself to "have no connection whatever with any secret society, nor be present at the meetings of any secret society" while attending Princeton. There had long since grown up, however, not only the well-known upper class clubs, but freshman and sophomore eating clubs as well. Most freshmen, by the very fact that they were freshmen, were innocent of guile, and the result was that such politics as existed in the class usually left the control of these clubs in the hands of a few. Harold Medina never quite understood how to go about getting into such a club. Even when he managed to do so he did not understand just how it had come about. But even membership did not necessarily bring with it any sense of security. Sometimes those who had become members were thrown out, and that, in a way, was even worse than not having been accepted in the first place. This danger sometimes caused those who were not sure of themselves to live in a sort of terror, and freshman Harold Medina, for one, felt it constantly.

For the most part, the boys from the big preparatory schools were the dominant ones. The others—those from high schools and the lesser preparatory schools—had few influential contacts and knew little or nothing of what went on behind the scenes. Even the freshman clubs themselves—they were called White Hat, Green Hat, Dark Blue, Light Blue, and Red, perhaps from some earlier time when such hats were actually worn—were not only beyond the control, but also were often beyond the understanding, of those uninfluential and inexperienced members of the class.

Harold Medina had played a fair game of football at Holbrook Academy, and so went out for the freshman team at Princeton in the autumn of 1905. Early in the season, his back was hurt in practice—he got the impression that it was a kidney injury—and he was laid up in the infirmary for a couple of weeks during which the field house burned with all his football gear. He recovered—or thought he did—but, because of the injury and the coincidental loss of his equipment, he never returned to football. That in itself was of no major importance, but that injury has troubled him ever since, and was indirectly and by way of the ultra-Victorianism still prevalent at the time, to play its part in turning the following year into what Harold Medina still recalls as the unhappiest period of his life.

In the summer of 1904, when he was sixteen, he had accompanied his father on a trip to Europe, but the summer of 1905 was largely spent, in customary Medina fashion, at the old Pequot House at Morris Cove, near New Haven, Connecticut. A Canadian family named Burn occupied a cottage near the hotel, and Harold, who has never in his life been averse to feminine society, promptly met the family's five daughters. One of these, Phyllis, a girl about Harold's own age, had invited her good friend Ethel Hillyer, of East Orange, New Jersey, to come to Morris Cove for a visit, and Harold Medina was more or less constantly about the Burn cottage while the guest was there. That autumn, too, after he had entered Princeton, he found—or created—an opportunity while visiting friends in East Orange who knew Ethel Hillyer, to call on her in their company. She was away from home at the time—was out walking, in fact, with another boy—but Harold, though he missed seeing her, was nevertheless quite properly introduced to her mother.

It is on such minor events that greater ones sometimes turn. It must be remembered that the year was 1905, and that Victorian manners, though beginning to undergo some modification, were still dominant among a good many of the parents of that day. Had that introduction not been made, for instance—had Harold Medina, the seventeen-year-old freshman from Princeton, not been presented to Mrs. Hillyer by her daughter's friends, the Misses McKelcan—the next development might very well not have taken place. As it was, however, when Ethel Hillyer returned and expressed her disappointment at missing the young man's call, her mother suggested that it might be correct, and even desirable, for her to invite him to spend a week-end at the Hillyer home—a suggestion Mrs. Hillyer later came to wish she had never made.

The invitation was sent and was accepted, and Harold came in October—a young man who was attending Princeton—who had been to Europe and who, with his father's approval, actually smoked cigars. His visit was an event, not only for seventeen-year-old Ethel, but also for Mrs. Hillyer, for the family's maiden aunt, for the small sister and two brothers.

Mrs. Hillyer's responsibilities, it should be pointed out, were heavy. As a member of an old Philadelphia family, she had been given such training as was considered proper for young ladies in the 1880's, and her husband had died about three years before Harold Medina's visit, leaving her with four children, the eldest of whom was fifteen, and very little in the way of this world's goods beside an insurance policy for two thousand dollars. Compelled to go to work, she found that few openings were available for inexperienced ladies. Nevertheless, she obtained a position in Wanamaker's newly opened "shopping guides" office, and by means of it succeeded in holding her family together and in supplying them with their essential needs. It is not surprising, in view of this background, that she seems to have studied young Harold Medina closely from the very first. And his suit, which from her point of view may have appeared somewhat juvenile, got off to a very bad start.

At dinner on the evening of the young Princetonian's arrival, the conversation began readily enough, though probably with the maiden aunt and the young brothers and sister more than ordinarily silent. Harold Medina has never been backward as a conversationalist, and Princeton was a welcome topic to him. Football ultimately followed, too, and Harold, who has never had much of the Victorian about him, admitted not only that he had given up football, but that he had done so because, in practice, "I injured my kidney."

Horrified silence fell upon the table, and though conversation was ultimately resumed, it was only with difficulty. Nor was this merely a matter of momentary embarrassment. All that night, apparently, as Mrs. Hillyer awakened and found it difficult to go to sleep again, she brooded over this remark, which, to her, was so rude, so ungentlemanly, so utterly inexcusable. Early the following morning, in dressing gown and slippers, she went silently to Ethel's room and sat down on the edge of her daughter's bed.

"Ethel dear," she whispered. "This young man is simply impossible. We can *never* have him inside the house again."

But Ethel had been little troubled by the remark that had so disturbed her mother, and when, a week or so after Harold had returned to Princeton, a letter came from him asking her to go to New Haven for the Princeton-Yale game, she accepted.

It is entirely clear that at this period in his development Harold Medina was not making the best possible impression at Princeton. In his association with his classmates he obviously lacked both ease and confidence. This, as much as anything, seems to have been the cause of the self-assertive loudness to which, as of that day, he now pleads guilty. But though he succeeded in making himself more or less objectionable to many members of his class, he seems not to have done so, and even to have done the opposite, where young ladies were concerned.

He had asked Ethel Hillyer to go with him to the Princeton-Yale game, and as it was to be played in New Haven she arranged to stay with her friend Phyllis Burn while she was there. And Harold, promptly recognizing his social duty in the matter, asked Phyllis to go also, and even asked her sister as well. This was before the present Yale Bowl was built, and the field was smaller and less well arranged than now. Nevertheless, this Princeton freshman somehow managed to obtain four excellent seats almost exactly on the fifty-yard line; and when he arrived at the Burn home before the game, he was almost lost behind three bunches of orange-colored chrysanthemums which he had purchased for the three young ladies whose escort he was to be.

It was unfortunate, no doubt, that Yale won by the somewhat unequal score of 23 to 4, but that was not enough to ruin a day that must otherwise have been very nearly flawless. Despite the score, Harold remained so enthusiastic and uninhibited that a lost kitten he and the girls came upon was adopted on the spot. In fact, it was decorated with a large orange bow, was immediately named Wow Wow, and was taken by train to Princeton the following day, when Harold escorted Ethel Hillyer back to East Orange. When they reached New York, the two had lunch—with Harold still carrying the decorated kitten—in no less a place than Mendel's Restaurant which, in those days, attracted its select clientele to the space it occupied in old Grand Central Station.

It is Harold Medina's feeling now that scholastically he got very little from his freshman year at Princeton. He may be mistaken in that belief. The fact is that he had fallen deeply in love, and from the very beginning of his freshman year, his mind was given less to his studies than it might otherwise have been.

Certainly he seized every opportunity to go to East Orange, and the forty-six miles he had to travel to get there have probably seldom been traversed more often by any Princeton freshman. Nevertheless, he managed to stand well in his classes, though even in the classroom he was sometimes misunderstood.

In Professor "Pop" Long's English class that freshman year, early in the study of Chaucer's *Canterbury Tales*, the students were called upon to read the poet's descriptions of the various Canterbury pilgrims, one of whom, it will be remembered, was:

a Prioresse,
That of hir smyling was full simple and coy.

To a freshman class, of course, Chaucer requires some explanation, and on the day in question it may be that Professor Long was not at his best—perhaps was less patient than professors often have need to be. To young Harold Medina, Chaucer was far from clear when he wrote of the "Prioresse" that:

Hir over lippe wyped she so clene,
That in hir coppe was no ferthing sene
Of grece, when she dronken hadde hir draughte.

He asked, consequently, what it meant, and Professor Long explained that in modern terms it meant that:

She wiped her upper lip so clean
That in her cup no floating particles were to be seen
Of grease when she had drunk her draught.

Still the passage remained unclear to Harold, who apparently could not imagine anyone's lip—and especially a woman's—so greasy as to leave any sign of it floating in a cup from which she had drunk. So he asked again, and still getting no completely satisfactory explanation, continued to ask for one. Professor Long, impatient and apparently under the impression that the insistent freshman was making fun of him, abruptly ended the incident by ordering Harold to leave the room.

Such occurrences were infrequent, however, and Harold, so far as his classes were concerned, did well that year. This is amply proved by his standing when the second term ended.

Class records at Princeton were averaged in those days, and

at the end of each term those students who had passed were listed in five different general groups. The names of those in the First General Group and in the Second were publicized, for such records were high and worthy of commendation. How high these groups stood is demonstrated by the fact that in Harold's class of 383, only six students were named at the end of the year as belonging in the First General Group, and only twenty-two in the Second. And Harold Medina, despite the horsing and the distracting influence of the young lady in East Orange, was one of those in the Second General Group. In college activities outside the classroom, however, he was much less fortunate.

Just as there were freshman eating clubs, into one of which, though without ever knowing how or why, Harold Medina had gained admittance, so there were sophomore clubs, the members of which were chosen from the freshman class each spring for membership the following year. When that time arrived the freshmen had come to be conversant with university customs, and there was something of a scramble to get into the established clubs. Always—and this was a weakness of the club system that often came under attack—a measurable percentage of each class failed to "make" any of these clubs, which resulted in heart burnings and disappointments that often left their mark for years.

In the spring of Harold Medina's freshman year, as usual, this selection of members for the sophomore clubs took place. After two semesters together, the members of the class knew each other reasonably well; and there is normally some realignment of friendships in almost any such class. That was true here, too, and it undoubtedly had its effect on the membership of the various clubs. When April or May came around and the memberships were decided, some fifty or sixty of the 383 members of the class found themselves without invitations to join any club. Some of this group would undoubtedly still have found their way in, and this might very well have applied to Harold Medina himself. He was impatient, however, and not yet having been chosen by any club, he assumed that he had been definitely rejected.

It was a blow to his pride. Such matters always strike there. But Harold Medina's stubborn determination was too great to permit him to accept any such situation, half-imagined though it may have been, without doing anything about it.

An old dormitory then stood at University Place and Nassau Street, where the Commons was built a little later, and Harold Medina called a meeting there of those members of his class who, like himself, had not yet been invited to join any sophomore club. He made a speech—an effective speech, apparently. As a result of that meeting, those who had assembled organized a new sophomore club which they named the Vikard. The name had no meaning and no significance, but the club had. It operated throughout sophomore year, and though it was unable fully to salve the hurts its members had received, it nevertheless served to take much of the sting away.

Mrs. Hillyer, meanwhile, was growing more and more perturbed over her daughter's affair with "the impossible young man." She was constantly concerned with economic problems that were not easy to solve. Seeing that what she may at first have thought was mere infatuation was developing into something much more serious, she began to wonder about this young man's prospects. She soon reached the conclusion that he had none; and with less judgment than feeling, she sat down and wrote Mr. Joaquin Medina a letter phrased in unflattering terms. The letter has long since been destroyed, but there were references in it to this boy with "no prospects," and to other matters that could not be overlooked by so meticulous and considerate a gentleman as Joaquin Medina.

Up to this point there had been no restraints placed either on Harold or on Ethel, but now, Mrs. Hillyer laid down a number of positive edicts, and Mr. Medina, though undoubtedly not in sympathy with this method of control, saw to it that his son recognized that lady's authority in the matter. Visits to East Orange were limited to one every second weekend. Letters were limited to one a week. Lesser restrictions were also placed in effect, and in June of that year Mr. and Mrs. Medina, with their two sons, left for Europe. Supplied with a *Baedeker*, Harold and Richard were alternately assigned to guide the family party as they strenuously and continuously visited museums, art galleries, castles, and palaces. Harold, however, was much more interested in the letters he expected from Ethel Hillyer, and even today is averse to such sightseeing as engaged the Medina family that summer.

If that trip to Europe was intended to break up the love affair that had so upset both families, it failed of its purpose. The affair may actually have been furthered by it and by the restrictions that now were supposed to govern the two who were most concerned. The letters which could be mailed only once a week could at least be *written* every day, and they were. The result was that they assumed enormous proportions. One of Harold's letters still in existence actually covers seventy-two pages. In fact, these "once a week" letters started a daily correspondence between the two which lasted without interruption for five years. Even now, after most of them have been destroyed, a large box filled with the remainder occupies a corner in the Medina attic.

The restrictions that limited visits to one in two weeks promptly broke down. Ethel had now graduated from Miss Jennie Hunter's Kindergarten Training School on West 127th Street, New York, and was teaching the younger children who attended Parsons' Preparatory School in Ridgewood,

New Jersey, some eighteen or nineteen miles from East Orange. All week she remained in Ridgewood, but each weekend she spent at home, returning to Ridgewood late each Sunday, and going by way of Newark. Here was an opportunity too good to be missed, and the school year had no sooner begun in the autumn of 1906 than the two young people began to meet in Newark for supper late every Sunday afternoon. Their meeting place was the corner of Broad and Market streets, where Ethel came by trolley. Though these meetings were entirely unofficial, they were not clandestine. Mrs. Hillyer never approved of them, but she knew they were taking place and never issued any orders against them, which was permission enough for the two who were most concerned.

Nevertheless Mrs. Hillyer's opposition was a powerful influence. The two young people were very much in love and considered themselves engaged. They were so young that they did not realize how effective a solvent time can often be, and they were unhappy accordingly—painfully unhappy and almost despondent, as only youth can be. Harold Medina vividly remembers that year as the unhappiest of his life.

His classes and his other school activities occupied most of his time. He came to know Pompeo M. Maresi, the son of a successful Italian caterer of Brooklyn, and with the opening of sophomore year, when drawings were made for rooms in the campus dormitories, the two decided to room together and were so fortunate as to draw Number 72, Patton Hall, though a good many members of their class could not be accommodated on the campus at all.

So far as his studies were concerned, Harold's sophomore year logically followed his freshman one, during which he had specialized somewhat heavily in languages. He gave up Greek, registered for a course in beginning Spanish, and took no mathematics. He continued his French, Latin, and English, however, and took a course in medieval history. He busied himself, too, with athletics, but without much success. He even raised a mustache—the only one in his class—perhaps because of his admiration of his father who wore one.

"I tried to inflate my ego," he has explained, "by going out for the gun team, for fencing, and for swimming, but I didn't make any of them. I was running around all the time, but I wasn't getting anywhere."

It would not have been surprising if he had failed completely in his studies. Certainly his mind, for the most part, was elsewhere, and his classwork must have suffered. But he found himself, at the end of sophomore year, in the Second General Group again, just as he had been at the end of freshman year. That must be accepted, too, as saying a good deal for his mental equipment, for there is no doubt that he gave his studies far less attention than they should have had.

The very real trials he faced that year were playing an important part in the evolution of Harold Medina's character. His "loudness" had not been softened into shyness or silence. Nevertheless, the objectionable qualities that so clearly marked his freshman year must have undergone some modification. Two years at Princeton had done much to develop in him some of the manners and mannerisms that ultimately made him the genial, friendly person he later came to be. That some change had clearly taken place was proved in the spring of his sophomore year.

The freshman and sophomore clubs at Princeton, as Harold Medina knew them, were important to the members of those two classes, but were clearly secondary to the upper class clubs. These, to which only juniors and seniors are eligible, are even yet dominant in the social life of the university, and membership in some one of them is almost essential to anything like real undergraduate success. As in the case of the freshman and sophomore organizations, the upper class clubs were originally organized merely as eating clubs, but because membership could only be attained by invitation, they were selective from the first. Then, as their social importance grew, they came to be select, and ultimately exclusive. In recent years this exclusiveness has come so heavily under attack that it has been much modified. When Harold Medina was an undergraduate, however, no such liberal ideas prevailed. Woodrow Wilson, who was then president of the university, and who tried to break down this exclusiveness, suffered a resounding defeat in the matter—a defeat, incidentally, which so dramatized his liberalism as to play a part in making him governor of New Jersey and, ultimately, President of the United States.

Sophomore Harold Medina, already unhappy enough over other matters, could not look forward with any assurance to membership in any one of these all-important clubs. He had failed, at the end of his freshman year, to be invited to join a sophomore club, and had little confidence in doing better where the more important ones were concerned. A considerable minority of juniors and seniors—perhaps as many as 20 per cent—always failed to get into any of the clubs and while some of these students were unable to belong for purely economic reasons, and a very few may actually have preferred not to join, it was a bitter disappointment—an almost tragic matter—to most of those who were left out.

Again the time for the selection of new members came in the spring, and members of the sophomore class, soon to be juniors, were those who were under consideration. Those chosen were selected each year in what had come to be called "The Bicker Session," and the various clubs frankly vied with each other in attracting the more prominent and popular members of the sophomore class. Each club had its Bicker committee, and the most desirable prospects were approached by these, with the result that the better known and more popular classmen—athletes, socialites, and others—sometimes received more than one invitation and were able to choose which of several memberships they cared to accept.

Harold Medina was not approached. No Bicker committee seemed interested in him, and the exciting activities of the Bicker Session appeared to be passing him by. Again, it seemed to him, his classmates were about to reject him. Once more he seemed certain to be excluded, and this time the blow would be even more bitter than the one he had suffered the year before. But the blow never fell. Although no Bicker committee had seemed to recognize his existence and no club had solicited his membership, he found to his immense relief and pleasure that he had been elected a member of the Terrace Club. How it had come about he did not know, and in his relief he never asked. Some friend might have put in a word for him, and he himself must have appeared more acceptable to those who controlled the membership of the Terrace Club than he had appeared to many of his classmates the year before.

Even if Harold Medina had gained no wide popularity among his fellows, he nevertheless no longer felt himself to be an outcast, as he had been inclined to feel when he failed to make a sophomore club. He was now at least "in with the mob." But more than that, his development was continuing. He had passed his nineteenth birthday only in February of that sophomore year—was definitely younger than most of his class—but his youth was less apparent. He was developing, expanding, growing, and above all, was beginning to take on those characteristics which, as his classmates also underwent their own evolution, were to bring about so great a reversal of their attitude toward him.

Not long after his election to the Terrace Club, his name again appeared in the Second General Group of his class. But these two welcome and gratifying successes almost faded from sight in the light of still another happening that marked the end of that eventful semester: after more than a year of most discouraging opposition, Mrs. Hillyer relented, and "the unhappiest year" of Harold Medina's life came to a very happy end.

There is no doubt in Judge Medina's mind that the events that marked the close of his sophomore year constituted an important milestone in his life. Scholastically he had done well even before this point was reached—remarkably well, considering the adverse influences that had affected him. He was capable of doing better, however, and during his junior year he began to demonstrate that fact.

It was still his intention to study law, and in selecting his subjects for his junior year he did what most of the other prospective lawyers did. He chose the Department of History, Politics, and Economics, but within two or three days, he began to feel some qualms in connection with that decision, and went to talk the matter over with Dean "Andy" West.

Dean West was a very learned man and a famous Princeton character. It was he who played a most important part in opposing—and defeating—Woodrow Wilson in the matter of the clubs.

The Dean was at his desk when his caller entered; he listened silently while Harold explained that he was a little afraid he had picked the wrong department.

"What department do you think you ought to be in?" the Dean asked.

Harold was doubtful, but admitted that he thought that *possibly* he should have chosen the Modern Language Department.

The Dean was busy writing while Harold was expressing his somewhat doubtful conclusion, and now, rather abruptly, he handed the student a card.

"Well," he remarked. "You're in it."

"But, Dean," the young man objected. "I expected to discuss it with you—"

"You have discussed it," snapped the Dean. "Now get the hell out of here."

Sudden and perhaps half-unexpected though this change was, it seems to have been wise. Harold Medina was already beginning to learn that he had a gift for languages, and now he began, scholastically, to do what he was really capable of doing. Throughout his first two years he had regularly made "first groups" in French, and, with his various marks averaged, had consistently made "second groups." Throughout his junior year he made "first groups" in all his studies. To use his own term, he was still "a little guy" in other class activities, but he was no longer out of the running. He made the swimming team, the gun team, the fencing team. He was given a position on the board of *The Tiger*, the undergraduate humorous publication, and wrote jokes and other contributions for it.

Success, in varying degrees, was now coming to him after an extended period of discouragement and lack of success. As a result he was undoubtedly beginning to build up some belief in himself—beginning to break down the lack of confidence which had brought about the loud, assertive cockiness that had formerly so antagonized his fellows. Harold Medina would not have been Harold Medina had he suddenly reverted to softness and to silence. He is, and apparently has always been, a hearty, robust person, inclined to be impatient, especially in small matters, and apt to be didactic and even positive in statement.

Throughout both his junior and his senior years he applied himself constructively to his studies. He was not, to use a Princeton term, a "poler", that is, a grind. Instead, he developed, or possibly always had, a real capacity for concentration. Unlike many an undergraduate, he did not dawdle over his books.

"When I studied," he has said, "I *studied*." His marks confirm it.

With Mrs. Hillyer's change of attitude toward the once "impossible" young man, thoughts of marriage came to the fore. Harold Medina and Ethel Hillyer had long considered themselves as being engaged, but that status had not yet been recognized by their respective families. Furthermore, an engagement ring was a more or less essential part of the announcement they hoped would shortly be permitted.

Engagement rings are apt to be expensive, and Harold Medina had only the allowance his father gave him. Unasked, his father now even increased the amount but, somehow, an engagement ring simply *had* to be purchased with money he himself had earned—a point of view with which Ethel, who was to wear the ring, was in complete sympathy. So, looking about during his junior year for ways to make money, Harold turned to tutoring, and this went so well that he was now and again recommended by members of the faculty when some of their faltering students needed help. But Harold did not stop there. He looked back over some of the courses he had taken and saw that well-prepared notes and abstracts of those courses would be useful to later students. With this in mind he prepared several syllabi—one covering a course in history and a couple covering courses on politics—and had them printed. These he sold to students who had need of them.

By these methods he made money enough to buy the ring, and in the spring of 1908, he and Ethel Hillyer went together to Tiffany's and very seriously picked it out. Oddly enough, their memories are not in accord as to its cost, though the Judge clearly remembers that he earned every penny of it. They both remember, however, the thoughtfulness and consideration of the clerk who helped them select that diamond. He, too, seemed really to understand that it was an unusually important stone.

Two dates were engraved in that ring: September 11, 1906, and June 11, 1908. The first is the date on which they had actually become engaged. The second is the date on which, with parental permission, it was announced as a fact.

During his junior year, Harold Medina had taken a course in the lyric poetry of the Augustan Age, the period that coincided with the reign of Augustus Caesar and which marked the golden age of Roman literature. The course was given by Professor David Magie, and though the freshman and sophomore Latin courses had failed to arouse much interest in young Medina, this course—and this professor—made a deep impression on him. Professor Magie brought the words and phrases of a dead language to life and succeeded in dramatizing as well as explaining Latin rhetorical devices and combinations of words that had theretofore been little more than words and phrases to the students. It was because Harold Medina so greatly enjoyed the poems he studied in this course—the poems of Ovid in particular—that he has to this day retained his interest in Latin. Many years after he graduated from Princeton he resumed his study of the language, and even yet, is continuing it, especially in connection with the study of Latin poetry.

The late Christian Gauss, who was to become Professor of Modern Languages, then Chairman of the Department, and later still Dean of the College, was "one of those preceptor guys" when Harold Medina first came under him. But from the first this unusual character was more than merely another teacher to the young man from Brooklyn. Four men, the Judge feels now, have influenced his life more than any others. His father was one of these: another was Harlan Fiske Stone, who did not come into his life until the second year after he graduated from Princeton. The other two were on the staff at Princeton: one was David Magie, who so effectively dramatized the beauties of Latin verse; the other was Christian Gauss.

The field of American education has produced its full share of eminent figures, and Dean Gauss of Princeton must be ranked high among them. He came to be one of Judge Medina's close friends, but had also known him when he was "loud and objectionable" as a freshman, when he was depressed and clearly less than popular as a sophomore, and when, in his junior and senior years, he came to occupy a more acceptable place among his fellows. Undergraduate popularity, or the lack of it, is a somewhat unsure foundation on which to base a sound opinion of any person's character, and this may be true even of the casual opinions of most professors. Harold Medina's character, however, as it was during his years at Princeton, begins to appear in a new light, when viewed through the eyes of so clear an observer and so rare a character as Christian Gauss. Only a few weeks before his death, which occurred on November 1, 1951, he replied at length to a letter from me in which I had asked what his recollections were of Harold Medina as an undergraduate. Along with a short hand-written note he sent the following:

Harold Medina as Undergraduate

Harold Medina entered Princeton as a freshman in 1905, the year that Woodrow Wilson introduced the preceptorial system.

As he was enrolled in French classes and I was one of the preceptors in Romance Languages, I occasionally taught the small group of which he was a member. As he specialized in modern languages, he later took several courses with me. I came to know him as well and as favorably as any member of his class. As he was the only student who was awarded "highest honors" in our department, the record confirms my recollection that he was the ablest student in his class in the general field of French language and French literature.

He was as remarkable as a person as he was as a scholar, but these remarkable personal qualities were a handicap to a freshman in 1905. At that time eastern colleges were still in the hey-day of the "College customs" era. The rights and privileges of seniors, juniors, sophomores, and freshmen were still clearly prescribed, and descended sharply from seniors, who possessed all of them, to the freshman who possessed almost none. It was the freshman's duty, and usually his habit, to conform. He must know his place, he must not run it out, and he must not be a "sad bird."

Harold Medina has told me that these dire warnings against being a sad bird came from so many sides that they troubled him and he occasionally wondered whether he might not be one of them. He could have spared himself any concern on this score. A "sad bird," in later college slang, a "meat ball," was an undergraduate with no inner focus of radiation. He took no part in athletics, or in extracurricular activities. He usually lived by himself and was classified as a gloomy Gus. He was, in short, an introvert. Harold Medina's vulnerability lay in the opposite quarter and if during his undergraduate years his classmates never elected him to any of those important offices which go to the Big Man in the College, it was because many of them could not quite fathom him and suspected him of running it out. Here they were mistaken for running it out meant playing to the grandstand, and this he never did, then or later. If he was so unusual a person that during his college years many of his classmates could not quite make him out, his circle of friends was an ever-widening one. If you asked his classmates now: Who has done most for the Class of 1909?—the reply would certainly be Harold Medina, and it is gratifying to note that he became the recognized leader of his class years before he achieved his national prominence in the Communist Trial. When I ask myself which undergraduate did most to make French studies attractive in his upper class years, my answer would have to be the same.

In his junior year we had an undergraduate French Club that was dying on its feet. It offered extracurricular classes in French conversation and conducted social evenings which no one attended. We persuaded Harold Medina to accept its presidency and it became one of our liveliest organizations. When the public presentation of a five-act French comedy threatened to fall through for lack of an actor willing to take over the time-consuming role of the dumbbell hero, Medina was persuaded to take it over and made it an hilarious success.

There was something about him that couldn't help arresting your attention. It attracted mine the first time I met him in a group of freshmen gathered for a preceptorial discussion. Even on the side of physique, this stocky, broad-shouldered young fellow with the swarthy complexion and dark hair, stood out. But what set him off most sharply from his fellows was his animation. There was something particularly hale and hearty about him in the very best sense. He was not a bookish student for his interest in persons was as keen as it was in ideas. His good sense and good nature are rooted in the fact that then and later he kept persons and ideas in balance. He had a keen sense for human foibles and when in our reading or discussions something really amusing turned up, he did not meet it with a thin Chesterfieldian smile, he laughed heartily as he still does. But it was ideas that excited him most. They were meat and drink to him, and his teachers had the unusual satisfaction of watching him think. When a challenging idea was put to him, you could see him knit his brows and shake his head. His mind worked swiftly. In a moment his brow would clear and his eyes literally sparkled and you could see that he had reached his conclusion. The amazing thing was that in spite of the rapidity of the process and the animation of his presentation his conclusions were never jumbled but clear cut and presented in logical sequence.

In his upper class years when he became an advanced student in my department it was my privilege to spend six hours a week in classes and conferences with him. I still look back upon those years as among the happiest in a long life as a teacher. His rich intellectual gifts were a part of personal qualities almost equally rare. He seemed to draw upon inexhaustible sources of intellectual and spiritual energy. He was so generous in heart and mind, so richly endowed with life, that he seemed to have more than one man needs. He had life to give away, and from the time I first knew him as a freshman he has been giving it away prodigally to friends and even to strangers in need.

I have had only one disappointment in nearly fifty years of acquaintance with him. He was so fine, friendly, and frank a person and had so promising a command of French literature and civilization that in his senior year I tried to persuade him to follow my own profession. For a time I believe he did consider doing so. To me then it seemed unfortunate that he should waste such talents on the law. Over the years in spite of his legal preoccupations, I repeatedly called upon him for services to individuals who needed his good offices, and, above all, for service to his alma mater. He never refused. Ten years ago, my department was looking for a Chairman to head its Advisory Council on Romance Languages. It would have been normal procedure to turn to a professor in this field. But my older colleagues and I could not forget that one of the ablest students we had ever had was Harold

Medina. He has served ever since in that capacity with such profit to our work that I for one am reconciled that my favorite pupil and perhaps my most gifted student should have found his avocation in the law.

(signed) CHRISTIAN GAUSS

Harold Medina's senior courses had principally to do with French and Spanish, though he also took a course in history, a minor course in jurisprudence, a series of lectures given by Visiting Professor Ford on the referendum and recall, and a course on politics under Woodrow Wilson.

He had come to be intimate with many members of the Terrace Club, and now found them more congenial and companionable. His acceptance by his fellows is additionally demonstrated by his success as president of *Cercle Français*, the French club to which Dean Gauss referred, and by his selection, though he was not the best fencer in the world, as captain of the fencing team.

"Probably on that account," he once told me, "I became less noisy, less pushing, less objectionable."

It may be more accurate to say that his confidence in himself was growing, and, as a result, he felt less need to be overly assertive.

In attempting to trace the development of the character of Harold Medina one not infrequently encounters what appear to be conflicting facts. Those who know him best realize that he can be abrupt and sometimes violent, as well as gentle; vain as well as modest; sharp, cutting, and impatient, as well as thoughtful and considerate; indecorous and even ribald, as well as delicate and deeply religious. With traits so apparently at odds with each other, it is difficult to present Harold Medina "in full color."

He was baptized in the Episcopal Church that stands at the corner of Marcy and Gates Avenues in Brooklyn, and confirmed in the Episcopal Church at Ossining, while he was a student at Holbrook Academy. He has always remained a church member and has attended services with more than usual regularity. Even as a boy he made up his mind to study law, and at no time does he seem to have considered the idea of entering the ministry. Nevertheless, he has on occasion played the part of lay preacher.

His memory is often very detailed and accurate where his Princeton experiences are concerned, but he can recall only vaguely, and seems unable to explain at all, an experience he must have had during the month of June that followed his freshman year. In discussing this matter with me, he remembered that he went to a place called Northfield, though he could not be sure whether the town was in Connecticut, Massachusetts, or some other state in that general region. Why he went he did not know, or how long he remained, and he only vaguely recalled that during the ten days or two weeks he stayed there, his activities had largely to do with lectures, discussions, prayer meetings, and tennis.

This was somewhat vague, but a little additional investigation somewhat plainly suggested that he had attended the Northfield Students Conference, in Northfield, Massachusetts, which was usually held at the end of each college year and normally lasted about ten days. Originally organized in 1887 by the evangelist, Dwight L. Moody, this annual conference was attended by college undergraduates who were interested in religious education and related matters. The lectures and the group work in which the participants engaged were entirely religious in background, and the young men and young women who attended came mostly from eastern colleges.

Judge Medina has long since forgotten the details of the

conference, and he never attended another. His activities during his sophomore and junior years were apparently unaffected by whatever it was he learned there. In fact, the Judge is not sure that his attendance at the Northfield Conference had any real connection even with a decision he reached in his senior year when he agreed to conduct religious meetings in a number of crude little chapels that lay in the backwoods in the general vicinity of Princeton. He simply cannot explain it and does not even know now who, if anyone, encouraged him to do it. He remembers only that on a good many Sundays during his senior year he got a horse and buggy from some person now unknown, and, armed with a large book of sermons that had a light green cover, went to three or four of the little backwoods chapels and conducted services.

The number of people who attended these services was always limited. Sometimes there were as many as fifteen or twenty, but sometimes there were fewer. In no case was there any regular minister, and sometimes there was no one even to play the organ. Neither were the services cast in any regularly accepted form. He merely offered a prayer, gave a sermon selected from the book with the light green cover, chose a hymn, and then went on to the next backwoods chapel in order to conduct another simple but entirely sincere and reverent service.

This activity began and ended for no reason that the Judge can now recall, but it strongly suggests the sincerity of Harold Medina's beliefs—a sincerity that is equally evident today.

Throughout his senior year Harold Medina's scholastic standing duplicated the record he had set in his junior year, and in his language courses he was especially brilliant. Indeed, Professor Vreeland, who was then head of the Modern Language Department, and Professor Gauss came to him, as the final semester approached its end, in an effort to convince him that he should accept a fellowship, attend the graduate school, and devote himself to teaching modern languages. It was to this that Dean Gauss referred when he said that he tried to persuade Medina "to follow my own profession." He had an attitude toward modern languages, he was told, that was most uncommon, and had abilities that it would be "criminal" to waste.

Here, obviously, was a critical moment in his life. He was deeply interested—was almost steeped—in the subject they wished him to pursue. He was fascinated by Old French, by Old Spanish, by the history of languages, by the methods used in conveying thought. Nevertheless, he recognized that life requires the solution of many purely practical problems which, in large part, become a matter of dollars and cents. He was especially conscious of the responsibilities his engagement to Ethel Hillyer entailed. If they were to be married, as they hoped to be at the earliest possible moment, he had need to begin to earn what they would require. Nevertheless, the suggestion the two professors made interested him, and he discussed it seriously with his father.

The older man stressed the practical side of the matter.

"What would you get?" he asked.

Harold admitted that it would be only six hundred dollars the first year.

"What could you ultimately expect?"

It seemed likely that he might ultimately earn three or four thousand dollars a year.

His father stroked his big mustache and shook his head.

"That's all right," he replied, "for these fellows who have money of their own, but if you're going to get married and bring up a family you just can't do it."

Harold Medina had to acknowledge the force in that reply. It was clearly necessary that he give up the idea.

As the end of his senior year approached, it was clear that he would graduate high in his class, and yet he was fearful that he would not make Phi Beta Kappa, membership in which is conferred only on students who have attained unusually high scholastic standing. Harold Medina had no need to worry about the marks he had earned in his final two years, but his record during his freshman and sophomore years, though well above the average, had been less spectacular, and it was this fact which troubled him. He need not have worried. The gold key that is the sign of membership in Phi Beta Kappa is still one of the Judge's prized possessions.

It has been said that he graduated from Princeton *summa cum laude*, but that is not true. In error, this statement was once included in his write-up in *Who's Who in America*, and though it was corrected in the next edition of that volume, it still occasionally appears in print here or there. The fact is that in Princeton usage there is no such thing as graduating *summa cum laude*, though Harold Medina, to whom the phrase might elsewhere have been applied, graduated at Princeton with a standing that was recognized as being among the highest of his class, and actually "with highest honors in French." In this connection, too, his character becomes a little clearer when it is pointed out that his pleasure in attaining this honor in French was greatly enhanced—and is to this day—by a happy letter of congratulation he received from "Prof" Nagle, who had been his genial, bearded teacher of French at Holbrook Academy.

It can be seen that Harold Medina graduated with a scholastic record that was outstanding. Despite the bitter disappointments of his first two years, when he felt himself rejected by so many of his classmates, he had made close friends in the Terrace Club and elsewhere. He had even attained a kind of minor recognition, as president of *Cercle Français*, as captain of the fencing team, as a member of the editorial board of *The Tiger*, and elsewhere, though he was far from being pre-eminent among his classmates. In his own phrase, he was still "a little fellow hanging around the edge."

"Little fellow" though he still felt himself to be, he was graduating with honors such as many of his classmates must have envied. He was engaged to the one girl who had ever held a place in his heart. He was about to begin the study of law. He was only twenty-one when he was handed his diploma in June, 1909, and had much still to do in order to prepare himself for life. But he was growing up—could see more clearly the path he was to follow. Difficulties and disappointments still lay ahead. His character was still evolving. But Princeton, with its invaluable contributions, now lay behind him, and he was young. To what degree his self-confidence had developed even he, no doubt, could not have told, but it had grown, and that was just as well. He would find much need for it in the years that lay ahead.

3

COLUMBIA UNIVERSITY AND THE LAW

UNTIL LATE IN HIS SENIOR YEAR AT PRINCETON, HAROLD Medina had not decided on the law school he wished to attend. Most of his classmates who planned to study law had chosen Harvard, though some made other choices, or, like himself, had not made up their minds. Before the year ended, however, representatives of several law schools arrived to tell of the advantages of the institutions they represented. Among these were Professor Alfred G. Reeves, of the New York Law School, and Dean George W. Kirchwey, of Columbia University Law School. Having listened to what these men had to say, Medina began to see that if he were to choose a law school that was situated in New York, he could live at home and could complete his education at much less expense than otherwise. At no time had his father made any such suggestion. The son understood, however, that another three years away from home would be costly, and he knew, too, that in selecting Columbia he would be choosing from among the best. But another influence was at work. Columbia was convenient to Ridgewood, New Jersey, and East Orange, and this fact no doubt influenced his decision.

It was in the autumn of 1909 that Harold Medina began his law course at Columbia. He was living at home once more, in the brownstone front at 273 Jefferson Avenue in Brooklyn, and was occupying the familiar third-floor bedroom that had been his since his earliest recollection. Here, in the little alcove that separated his room from his brother's, he set up a table, selected a gas lamp with a mantle and a green glass shade, and began the almost endless reading that is so important a part of the study of law.

In order to get to his nine o'clock classes at Columbia he had to leave home each morning at 7:30. Catching a Long Island Rail Road train at the Nostrand Avenue station, he changed at the Flatbush Avenue Station two miles farther on, and took the subway for an additional ten-mile ride to 116th Street and Broadway in New York. Here, high up under the dome of the "old" library of Columbia University he attended classes.

No entrance test was necessary in order to be admitted to this graduate school of law. A graduate of any good college was eligible. Each student had merely to register and pay the moderate fees that were required, and the class of which Harold Medina was a member numbered about two hundred.

From the first, the young man from Brooklyn found that his status differed sharply from what it had been at Princeton. Four years earlier he had made a poor impression on many of his classmates, and had been held at arm's length by some of them, but here at Columbia he was accepted from the first. He had developed at Princeton. His manner was more acceptable. He was more at ease in his personal contacts. "I was not so damned obnoxious," he once remarked in an oversimplification of what had taken place. Aggressive still—for that is an immutable part of Harold Medina's character—he was less objectionably so. Naturally irrepressible, he has only to be present in order to defy being overlooked, and he was never overlooked at Columbia. Within a few days of his arrival, three different fraternities were "rushing" him, and that in itself was a new experience—one that had no counterpart in his four years at Princeton.

A little earlier he might have found those fraternity invitations irresistible, but that was not true now. His mind was on his studies. He was anxious to establish himself in the world, and had no intention of delaying in the slightest the day when he and Ethel Hillyer were to be married. Consequently he thanked the fraternity men who were urging him to join, declined their invitations, and turned resolutely to his studies, though later he became a member of Phi Delta Phi, the law fraternity.

He took to the law like a duck to water, but he worked as he had never worked before. He studied almost constantly, even on the long subway and train trips from and to his home in Brooklyn, and during his three-year course he never missed a class. He was a consistent asker of questions, a demander of explanation. Professor Charles Thaddeus Terry, who gave the course in contracts and who was most expert in utilizing the Socratic method, actually called on Medina every day for four solid months, obviously glad to make his points at the expense of this disputatious student.

"Whatever I said, he would prove wrong," the Judge has admitted. "I dreaded it, but it was great training."

Many of his classmates were well founded in the law. Some were the sons of successful attorneys or of judges and had been reared in an atmosphere that greatly aided them in their studies. Nevertheless, when that first year reached its end and the marks were in, Harold Medina was one of only three or four among the two hundred members of the class who were given A's in all their courses. The second year, too, was much the same, except that the Law School established itself in newly completed Kent Hall, and Professor Harlan Fiske Stone was made dean.

During his first year at Columbia, Harold Medina had not come in contact with Professor Stone, but during the remainder of his course he not only attended Stone's classes but had long and frequent talks with him in his office. Judge Medina credits Harlan Fiske Stone with having been one of the four most influential men in his life, and feels that those long, quiet personal talks were an important part of his legal education. Stone's rugged simplicity and utter integrity are even yet a perennial influence with the Judge.

"To do the right thing is good," he once remarked in referring to Stone, "but to do it as he did, without even a thought of the opposite, is better."

In his classes, Stone could be difficult to follow, and only those students who seriously applied themselves got any great benefit from him. His close reasoning was more than could be wholly grasped by dull or daydreaming listeners. Harold Medina, however, applied himself wholeheartedly and absorbed much of what this unusual character had to impart.

But that was true of his other classes as well. At the end of his second year, he again got A's in all his courses, and this time only one of his classmates succeeded in doing as well. As he once put it, "I was catching on."

Ethel Hillyer, to whom, by now, Harold Medina had been engaged for nearly five years, was no longer teaching at Parsons School in Ridgewood. Instead, she was a substitute teacher in the public schools nearer home, where Harold saw her every Sunday. The difficulties that had attended the first two years of their acquaintance were long behind them now, and for several years Ethel had even been permitted to spend a month or so each summer as a guest of the Medinas, twice at Orient, once at Greenport, and once at a hotel on Shelter Island.

Not for a moment had the two ever modified their intention of getting married at the earliest opportunity, and Harold's father was not averse to the idea. At any rate, it was he, as Harold approached the end of the second year of his three-year course at Columbia, who made possible the hoped-for wedding that had been so long delayed.

One more year of study lay ahead before Harold Medina could actively begin his career as an attorney and seriously enter upon the task of earning a living. That he would ultimately be successful in his chosen profession was already beginning to be as evident as such matters can be in advance, and his father, who was as confident of his son as Harold was of himself, agreed not only to advance the money to enable Harold to complete his education, but also a modest amount in addition to enable him to marry Ethel Hillyer at once and support her at least until his graduation.

The American dollar of 1911 was immensely greater in purchasing power than it is today, and Harold Medina, even with one more year of concentrated study ahead, was confident of his ability to earn more than a little in ways that had already occurred to him. His father, therefore, was asked to advance only fifteen hundred dollars in order to make it possible for the young people to be married, to establish themselves in their own apartment, and for Harold to complete his final year at Columbia.

The wedding was at Grace Church in Orange, New Jersey, on June 6, 1911, and was followed by a small reception in the little Hillyer home. Throughout the morning of that day it rained, and Mrs. Hillyer was in something of a dither over leaks in the awning. Late afternoon, however, brought clearing skies and a perfect sunset, and with four bridesmaids and Ethel's sister Lillian as maid of honor, the wedding party made its way to church.

Harold's brother, Dick, together with the other ushers, went to Summit, a few miles distant, for supper and to dress. Dick, however, had somehow failed to bring his Tuxedo trousers, and before some helpful person managed to replace them with a pair of dark blue trousers—the best substitute that could be found—guests were already beginning to arrive at the church in Orange, and were being escorted to their seats by a group of "extemporaneous" ushers, unexpectedly called to serve until the official ones arrived.

The wedding trip led to Boston and Montreal and, after spending the rest of the summer at Shelter Island, the young couple established themselves in a first floor, five-room apartment in the rear of an apartment house at 527 West 143d Street. It was convenient to Columbia University, but there was an additional reason for their choice of that apartment; a Princeton classmate, Joshua Brush, and his wife were living in the apartment house next door.

When Harold Medina was attending Columbia, any college graduate was permitted to take the New York State bar examinations at any time after he had completed his second year at law school, and in October, 1911, Medina took advantage of that opportunity. Furthermore, he passed, the notice of his success ultimately arriving by mail at the apartment in 143d Street.

"It was the most impressive communication," the Judge has said, "that I had ever received."

Passing the examinations, however, was not the only requirement. Before becoming an actual member of the bar he had to satisfy the character committee, and to do that had to obtain from lawyers personally known to some member of the committee, two affidavits attesting his good character. At first glance that may not have appeared difficult, but it was, for Harold Medina, despite the progress he had made in the study of law, knew no lawyers. Even his father did not, or knew so slightly those he had met as not to feel free to approach them in the matter. In thinking it over, however, he remembered that he had had some business contact with the legal firm of Cadwalader, Wickersham & Taft, and had come to know that firm's managing clerk, a lawyer named Charleton. And Mr. Charleton, to whom Mr. Medina mentioned the matter, agreed that, if Harold were brought down to meet him, he, knowing Mr. Medina, would supply one of the necessary affidavits. This was done, but the second affidavit still remained a problem.

At the beginning of that final year at Columbia, Harold Medina was one of the first three members of his class chosen to serve on the 1912 board of the *Columbia Law Review*. It was an honor to be connected with that publication in any capacity, but the board, which consisted of about twelve members, had to choose, from among themselves, an editor-in-chief and certain other officers. A meeting was called for the purpose, and those who were nominated withdrew from the room as their names were presented.

The choice for editor-in-chief lay between Harold Medina and Paul Shipman Andrews. The board found it impossible to decide between the two, ultimately reaching the conclusion that the matter should be left to the members of the 1911 board, who were also authorized to choose the other officers as well.

In the hierarchy of the *Law Review*, the most important post is that of editor-in-chief, with the note editor second, the decisions editor third, and the secretary fourth. To be chosen editor-in-chief is to be honored especially, for the position carries with it such kudos as to add measurably to any person's stature, and Harold Medina could hardly imagine any position which, at the moment, he would have preferred. Still, he acknowledged to himself that Paul Andrews, the son of a judge and a most excellent student, might very well be the better choice, and was willing that Andrews be selected. After all, even to be note editor would be a distinction, and, since only he and Andrews were being considered for the first place, it seemed reasonable to suppose that the one who failed to get it would be given the second position.

The 1911 board, however, reached quite another conclusion. Andrews was made editor-in-chief, as Medina had felt he probably should be, but Medina was not made note editor, nor was he even made decisions editor. To his dismay he was chosen merely to be secretary, a post far removed from the one he had hoped to attain.

Here was a real disappointment. Time and again this sort of thing had happened in the past—in eighth grade, at Holbrook Academy, at Princeton. And now it was happening at Columbia. He had once more *almost*, but not quite, reached the top; and, though he could not know it at the time, that kind of thing was to re-occur in other forms more than once in the years ahead.

He said nothing, for he had learned to keep such disappointments to himself. Already he was beginning to evolve a point of view that later was to become a fundamental part of his philosophy. He made no complaint. He merely accepted what had come to him, and in doing so, he no doubt grew at least a little in determination and in character. That disappointment, along with others, past and future, must surely have played a more constructive part in his evolution and his growth than easy success could possibly have done.

The funds that made possible Harold Medina's marriage were intended to see him through his final year at law school as well, but some additional income would clearly be necessary. Even in 1911, fifteen hundred dollars could hardly be expected to cover Harold's school expenses, and pay, as well, the expenses of a young married couple in New York for a year. Though their tastes, fortunately, were modest, and their expenses were kept reasonably low, nevertheless more money was essential.

Medina had learned at Princeton that tutoring could be remunerative. So, needing the money, he again turned to tutoring, and before long, members of the Columbia faculty began suggesting him to students who needed such help.

He had had some success at Princeton, too, in preparing and selling notes and abstracts of several courses, so he now began to prepare such notes on several law courses. He half learned shorthand, and set himself the task of picking out the essential facts of various courses and getting them down accurately, compactly, and in their proper order. In this work, for which he had a natural aptitude, he soon began to develop a real skill, and having progressed this far, he invested in a typewriter and a mimeograph. Night after night in his little cubbyhole of a study in the 143d Street apartment, he carefully cut his stencils and operated his mimeograph, preparing copies of the notes he had made, and for which he found a somewhat ready market. It was early in that year, too, that Professor Kirchwey recommended Medina for the task of revising all the legal definitions for the forthcoming second edition of the *New International Encyclopedia*.

Here, then, along with his class work and his work on the *Law Review*, were three additional and somewhat pressing tasks: tutoring, preparing and selling his mimeographed notes on a number of law courses, and the revision of hundreds of legal definitions and references that were sent him, from time to time, by the *New International Encyclopedia*.

Tutoring demanded less of him than the other tasks he had

assumed. It took time, but otherwise he did not find it difficult. In fact, it was helpful, for it forced him not only to understand what he was helping these other students to learn, but also to find clear ways of putting his knowledge and understanding into words. This was true, also, of the mimeographed notes he was preparing, for in getting them together he was forced to develop real ability in condensation, as well as in clear and orderly arrangement. At the time, the work no doubt seemed merely to be a chore necessitated by economic needs. It must have been obvious that the more completely, accurately, and clearly those notes were prepared the better they would serve their purpose and the more law students would buy them, but in many ways the work was nothing more than drudgery. It was quite beyond anyone's power to guess that the orderly accuracy he developed doing this work was to make it possible, nearly two score years later, for Harold Medina to keep an accurate, detailed record of a nine months' trial of eleven Communists—a trial of nation-wide, and even world-wide, interest—on one hundred sheets of paper—a hundred sheets of paper that played an invaluable part in the Judge's handling of that trial.

Similarly, the task of revising the almost endless legal references in the *New International Encyclopedia* clarified in his mind hundreds of legal definitions and acquainted him with many legal facts. Most of these references were short—mere bits and pieces, ranging from a few lines to a column or two—and the work was hard and very poorly paid. Nevertheless, it impressed on Harold Medina's mind an extensive series of legal facts that added immensely to his understanding of the law.

With so many tasks pressing heavily upon him, Medina had little time to spare. He and his bride had almost no social life at all. They went occasionally to the movies, and soon after they settled themselves in the 143d Street apartment, they became parishioners and regular attendants of St. Luke's Episcopal Church on Convent Avenue at 141st Street. Otherwise, however, Harold Medina worked early and late over his studies, his tutoring, his notes, his mimeographing, and his revision of the encyclopedia's legal definitions. There was almost no time for anything else whatever.

His success in passing the bar examination had naturally delighted him, but he was still troubled about the second affidavit that had to be sent to the character committee. His classmate, Paul Andrews, however, who was now editor-in-chief of the *Columbia Law Review*, thought he saw a way to solve that problem. His father, who was a judge, had a wide acquaintance among lawyers, and an especial friend was Charles C. Burlingham, a member of the law firm of Burlingham, Veeder, Masten & Fearey, later president of the Association of the Bar of the City of New York and one of the city's most eminent attorneys. And it was to Mr. Burlingham that Paul Andrews took his friend, Harold Medina. It was not easy, however, on such short acquaintance, for Medina to ask so eminent a member of the bar for the needed affidavit, and it was only indirectly that the subject arose. Mr. Burlingham, however, quickly saw his young caller's predicament.

"Why, Medina," he remarked. "I'll give you an affidavit."

He called a stenographer in at once, and the statement he dictated and signed played its part in assisting Harold Medina to become a member of the New York bar months before he graduated from Columbia Law School.

Each year at Columbia the Ordronneaux Prize is awarded to the third-year law student whose scholastic standing has been best throughout the entire course, and, oddly enough, it was awarded in the spring of 1912 before the final marks were all in. Furthermore, it was awarded *jointly* to two students—Harold Medina and Jerome Michael. Michael, incidentally, had earlier been made note editor of the *Columbia Law Review*, the position that Harold Medina had hoped—had even expected—to attain, and there was no question that he also deserved the honor he now shared with Medina. Medina, in fact, considered himself fortunate even to be sharing the Ordronneaux Prize, for he had the greatest respect for Michael's ability, and *this* time, at least, he did not stand second.

Up to now, both Medina and Michael had earned A's in every course they had taken, and at the beginning of their last term they had each signed up, along with their other courses, for a one-hour-a-week course on trial evidence given by Goldthwaite H. Dorr. The course was not essential, and Medina, who had enough points to graduate without adding the credits he would obtain for this minor course, was tempted to drop it. He did not do so, however, and attended class regularly throughout the term. As the term ended, and he took his final examinations, he was gratified to learn that his marks were again all A's, except in this inconsequential course on trial evidence. Mr. Dorr had decided not to give any examination, but had merely based the marks he gave on his students' classroom work, and to Harold Medina's enormous disappointment, he was given a B.

The Ordronneaux Prize, of course, had already been awarded, and this contretemps would have no effect upon it. Nevertheless, Medina's commendable and unbroken series of A's had been shattered by that B, given in an unimportant and quite unnecessary course. It not only hurt his pride, but it also offended his sense of justice, for he firmly believed that he had done at least as well in the course as several to whom Mr. Dorr had given A's. Nor could he help wondering what

Jerome Michael would now think about that shared Ordronneaux Prize.

It was not until fifteen years later that Medina learned that this prize had been fairly shared after all. It was only then, when Michael, having served for a time as Special Assistant to the United States Attorney General, returned to Columbia to become a professor of law, that he thought to mention to Harold Medina that he, too, had been given a B in that course under Mr. Dorr.

Medina graduated from Columbia in the spring of 1912. He had worked hard and had had his share of disappointments, but he was far more confident and more at ease in his associations than he had been when he graduated from Princeton. At Columbia he had undergone no such period of depression as he had known at Princeton, and from the first he had been accepted by his fellows. But now his period of scholastic preparation was behind him, and he was faced with the task of putting to use what he had learned.

It was still widely customary for such young attorneys to go to work as law clerks for established law firms, and to be paid either nothing at all or as little, perhaps, as six or eight dollars a week. It was understood, of course, that such pay was only a token wage for any person of training and ability. Such arrangements were an outgrowth or a survival of the earlier apprentice system under which young men acquired their legal education by "reading law" in the offices of practicing attorneys, performing minor duties and even paying for the privilege. All this was breaking down, and salaries of reasonable consequence were sometimes being offered law graduates whose scholastic standing had been especially good. It is an odd fact, however, that Harold Medina, despite his record at Columbia, made no attempt to get one of these well-paying jobs. Here is further evidence that he has always combined a certain lack of confidence with his assertiveness, and has always been somewhat strangely diffident despite his bluster.

"Even today," he admitted after he had been appointed to the Court of Appeals, "I still can't get away from feeling that some day folks are going to find out that I don't know half as much as they think I do."

Throughout his final year at Columbia both Medina and his wife had been regularly attending St. Luke's Episcopal Church, and Mrs. Medina, at meetings of the Ladies Auxiliary, came to know a lady much older than herself, Mrs. H. Crosswell Tuttle. The bride, of course, was not averse to telling how wonderful her husband was, and Mrs. Tuttle, in turn, found it easy to enlarge upon her son. That both these subjects of conversation were attorneys—one about to graduate from Columbia and the other a member of the law firm of Davies, Auerbach & Cornell—soon became evident, and ultimately Mrs. Tuttle's son Charles and his wife were invited to dinner at the Medina apartment. The invitation was accepted and a job for Harold Medina was the result—a job with the firm of Davies, Auerbach & Cornell. He was to be a law clerk, and was to be paid eight dollars a week!

It was in June, 1912, that he went to work at that new job in the firm's offices at 34 Nassau Street, far down toward the tip of Manhattan Island. He was filled with ambition, of course, but his enthusiasm was especially concerned with trusts and estates, with wills and future interests in property. He had studied these subjects under Professor Nathan Abbott, of whom he was particularly fond, and this field appealed to him so greatly that he readily imagined himself as ultimately becoming a great conveyancer, an expert in matters having to do with deeds and leases, with wills and trusts, and future interests in property of every kind. He recognized the importance of trial lawyers, of course, but the idea that he himself was to develop into an especially successful one was far from his thoughts in those days.

"I am persuaded that a man is not the best judge of his own capabilities," he once remarked in discussing his early attitude toward the law. "But the world, I believe, is apt to shake a man down into about the position in which he belongs."

He knew, of course, when he first went to work for Davies, Auerbach & Cornell, that he would have little opportunity, for some time at least, to perform any but minor tasks. Still, he had been a person of some consequence in his class at Columbia, and he was not prepared to be received as he was when he went to work on that new job.

"I walked into that law office in June," he once told me, "and it was a full week before anybody said a word to me. There was a receptionist, and he told me where to sit, but otherwise no one even seemed to look at me. Odds and ends began to come to me by degrees, of course, and finally I was set to looking up the law. In six months or so I began to act as Mr. Tuttle's assistant, but in the meantime I spent most of my time looking up the law and finding cases."

There were a dozen or so other clerks in the office, and all of them—Medina included, ultimately—were kept fairly busy getting the information the members of the firm required. Altogether there were ten or a dozen partners in the firm, but for the most part the requests they made for information were less clear than they might have been. Demands were forever being made that something or other be looked up, but ordinarily so little was done to give any background to these demands that it was impossible to guess just what was wanted. Medina was usually insistent enough to get some idea of what was required before going to work, and so he saved himself much aimless, fruitless labor. He soon learned, too, that the same requests—or closely related ones—were often repeated, so he began to file away what he learned in these searches and so had it readily availabe for future use.

Mr. Joseph S. Auerbach, one of the senior members of the firm, was especially given to asking the same questions over and over. Every few weeks he would again demand information that had already been found for him, and Medina, with his card-index system, was often able to reply almost at once.

"That fellow Medina," Mr. Auerbach once remarked to an associate, "finds things so fast that I don't know how he does it. He's a perfect genius."

The "perfect genius" was forever begging for something else to do, especially something, no matter how small, that would give him an opportunity to appear in court. His eagerness and impatience came to be one of the office jokes.

On one occasion Roswell H. King, the managing clerk, called him in. "Look here, Medina," he began. "We've got a motion coming up in Municipal Court next week. You take it and handle it."

It was a landlord-tenant matter in which Davies, Auerbach & Cornell represented the landlord, to whom some rent was due, and the problem at the moment had to do with a motion, which had been made by the lawyer for the tenant, to vacate the service of the summons.

In those days, when an action was to be started in Municipal Court, it was necessary to go to the clerk for a summons. Then, the summons having been issued, it was necessary "to make the service"—that is, to hand it to the defendant—within a certain number of days. If, within that time, it could not be served, it was possible, if the request was made before "the return day," to get an "alias summons" which, in effect, extended the time. In this case, however, the managing clerk, who had obtained the summons, had neglected to ask for the alias summons within the stated period.

With the matter in his hands, Medina promptly looked up the law and learned that his opponent was entirely right in applying "to vacate"—that is, to annul—the summons. It was perfectly clear that "where there is a gap in the aliases, the service is void." But it also began to be clear that the office knew nothing could be done, and that a joke was being played on the new clerk. Still, the time came to go to court, and there was nothing to do but go. As luck would have it, the attorney who had made the motion, instead of merely calling the judge's attention to the technical point upon which his motion rested, launched into a furious criticism of the firm of Davies, Auerbach & Cornell. He even insisted that they were attempting "to commit a fraud on the court"—that they must know the situation as well as he.

Medina, who was in no position to argue very effectively for a decision in his favor, naturally felt called upon to defend the reputation of the firm, and in doing so said very little indeed about the matter at issue. And the result was that the judge—though for what reason did not appear—actually denied the motion that was before him, though Medina had not seriously attempted to attack it.

The office was almost openly chuckling over their joke when Medina returned. He carefully refrained from making any report, however, until he was asked about the outcome of his first appearance in court.

"What happened, Medina?" Mr. King asked.

"Oh," Medina replied carelessly, as if the outcome had been only what should have been expected, "motion denied."

There was more to the matter, of course. The opposing lawyer called up to say that he was going to appeal. Medina, in turn, entered judgment against his opponent's client for the rent. Next, the opposing lawyer served notice of appeal to the Appellate Term of the Supreme Court which, in New York, hears appeals from the Municipal Court. He failed to remember, however, that no appeal from an interlocutory order of the Municipal Court is possible without first obtaining permission to appeal, which he had neglected to do. Medina waited, therefore, until it was too late for the request to be made, and then, in his turn, made a motion to dismiss the appeal, which was granted.

The whole affair was relatively minor. Nevertheless, it accomplished two results. First, the client collected the money that was due him, and second, the office learned that the new clerk had more than average understanding of the law. Even Mr. Julien T. Davies, the very "tough" head of the firm, of whom everyone was frightened, sent for the new young man.

"'Medina," he remarked. "I've just heard about this case you won in the Appellate Term. That's good work!"

"The only job I ever had was with that firm," Judge Medina once remarked, "and I think those were the happiest days of my life. I was working hard and getting nothing much for it, but I liked it and, in addition, I had no responsibilities of consequence."

Medina's eight dollars a week had to be supplemented somehow, and the young lawyer consequently obtained permission to handle cases of his own. Such matters as came to him were minor and the fees were small. His first case had to be argued in the Appellate Division, and the fee he received was twenty-five dollars. He represented the widow of Caspar B. Ughetta, a relative of Pompeo Maresi, with whom he had roomed at Princeton, and he went to much work to prepare himself adequately. In court, however, he had no sooner begun his presentation—had spoken only two or three sentences—when the presiding judge growled something at him. Medina failed to understand what had been said and could not imagine. The judge's voice had seemed to be little more than a mumble to the nervous young lawyer. It frightened him—frightened him so much that he forgot everything he had intended to say, and he abruptly sat down. And yet he won that case. He never succeeded in offering any argument at all, but the brief he had submitted was entirely adequate.

Beginners are seldom given much legal work of consequence, and that was true of Harold Medina. Little by little, additional cases came to him, but all of them were small, and in referring to this period in his career he admits that he was just "a typical little guy trying to get on." His first jury trial in the Supreme Court, however, was not long in coming, and it had to do with a matter of some consequence.

H. Gray Treadwell, a former classmate at Princeton, recommended Medina to a Mrs. Mary Middleton, who had been injured while riding on the open top of a Fifth Avenue bus in New York. The bus, having been deflected from its regular route by a parade, passed under the old elevated railroad structure at 57th Street and Ninth Avenue, and there, because of some inequality in the pavement, was jolted so heavily that Mrs. Middleton's head struck the steel framework. Medina was retained to represent her and here, at last, he had an important case to handle.

In getting ready for the trial he especially prepared what he believed to be an important series of hypothetical questions that he intended to ask a doctor who was to be put on the stand as an expert witness. He was inexperienced in such cases, of course, and was now before the Supreme Court for the very first time. He knew the technicalities of the law and he understood court procedure, but he was naturally ill at ease. He later came to be completely at home in court, able to think clearly on his feet, to present his arguments and to time his questions almost perfectly, and to keep every rule in mind. But here, with an important expert witness on the stand, something went very wrong.

On no part of his preparation had he worked harder than on the questions he planned to ask the witness. They were important, and were to play what might be the decisive part in his whole presentation. His opponent, however, objected to every single question he attempted to ask, and for some reason that he simply could not understand, the judge sustained the objections.

Over and over again he tried, but always he came up against those reiterated objections, and finally he turned to the judge. He pointed out that he had worked out those questions carefully, that they were important to his client's case. And he added that he did not know the grounds on which his opponent's constant objections were being sustained.

"Well, who is this man?" the judge demanded, pointing to the witness.

The jury laughed, and Medina suddenly realized that in his eagerness to get to the all-important questions he had completely forgotten to "qualify" the doctor as an expert witness —to ask the questions that would establish this man's qualifications to answer the hypothetical questions necessary to establish by medical proof the extent and duration of the injuries.

The matter was set straight and the witness was now properly qualified. Medina's case, however, had been immensely weakened by that fiasco, and he was unable to gain what he had lost. The jury brought in a verdict for the bus company.

The disappointed young attorney promptly made a motion to set aside the verdict and for a new trial on the ground that the judge had refused to instruct the jury in accordance with certain written requests, Medina having taken proper exceptions to the judge's refusal to charge. He felt that this motion might be granted.

Now, however, Mr. Julien T. Davies, Jr., who, as well as his father, was a member of the firm of Davies, Auerbach & Cornell, called Medina in. Mrs. Middleton, it appeared, had called and said that young Mr. Medina had proved to be incompetent—had said, too, that she wished to have him discharged.

The young lawyer, quite naturally, was stunned. He had already been sharply critical of himself, and had made preparations to do what he could to carry the matter to a successful conclusion. Furthermore, he did not feel that he was in any way responsible to Davies, Auerbach & Cornell in the matter. It was not their case.

He admitted his error in failing to qualify his witness, but he pointed out that his motion for a new trial seemed likely to be granted. And he added that it was his case anyway. So he was not discharged as Mrs. Middleton's lawyer, and the re-trial was granted. It soon began to be clear, too, that his case was a strong one, for it was settled out of court, and eighteen hundred dollars was paid by the bus company.

For a year or so after going to work for Davies, Auerbach & Cornell, Medina spent most of his time looking up the law, but little by little, members of the firm set him to writing memoranda or briefs for submission to the court. These had to be especially well done when they were called for by Mr. Tuttle, who, being something of a perfectionist, not infrequently consigned Medina's efforts to the wastebasket and wrote what he needed himself. Other lawyers in the firm were usually less difficult to please, but Mr. Tuttle, a very able lawyer of wide experience, more and more came to call on Medina for such work, and the training that resulted was of the best.

The year that followed the young lawyer's graduation from Columbia was not especially productive when measured in terms of income. His expenses, too, had very definitely increased. He and his wife still occupied the same apartment. Their tastes remained as modest as before. Their social life was still as restricted as it had been from the time of their marriage. Their first son, however, Harold, Junior, had been born on October 19, 1912, and the small salary that was paid by Davies, Auerbach & Cornell more than ever needed to be supplemented.

The New York State Board of Law Examiners in those days held examinations for prospective members of the bar four times a year—in January, April, June, and October. Later the January examinations were eliminated and the April ones were advanced to March; but then, as now, it was necessary to pass "the bar examinations" before being admitted to practice, and these tests were much more than mere formalities. A large proportion of the applicants—even many who had graduated from the best law schools—failed not only in the first attempt, but sometimes in later ones as well, and several "cram courses" were being given with the idea of helping prospective lawyers to pass this vital test. The best of these, probably, was one that was being given by Professor Walsh and Professor Bacon of the New York University Law School, but none attracted large numbers of students, and each time the bar examinations were given many who took them failed to pass.

It was this situation that caught Harold Medina's attention. He had passed the bar examinations even before he had graduated from Columbia, and had had no difficulty in doing so. It was clear, however, that a good many others found the examinations very difficult, and that their study of the law, while usually giving them most of the information they required, often left them inadequately prepared for this particular test. What was needed—or so it seemed to Harold Medina—was a bit of special tutoring which, given under more than ordinary pressure and just prior to the time the bar examinations were to be taken, would give the applicants the additional push that would make it possible for them to pass. This was exactly what the other courses were trying to do, but surely it could be done better. At any rate, it was worth trying. Medina had been successful as a tutor both at Princeton and at Columbia, and it seemed reasonable to suppose that he could do at least as well in this new field.

The average young lawyer, and especially one only a year out of school, might very well have hesitated to suggest that he was capable of teaching, or even adequately reviewing, not only all of substantive law, but procedure and evidence as well. But here again Harold Medina's characteristic assurance was uppermost, and he began to work out plans for the course he had in mind without so much as giving a thought to his presumption.

It was his idea to devote four or five weeks to each course, and because he was already busy all day the classes would have to be given in the evening. He had no reputation as an expert in such matters. He could not even claim to be a lawyer of real consequence. Still, he had had an excellent record at Columbia and, perhaps on that account, was able, in December, 1913, to get together a class of five young men who had already failed to pass the bar examinations but who were now planning to take those scheduled for the following month.

From the very first Medina found this new task difficult. He worked all day at the offices of Davies, Auerbach & Cornell. Then, at 5:30, he went to 96 Wall Street where his father, who was head of the J. A. Medina Company, had given permission for the class to be held in his private office. There the group went over their scheduled work until 7 or 7:30, when Medina himself hurried home to dinner, after which he found it necessary to study until very late in preparation for the next evening's lecture.

There were many problems to be solved in establishing that course, but the fee to be charged was not one of them. The other courses that had been established had already set a fee of thirty-five dollars, and Medina felt compelled to follow their example. That first group, consequently, brought in a total of one hundred and seventy-five dollars, from which, fortunately, few expenses had to be deducted. His father's private office cost him nothing, and as yet he had not prepared, or even evolved, the special material he later mimeographed, and, later still, printed for the use of the class. But what proved to be more important than the income he received from that first group with the fact that two of those who had come to him passed the examinations, and all of them felt that what he gave them was worth their time and money. It was because of this that eighteen students came to him in March, 1914, when his next "cram course" opened.

So large a group proved a bit too much for the older Medina's private office, and there was little money available to pay for a place in which to give the course. But now Mr. Tuttle, with whom Harold Medina was working more and more closely, offered to let the class meet, and without charge, in Davies, Auerbach & Cornell's committee room.

Eighteen students at thirty-five dollars each, it should be noted, brought Harold Medina a very tidy sum. Furthermore, the expenses of the course had still been held to a minimum, and most of that six hundred and thirty dollars remained to his credit. But once again, and even more important, a still larger class before long began to register for the course that was scheduled to be given two months later.

Medina, at the age of twenty-five, had turned necessity into opportunity and, without realizing it at the time, had laid the foundation for the fortune he was somewhat rapidly to create.

"It was like stumbling on a brick of solid gold," he once told me in an uninhibited moment. "It soon became apparent that I had a genius for this kind of thing. I had a gift for getting such stuff over, especially procedure."

How much the success of the bar examination course was due to Harold Medina's "genius" and how much to plain hard work, it is impossible now to tell, but Harold Medina is especially characterized, when his interest is aroused, by energy and effective action. He has a talent for application and hard work. Work is of no interest to him merely because it is work. The end to be attained must capture his attention, must serve his purpose, must intrigue his interest. Otherwise he is just as capable of avoiding the work that would be entailed as he is of welcoming it when his interest is aroused.

All this undoubtedly had its application to the bar examination course. He had to make more money, and from the first the course proved it could be profitable. Always, deeply imbedded in his nature, Medina has had a desire to instruct. Even as a student he had turned to tutoring. As a lawyer he later developed a you-just-listen-and-I'll-tell-you manner which frequently led him to be something of a teacher even in court. Nor has he lost that attitude as his years have increased. He is far mellower than he was as a younger man, but he nevertheless sometimes seems to be most in character when he is able to seize some opening to be the schoolteacher even on the bench, a tendency that has led some observers to say that he talks too much.

The bar examination course served Harold Medina's practical as well as his psychological needs. At the office of Davies, Auerbach & Cornell he was being paid only a small salary, but the course, even in the first year of its existence, gave him an income of modest consequence which later was to grow enormously.

At Davies, Auerbach & Cornell he was credited with being little more than a tyro, but in the bar examination course he stood before his classes as teacher, director, expert.

From the very first he made good with those who took his course, though he could be sharp and was not invariably thoughtful of tender feelings. The more able the student, it would seem, the better his opinion was likely to be of Harold Medina. No doubt that was largely due to the fact that mediocrity and the kind of inattention that often accompanies mediocrity were apt to arouse his indignation and his sharpest comments. But even some who felt the sting of his remarks are willing yet to credit him with unusual ability at imparting knowledge. This belief was widespread, too. Mere word of mouth advertising was what caused the early increases in the number of those who came to him. His first class of five young men was succeeded three months later by a class of eighteen, and two months after that by a class of forty-six. Ninety-two attended his classes during the first year of their existence, 228 registered the second year, and generally a very healthy majority of them passed. From then on for fifteen years, each year's total usually surpassed that of the year before, and before the course ultimately came to an end under the impact of World War II and Harold Medina's own growing responsibilities in other fields, most of the lawyers practicing in the State of New York, and many who practiced elsewhere, had come at some time or another under his tutelage.

At no time during the twenty-nine-year existence of the bar

examination course did Harold Medina ever give it his full time. His law practice took more and more of his attention. He began the course by giving all the lectures himself and by keeping all the business and scholastic records as well. Little by little, he began to prepare written material for the use of the students, and in order to be able to distribute this at the least possible cost to himself, he turned once more to his typewriter and his mimeograph.

During the summer of 1913, when the first bar examination course was no more than an idea that might or might not develop further, Medina rented a house at 42 Washington Terrace, East Orange, New Jersey. Mrs. Medina was as willing as he that a house should be rented—more willing, perhaps—but she had no part in its selection. She and Harold, junior, were spending the summer at Bayhead, New Jersey, when her husband found the house and signed the lease, and she had no knowledge of it except what he told her. Even when she first saw it she was not conscious of its shortcomings, for it was roomy, attractive, and surrounded by a yard that seemed unusually spacious after the limitations of an apartment. With the coming of winter, however, that somewhat pretentious house began to appear in a much less favorable light. There was no lack of space, but it was all but impossible to keep the house comfortably heated. It was as cold and as uncomfortable as the proverbial barn; and the attic which was exceptionally roomy and had appeared in midsummer to be an excellent spot in which to set up the mimeograph, turned out to be an utterly frigid place in which to work.

Throughout that winter and the next, as Harold Medina added to the written material he was preparing for his bar examination course, he typed out his original copy, cut his stencils, and, amid the discomforts of that too-airy attic, operated his mimeograph on many a cold, late winter evening.

In its early phases the bar examination course consisted of twenty-two lectures, given, for the most part, one a day at about 5:30, and lasting for an hour and a half or thereabouts. Later the course grew to thirty-one lectures, and often the period was longer than an hour and a half, but rarely was it ever shorter than that. From the first, each lecture was given either without any notes at all, or with a minimum of such reference matter. It was apparently instinctive with Harold Medina to steer clear of notes, as if he subconsciously understood their deadening effect on almost any presentation. It meant much greater care in preparation, and a better understanding of the subject under discussion was required of the lecturer. Furthermore, this absence of notes gave him added authority in the eyes of his listeners, and, because it forced him to speak extemporaneously, it developed in him a real ability to take advantage of such opportunities as gave color and interest to his talks.

Harold Medina is a tense, high-pressure worker, and much nervous energy goes into any lecture that he gives. This tenseness could easily make his presentations difficult to grasp—devoid of lightness—and the seriousness with which he often approaches a subject could easily weigh it down. Fortunately, however, he has a well-developed sense of humor, a human touch, a down-to-earth simplicity, and a sense of the dramatic that adds greatly to the interest and the human quality of what he has to say.

Along with all his bar examination course lectures there was an executive job to do. As the course expanded it became necessary to hire someone to enroll the students, to take the money, to keep the records, even to give a few of the lectures. Medina did all that alone at first, and never, throughout the existence of the course, left it more than partially in other hands but it gave him very little spare time. All this work, in addition to that required of him at Davies, Auerbach &

Cornell, and that necessitated by such private practice as he had, resulted in an almost utter lack of social life. "I don't see how my wife went through those first ten or fifteen years," he once remarked in reference to their early married life.

Certainly both he and she were largely cut off from ordinary social activities, and there was little opportunity for diversions or relaxations. Nevertheless, his willingness to work so constantly goes far to explain his success.

When he first began work on the bar examination course he probably appeared to be no more than another aspirant in a field that offered only limited opportunities at best. Late in 1914, however, when Medina was about to launch the fourth and last class of his first year, Professor Walsh, who was by far the most important of his competitors, decided to capitulate. He had been able to attract only eight students for his own October course, and rather than carry on what must have seemed to him an unpromising activity he acknowledged his inability to continue and very considerately sent his eight students to Harold Medina, thus bringing to ninety-two the number who attended the young man's new course during its first year.

Mrs. Medina, following the birth of Harold, junior, in the autumn of 1912, had suffered an attack of puerperal fever, and for a time her life had been in danger. Her doctor was quite properly concerned, and told Medina that he wished to consult a specialist, a certain Dr. Cregin. Medina was quick to approve and Cregin was called. When he arrived, he insisted on being paid twenty-five dollars before he would even look at the patient. Medina, not having that much in the apartment at the time, had to hurry around the neighborhood in order to raise it. It was paid over presently, and the specialist finally entered the sickroom.

When he emerged a few minutes later, he was clearly lacking in optimism. Yes, he admitted, her condition was serious. Quite serious, in fact. She might die. No. There was very little that could be done. Nothing, really. Nothing but wait. That was all.

It was a badly harassed Harold Medina who awaited the outcome, but fortunately his wife recovered, though for a time her health remained far from good. This period of heavy anxiety on his wife's account had been added to Harold Medina's financial difficulties, but with the completion of the October course in 1914, it began to be apparent that he was getting on his financial feet.

Harold Medina's first little class had been held in his father's private office, and his second in the committee room at Davies, Auerbach & Cornell. His third class had outgrown even these quarters, and in looking about for a place in which it could meet, he rented a street-floor lecture room at the American Institute of Banking which was then located at 34th Street and Lexington Avenue. The room was adequate for his purposes, but it was somewhat less than ideal, for its large windows looked out onto Lexington Avenue, and during the course of every lecture street urchins of the neighborhood were forever climbing up and peeking in.

The bar examination course classes held in June were usually best attended, but as autumn approached in 1915, it began to appear that the October class that year would also do well. That fact was welcome, too, for on their fourth wedding anniversary, June 6, 1915, a second son, Standish Forde, had been born to Harold and Ethel Medina.

The October course of the year before had attracted only twenty-three students. Now, in September, registration for the October class was almost three times as large as that of 1914. It was on a September Sunday evening, about the time this fact was becoming evident, that the phone rang in Medina's East Orange home, and Harold Medina answered.

It was Harlan Fiske Stone who was calling—Dean Stone of the Columbia University Law School—and he wasted no time about what he had to say.

"How would you like to teach in the Law School?" he asked.

"When do I begin?" asked Medina in reply.

"Tomorrow morning."

"What's my subject?"

"Domestic Relations."

"Where do I get the books?"

Dean Stone replied with a minimum of detail, and added one or two more bits of information. He had called this late, he explained, because Professor Nathan Abbott had been taken ill—might not be able to return.

"I'll be there," Medina replied.

He was still employed by Davies, Auerbach & Cornell, and his two-year-old bar examination course was expanding far beyond his expectations. Already he was busy during almost every waking moment, and his working day ordinarily extended from early morning until late at night. Nevertheless, he had no doubt about the advisability of seizing this new opening. He accepted it with no more than a moment's thought, but that is characteristic of Harold Medina. Throughout his career his ability to make quick decisions has served him well. And it did in this case.

No sharp line can be found to mark the end of his period of preparation and the beginning of his period of accomplishments. Nevertheless, that Sunday evening telephone conversation with Dean Stone opened a new chapter in Harold Medina's life. To that extent, at least, it marked a new beginning.

4

FOUNDATION FOR SUCCESS

BY THE TIME HAROLD MEDINA BEGAN TEACHING AT COLUMBIA his economic position had become a good deal easier. From the day his father had advanced the fifteen hundred dollars that made his marriage and his final year at law school possible, he had refused to ask for any further help, but at times it had not been easy for him to meet all his obligations. Davies, Auerbach & Cornell had increased his pay from eight to thirty dollars a week, and the law business he had been able to pick up personally had increased as well, but his income was still small. As a matter of fact, his income from the practice of law was to remain limited for some years to come. It was the bar examination course that started him financially on his way.

Each summer his wife had gone with their son to the country, where Medina joined them each week-end. At first they stayed at Bayhead, New Jersey, and in Greenwich, Connecticut, but in 1914 they went to Hampton Inn, at Westhampton Beach, Long Island. Harold Medina joined them not only for week-ends that year but for a full two weeks as well, and in 1916, now with two children, they chose the Apaucuck Point House where Medina, as a boy, had so annoyed his elders by climbing to the top of the windmill and to the roof.

When he had been with Davies, Auerbach & Cornell only

a year or two, and before his income had progressed beyond the precarious stage, some of Medina's fellow law clerks began buying stocks on margin. None of them had much to invest, and their knowledge of the market was limited, but for a time they seemed to be getting ahead, and Medina grew interested. The Jewel Tea Company somehow caught his attention and when he presently got around to taking a flier, it was a hundred shares of stock in that company that he bought. All he paid down was $150, and the stock advanced—for a time—but before long it started down. There was no doubt in the mind of the youthful investor that it would ultimately regain all it was losing, and he met several demands for more margin. Ultimately, however, he went to his father and borrowed eight thousand dollars to pay for the stock.

From that point on, of course, there were no further demands for margin, but the stock stubbornly continued to go down. What point it ultimately reached in its decline Judge Medina does not recall. Perhaps he never knew. He sold out at twenty-two, and what he remembers most vividly is the length of time it took him to pay back that borrowed money.

"I never did such a thing again," he once told me, "and I think my father loaned me that money in order to teach me a lesson. He never said a word, even when I was paying it back. Never a one. He was a very wise man, and merely accepted my payments as a matter of course."

That loan had not yet been paid off when he first began teaching at Columbia. The worst of his financial struggle was over, and he was justifiably confident, but he kept such matters to himself. It has never been his practice to discuss finances even with his wife. He did not do so when his income was limited, and he held to the idea when his finances began to improve. He felt that so long as he provided for his family, the rest should be only his business. Even to this day he believes that the head of a family is the one who should be essentially responsible for saving and for finances, and, surprisingly, his wife agrees with this idea.

During these early years, and for many years still to come, most of the fun he had, and most of the family life, was during the summer holidays. "The rest of the time I was working," he explains, and that is almost literally true.

The family did not travel, and their social life was limited. They bought an automobile—a Maxwell—while they lived in East Orange, and regularly went riding on Sundays, though this was a pastime that sometimes bordered on the adventurous. Tires, in those days, were not entirely to be trusted. Batteries often went dead. Motors, which had to be cranked by hand, often backfired, and rides were not infrequently prolonged by difficulties such as are now unknown. It was always possible to have an arm broken by a backfiring car, and on one occasion the crank, torn from Medina's hand by a backfire, struck him painfully on the jaw.

As a boy Medina had learned a lesson that his father had unintentionally taught, and even during the difficult days of his early married life he remembered it.

"When I was about nine or ten," the Judge once told me, "I saw that my father worried over a lot of things he couldn't do anything about, and I decided not to do that. And I never have."

This youthful decision has undoubtedly helped him in periods of stress, but another idea, which he evolved not so many years later, proved helpful also. While he was in college he began to keep track of his financial condition, and made it a habit, long before he read Samuel Pepys' diaries, to do as Pepys did. On January 1 of each year he sat down to determine just what his financial position was.

Harold Medina has never permitted his life to develop aimlessly. He has taken advantage of many unexpected developments, but his success has been largely the result of plan.

The offices of Davies, Auerbach & Cornell, where Medina was employed for the first five years after his graduation from Columbia, occupied two floors of a portion of the Mutual Life Building. The two floors were connected by their own private stairway, and were laid out around the large committee room that was centrally located on the lower of these two floors and the equally large library that was similarly located on the floor above. A skylight served, in the absence of windows, to light the library and, by way of a railed-in "well" that lay directly beneath it in the center of the library floor, even half-heartedly to light the committee room below. It was around these two big central rooms that the private offices were arranged, and in the library, against the railing on three sides of the central well, were the tables for those who were busy with the office's almost constant reference work.

It was in this library, for some months after he first arrived, and along with the other clerks, that broad-shouldered, mustached, twenty-four-year-old Harold Medina did most of the work he was called on to perform. With thirty or forty reference books arranged on the angled racks at the back of one of these tables, and with others stacked at his elbow or open before him, he studied cases or located references in his efforts to get together the information for which the firm's many partners were forever asking. Little by little, as the quality of his work improved, he came especially to be Mr. Tuttle's own particular assistant. He began to accompany that gentleman to court, doing little at first beyond sharpening pencils and putting in phone calls, but before long he began to play a somewhat more important part, even handling an occasional small case for the office on his own responsibility.

From the time he came to be accepted by the firm as a really useful member of the organization, Harold Medina was never at a loss for work. Even his own personal cases were increasing in number, and in addition, he had his classes at Columbia and the recurrent work of the bar examination course.

The economic developments of the preceding twenty years had changed under the impact of World War I. The entrance of the United States into the war in 1917, too, had furthered these changes, though that apparently did little at the time to affect Harold Medina's career. By then he had been with Davies, Auerbach & Cornell for five years. He was no longer a beginner, and was not interested in remaining indefinitely in a minor capacity with the firm. A partnership, no doubt, would some time have been forthcoming, but Harold Medina has never been one to interest himself in a "some time" future. He understood that difficulties lay in the way of establishing an independent law practice of consequence. Nevertheless, a few minor matters were already falling to him, and with his bar examination course as a trustworthy anchor to windward, he felt confident that the time had come to open an office of his own. The draft of World War I went into effect in 1917, but with a wife and two children Medina was exempt, even without considering the still occasionally troublesome back injury he had suffered during his freshman year at Princeton. As 1917 came to an end, therefore, he quit his job at Davies, Auerbach & Cornell, and, on January 1, 1918, opened his own office.

Harold Medina's first office was only a single room in a small suite on the seventh floor of the Mutual Life Building, next door to the much more extensive offices of Davies, Auerbach & Cornell. This modest suite, which consisted of one large room and two small ones, was occupied by another lawyer, Elbridge L. Adams, and the large room was Mr. Adams' own private office. It was one of the two smaller rooms that Medina rented, and he arranged for his stenographer to share the third room with Mr. Adams' stenographer who was already established there. He also hired as a law clerk a young man who had attended one of his classes at Columbia. This young man, Eugene A. Sherpick, had since graduated, passed his bar examinations, and gone to the firm of Cadwalader, Wickersham & Taft as a law clerk. He had not been there long when he began to realize that so dignified and conservative a firm was not likely to offer such opportunities as he wanted for really rapid advancement. When Harold Medina approached him, and especially when he tentatively agreed to a partnership in the reasonably near future, Sherpick accepted.

The final phases of World War I were about to begin in Europe, and conditions hardly favored any really rapid development of a new law practice. The recently opened office was able to do no better than to struggle along on very small pickings. Almost at once, however, Harold Medina was chosen to serve as chairman of Legal Advisory Board Number 141, which formed a part of a little publicized but very important wartime activity especially set up to make certain that draftees and others who had claims for exemption could without cost to themselves get proper advice as to their legal rights. Such boards were widely established, and their members served for more than a year, entirely without pay and often working late night after night after having been busy with their normal occupations all day long.

There were fifteen or twenty lawyers on the board of which Medina was made chairman, and all of them were older than he. Nevertheless, they served willingly and efficiently under his direction, groups of them meeting almost every night in a room that was assigned to them in one of the buildings of City College near Convent Avenue at 137th Street. Charles

Evans Hughes was an important figure in organizing this work, and as he knew of Medina's work at Columbia it seems likely that it was he who suggested the young lawyer for the chairmanship to which he was assigned.

At the time Medina began teaching Domestic Relations at Columbia University Law School, he and his wife and children were still living in East Orange. But with three classes a week, each at 9 in the morning, it soon began to be evident that they would have to move back to the city. It was not that the problem of commuting was so very difficult; many others went even farther every day and thought little of it. Medina, however, was finding it necessary to work at the Columbia Law Library until midnight or even later each time a class was in prospect for the following morning. Busy at the office, he could not do such work during the day, and it was essential that he prepare each lecture with the greatest care. After working so late, it was hardly wise to attempt to go home to East Orange for a few hours sleep before catching an early train back to New York in the morning. Throughout the autumn of 1915 and on into the winter, he made it a practice, whenever he worked so late, to go to Hotel Therese at Seventh Avenue and 125th Street in the very midst of Harlem, and from that quiet and conservative neighborhood—for Harlem, in those days, had not even begun to undergo the change that has resulted in its present condition—he was able to get to his morning class with a minimum of effort.

Fortunately, it was not necessary to continue this schedule for any extended period. In February, 1916, the Medinas rented a commodious ten-room apartment, for one hundred and twenty-five dollars a month, at 604 Riverside Drive, only a few blocks from the apartment they had occupied when they were first married. It was as well they did, too, for a month before they moved, Professor Henry S. Redfield, who taught

Common Law Pleading at Columbia, was taken sick, and Dean Stone asked Medina to take that course in the spring semester after he had finished the course on Domestic Relations. He accepted, for he had been a good student under the professor whose place he was now being asked to fill, and he still had the notes he had taken in class. Within a month of the time he began to teach that course, however, someone stole those all-important notes. Even with them, Medina had found it necessary to work hard in preparing his lectures for this new course, but, without them, he found the task immensely harder. The subject was technical, and he was attempting to replace a professor of unusual attainments. As a result, though he worked early and late, he was able for a time to do hardly more than keep one step ahead of the class he was teaching.

Despite this pressure, he was beginning to find time for more recreation. Mrs. Medina had a maid and a nurse. The Maxwell car had given way to a Buick, and now and again they found time for an all-day trip in the car. Sundays were usually given over to the boys, who often went on long walks with "Dadoo," or, in winter, were taken out with their sleds.

From the time Medina joined the staff at Columbia, he was successful in his teaching, as is proved by two developments. First, he was asked to teach Code Pleading and Practice, a third year subject, beginning with the autumn term in 1916, and second, having dropped the teaching of his earlier courses, he was made Associate in Law instead of being continued as Lecturer in Law, which, as the Judge now explains, is "the lowest form of academic life in Columbia Law School."

By the time World War I came to an end in the autumn of 1918, Harold Medina's life had taken on the essential pattern it was to follow for something more than two decades. Partly because of force of circumstances, but largely by his own design, he had come to be both a practicing attorney and a teacher, but he still had to prove himself as an attorney of ability and consequence.

The bar examination course had by now completed its fifth year. Because of the war its enrollment had dropped, the four classes of 1918 having attracted only 301 students as against 493 the year before. The coming year, however, was to double the 1918 enrollment, and the years ahead were to multiply it even more—were actually to double it not merely once, but three times; and in one instance, the 1918 attendance was to be multiplied by ten.

It was apparent to everyone that the bar examination course had no such atmosphere about it as that which surrounded the Columbia Law School. It had no collegiate connections of any kind, no institutional background, though those who attended it came to it from many law schools. It was actually nothing more than "the lengthened shadow" of Harold Medina; and though it was growing at such a rate that it was soon to attract many more students each year than attended the much more dignified law school at Columbia, there was always something about it that failed to please the narrowly academic mind.

Dean Stone was not to be influenced by this point of view. The bar examination course, to him, was apparently neither more nor less than it pretended to be: a high-pressure period of preparation so designed as to enable those who took it to face the bar examinations with somewhat greater expectations of success. Certainly he did not permit the course to influence his opinion of Medina as a member of the teaching staff at Columbia, though even he, as well as other members of the faculty, must have been impressed by the fact that the young man was merely a part-time teacher.

No one was more conscious of Harold Medina's part-time status at Columbia than Harold Medina himself. He understood, too, that teachers who had any hope for important advancement had need to do a certain amount of creative work above and beyond merely that which had directly to do with their classes. Already he was carrying a heavy, as well as a varied, load. His law practice, his bar examination course, and his classes at Columbia combined to fill his days to overflowing. In fact, any one of these three tasks was a full time job, though Harold Medina seems never to have concerned himself with any such idea. If a job was to be done, he did it, and if additional jobs of consequence required his attention, he almost always somehow managed to find the necessary time. So, seeing that if his reputation as a teacher was to grow, he must do some creative work in addition to his classroom duties, he unhesitatingly began it. In 1922 he published a book entitled *Pleading and Practice under New Civil Practice Act*, the first of several volumes that came to be of much real service to undergraduates in their study of the law.

This was work of a sort that is readily granted recognition in academic circles, and Dean Stone, perhaps in part as a result of this, came around to see the young Associate in Law.

"Medina," he remarked, "I've recommended you for a seat on the faculty with the title of Associate Professor."

Here, in other words—or so Medina thought—was the accolade, the academic recognition he had so sincerely wished to earn. To say merely that he was pleased is to understate the matter. He was delighted, and naturally assumed that such a recommendation, coming from such a person, would be acted upon favorably by the other members of the faculty. After some delay Stone came to see him again, and this time brought the discouraging news that the faculty had rejected his recommendation.

"They feel," he admitted, "that these bar examination classes of yours are *infra dig.*"

The disappointment Medina felt was no doubt the more marked because he had so confidently assumed that Dean Stone's recommendation would be adopted. It may even be that he had to take himself in hand in order to keep from saying just what he thought about such a point of view. It would have been easy for him to blow up, for such patience as he possesses sometimes seems to be a little more than a veneer, only thinly covering a somewhat tempestuous irritability. He restrained himself, however, and merely thanked the Dean for what he had done.

It is all but impossible to tell Harold Medina's story as a chronological record. He had successfully established his bar examination course by the time he first began to teach at Columbia Law School. He was well established with both of these activities when he began his independent practice of law. On the one hand he was a teacher, and on the other a lawyer, but even his teaching was divided into two such different parts as almost to suggest a kind of antipathy between them. Certainly the academic dignity that surrounded his work at Columbia was little apparent in the classes of the bar examination course; and as the course continued to grow, this difference became more apparent still. Nevertheless, both of these activities were successful. The students at Columbia were largely free to choose their own classes in the law school, and though Harold Medina was a strict disciplinarian and was often quick tempered and sharp in his remarks, the classes he taught were usually very well attended. His bar examination course, too, was attended only by those who wished to profit by it, and their numbers were growing at an ever-increasing rate.

These activities naturally had their effect on Medina's continued development, and undoubtedly had their effect on his ultimate, but more delayed success as a lawyer. His classes at Columbia necessitated the most detailed understanding of the legal subjects he was called upon to teach, and his bar examination classes not only kept his mind constantly refreshed on an infinite variety of matters having to do with the law, but also helped his self-confidence to grow, and even forced him to develop his voice as well. When he began those courses his speaking voice was weak, even a little squeaky, but in time it came to be not only strong and resonant, but resilient as well, thus permitting him to speak for hours at a time, day after day, with no bad effects of consequence. Even to this day his voice is strong and his diaphragm firm because of those years of training.

His career as a practicing attorney developed with less apparent promise. It was almost as if another Harold Medina had taken up the actual practice of law. Young men by hundreds listened as he taught, and an ever greater percentage of those who were beginning the practice of law in New York State had at some time benefited from his courses. But the clients who came to his law office were not numerous, and such cases as he handled were only moderately remunerative. Harold Medina was never one to refuse a minor case if he felt it had merit, and any fee was better than none. Spectacular fees, of course, were welcome, but by their nature they were likely to be rare. In the long run, enough small fees would bring the same result. It might necessitate more work, longer hours, less time at home. But Harold Medina seems never to have been impressed by such thoughts as these. Like his Yucatecan grandfather, he seemed to think that if there was work to do it should be done.

How conscious this attitude may have been, it is difficult to say. Nevertheless, it seems to have been the basis upon which Harold Medina's law practice was originally built. Later his growing reputation brought about a change. Spectacular cases and large fees ultimately came to him, but for some time after he began the independent practice of law he seems to have thought of himself as "just another little guy trying to get on."

Even during his first two years he managed to keep busy, but such practice as he had was very largely "junk"; the fees were small, and often he was not paid at all for what he did. He was still on good terms with Davies, Auerbach & Cornell, and had hoped that they would send him a little business now and then, but they rarely did. Even from the first, however, there was a gradual improvement, and on January 3, 1920, Eugene Sherpick, the law clerk who had come to him from the firm of Cadwalader, Wickersham & Taft, was made a partner and the sign on the door was changed to read "Medina & Sherpick."

By now the office was carrying itself, and when, after another year, Elbridge Adams decided to move to other quarters, the new firm took over the whole suite and hired Leander I. Shelley as a law clerk. Later Shelley became a partner, and later still, left to become assistant counsel for the Port of New York Authority, for which he ultimately became chief counsel.

From the first, Medina saw the advantage of building up his firm "from within." A law office, he insists, is a little like a family. Relationships are intimate—trust and confidence essential. The office's law clerks, if they were carefully chosen and put to work at minor tasks, could be trained in the methods of the office, and tested, before they were given real responsibilities. Later, too, when they came to be members of the firm, they could much more readily be shaken into place.

The early business that came to the office materialized from various sources, but little by little other lawyers began to bring negligence cases to the firm. Almost always these were being handled on a contingent basis by the lawyers who brought them to Medina, and usually they were on appeal. In other words, these cases had been tried, damages had usually been awarded, and it was now necessary, as they came up on appeal, to hold onto the awards if possible. The lawyers who brought these cases in were naturally anxious to keep at a minimum the fees they would be called upon to pay, while Medina saw that such appeals usually required comparatively little time. He was adept at writing briefs and, given the opportunity, could argue three or four such cases in a single day. He never asked for such business, for he considered it unethical to do so, but he knew that if he were to demand large fees when such case came to him, the lawyers would go elsewhere. By permitting them to pay him modestly, he realized he would be given more such cases to handle, and might very well earn more in the long run than higher fees would bring him.

This point of view was not what brought the first of such cases to him. They began slowly and came only at long intervals. When he had demonstrated his ability in this field, they came in greater numbers, and it was only then that he evolved any clear-cut ideas about them. It may even be that the low fees he got were originally due to his own low estimate of his value. Despite the surprising success of his bar examination course, he had no adequate idea of the value of his services as a lawyer. Other lawyers came to him only because they felt he could handle certain matters better than they could themselves; but he apparently had a fairly small opinion of his usefulness, and was so eager to build up his practice that he seems to have considered the size of his fees secondary. He preferred to get the cases at low fees rather than risk losing them. From the first he was reasonably successful, and his appellate work grew. Of the hundreds of cases he argued before the appellate courts, the great majority came to him in the earlier years of his career.

It did not take long for Medina's reputation as a specialist in appellate work to become established. The general public knew nothing about it, but many lawyers did, and a constant stream of appellate work came to him. One well-known trial lawyer, I. Gainsburg by name, was especially given to sending such work to Medina, and many of these cases were more than ordinarily important. Gainsburg would send over a record on some case or other, and Medina, with a minimum of lost time, would prepare the brief, argue the appeal, and send Gainsburg a bill. These cases, unlike many Medina was called upon to handle, were inclined to be substantial, but the bills he sent were never large. Usually they were for $200 or $250. The largest was for only $350. Gainsburg was not given to paying these bills one at a time. He would wait until he had five or six and would then ask Medina to call at his office. With Medina across the desk from him he would go over the bills one by one, and on about half of them he would "shade" the amount a bit.

Medina would sit and listen, invariably nodding in agreement, apparently unable, or unwilling, to argue in his own behalf. But he was also conscious of the fact that the fees, in a way, were less consequential than something else. These cases, for the most part, were important, and his reputation was growing as he handled them.

Harold Medina got ahead because, for one reason, he took everything "that had merit in it." It is his belief that he never once took a case that did not, and he firmly believes that if a case has merit a lawyer should take it. He made no attempt to limit the kinds of cases he would accept. Whether they were clean or dirty did not change his point of view. Matrimonial, negligence, or whatnot, he took them on their merits. Many lawyers are inclined to refuse certain cases for fear their reputations may suffer. Some especially dislike matrimonial cases because of the unreasoning emotion and bitterness—the weeping and genuine deviltry—that are often a part of them. Harold Medina is no fonder of this sort of thing than the next fellow. Nevertheless, when such a case had merit he was willing to accept it, feeling that every conscientious lawyer is duty-bound to do so.

Even during the early years of his independent practice Harold Medina had his fair share of successes, and in his appellate work even more than that. But he had his failures, too, one of which was on the occasion of his first appearance before the Supreme Court of the United States when the firm of Medina & Sherpick was only one year old.

The case had to do with an eight-year-old boy who, in an effort to reach a bird's nest, climbed the steel framework of a bridge that crossed the tracks of the New York, New Haven & Hartford Railroad, and in doing so touched a high-tension wire that was supported by a metal arm of the bridge. The boy was badly injured, and when the case was tried was awarded thirty thousand dollars damages.

During the trial it had been argued that because the framework of the bridge was naturally attractive to boys it should have been guarded so as to keep any boy from climbing it, and damages had been awarded on the theory that the bridge constituted an "attractive nuisance." Furthermore, this contention was upheld by the Circuit Court of Appeals, but the railroad took the case to the United States Supreme Court.

Medina had argued the case before the Circuit Court, and because his contention had been upheld there, he naturally assumed that he had an excellent basis for his argument in what was to be his very first appearance before the Supreme Court.

Any lawyer is eager to do his best before the Supreme Court, but that applies especially to any first appearance there, and Harold Medina was no exception. He even went to Young B. Smith, a Columbia classmate, who was then a professor teaching torts at Columbia Law School, explained that he had the case on a contingent fee basis, and asked Smith to help him. Smith agreed to do so, and together the two prepared a massive brief. They quoted every authority that had a word to say about the theory of "attractive nuisances," and when the time came, Medina made a most vigorous argument before the dignified justices of the Supreme Court. But all to no effect.

What he failed to realize was that his argument should have revolved about a decision that Justice Holmes had written, only a few months before, in a comparable case; he should have tried to show how the case he was arguing differed from that earlier one. But he failed to make this point—or failed to make it strongly enough—so his detailed discussion of "attractive nuisances" was wasted effort. The only question that had to be decided was whether or not the case he was presenting was in any important way distinguishable from the comparable case on which Justice Holmes had so recently written that "there can be no general duty on the part of a land owner to keep his land safe for children, or even free from hidden dangers, if he has not directly or by implication invited or licensed them to come there." With that principle already a part of a previous decision the "attractive nuisance" argument made no impression at all, and the thirty thousand dollar award was reversed in an opinion written by Justice McReynolds.

But that was not all. Harold Medina, "like a damn fool," as he himself once said, had taken the case on a contingent basis, and so he and Young B. Smith lost not only their first case before the Supreme Court, but their time and their expenses as well.

For the most part, as anyone familiar with the profession knows, the practice of law is lacking in color and excitement. Harold Medina, however, has always been inclined to dramatize matters if he could. On one occasion, for instance, when he was in the Appellate Division, representing a client who had a claim against an insurance company, he was able, by a surprising and unexpected demonstration, to turn the opponent's argument to his own advantage.

Medina's client had been the victim of a burglary, which a policy issued by the insurance company was supposed to cover. The burglars had entered through a very small hole that had been cut in the ceiling and the insurance company had based its refusal to pay the claim on the size of that hole. It was their contention that no one could make his way through it, and they insisted that Medina's client had cut the hole in an effort to explain a burglary that had never happened. In order to dramatize this contention the attorney for the insurance company, a small man, had had the hole exactly duplicated in a wooden frame so that he could show the court just how small the opening was, and as he addressed the Court he held the wooden frame up before them.

"Look at me, gentlemen," he said to the five judges. "I am small, but I can't get through this." And he wiggled the wooden frame about his head.

Medina rose from his chair at the counsel table.

"There's nothing to it, Your Honors," he confidently remarked, and with one firm push he slid that wooden frame down over his opponent's head and shoulders. And further argument did not change the matter. In that one moment he had won his case.

On another occasion when "a roaring lion" of an adversary was shouting and gesticulating dramatically in the Court of Appeals, he threw back his hand and struck Medina squarely in the face. It was unintentional, but the blow was so heavy and unexpected that Medina was knocked off his chair beside the counsel table. The overly dramatic attorney was startled, but what apparently quieted him most effectively was the fact that Medina got up without a word and resumed his seat as if being knocked from his chair was a perfectly normal part of the practice of law.

He was not always so calm. While representing the widow of a man who had fallen overboard from a tug and had been drowned, he appeared before the Appellate Division of the First Department. A lower court had awarded damages for the man's death, but the case was on appeal, and Medina had hardly begun what he had to say when one of the five judges—Judge Francis Martin, who later became presiding justice of the Appellate Division—slammed the record down on the bench and remarked to no one in particular, "There's nothing in this case."

The remark was most injudicious, and it made Medina angry.

"Judge Martin," he replied, "you have no right to say there's nothing in this case until you've heard my argument. I think it's outrageous for you to slam the record down and make such a remark."

There is no doubt that he was right, but even he admits that his reply was more strenuous than tactful. Judge Martin was a person before whom he frequently had to appear, and now the judge, as well as Medina, had been antagonized.

The case went on and Medina argued that the captain of the tug had been at fault. The man who had fallen overboard had been swimming strongly until he was drawn under by the propellor when it was reversed; and it was Medina's contention, in view of the captain's experience in such matters, that the jury might well have found that he was negligent and that the judgment of the lower court should be affirmed.

The case, however, went against him. In a decision written *per curiam*—that is, by the court as a whole—the judgment of the lower court was reversed, and Medina was compelled to take the matter to the Court of Appeals. And here he made his point so effectively that the reversal was unanimously reversed and the verdict reinstated. Medina, nevertheless, seems not to have reinstated himself in Judge Martin's good opinion. That jurist, apparently, was never able to forget his dislike of the outspoken lawyer.

It is difficult to appreciate the enormous pressure under which Harold Medina worked throughout the first ten or twelve years of his married life. He was commonly busy for twelve or fourteen hours a day and often worked longer. In 1922, the New York Board of Law Examiners changed the number of bar examinations held each year from four to three, and Medina, whose bar examination course was arranged to precede each of these examinations, changed his schedule accordingly. It did not change the total number of his students. They merely came to him three times a year instead of four. This made each of the classes larger, on the average, but actually reduced his own work as well as his overhead. Instead of scheduling courses for examinations to be held in January, April, June, and October, he was able, from 1922 on, to schedule them so as to precede examinations held only in March, June, and October. His other work was not affected by this change, but his classes at Columbia ran only from September to June, and it took him only a few years to learn that such law business as came to his office during the summer was for the most part inconsequential. It began to be apparent, therefore, that during the summer months, July and August especially, he could easily free himself from much of the load he had been carrying.

It must be remembered that though he was only thirty-five in 1923, Harold Medina had come to be a man of more than ordinary means. He had been practicing law independently for only five years, and his income from that source was still limited. Nevertheless, his practice, together with the salary he received at Columbia, made it possible for him to pay his living expenses. That had been true almost from the time he had left Davies, Auerbach & Cornell. His income from the bar examination course had been in large part clear. There had naturally been many expenses in the operation of the course. He had been compelled to hire assistants, the most important of whom, Milton P. Kupfer and William F. McNulty, were highly useful to him. He had to pay rent, to keep detailed accounts, and to prepare books, advertising, and other printed matter. But both attendance and income had grown enormously. In 1923 alone, 1,295 students paid more than forty thousand dollars in order to attend, and the total amount that had been received from the time the course had been inaugurated was in the neighborhood of two hundred thousand dollars. It had been a good many years since Harold Medina's income had been a hand-to-mouth affair.

The Medinas were now living at 90 Morningside Drive where they had taken an apartment more convenient to Columbia University. They had been married for twelve years, and eleven years had passed since Medina had graduated from Columbia. He was still a young man, but some two years earlier he had suddenly awakened to the realization that he had lost his ability to concentrate, and that tasks he had theretofore accomplished readily enough had suddenly become difficult.

Just what had happened he did not know. For years he had been working almost without pause. Month after month, from early morning until late at night he had been busy, and then, with no warning of which he had been conscious, his ability to drive himself so steadily had weakened. He had not consciously rebelled, but had apparently lost his ability to keep his mind uninterruptedly at any serious task. It had frightened him, and he had talked with Professor Ralph W. Gifford, of Columbia, about it.

"Harold," the professor told him, "you start walking home. It's a long way from 34 Nassau Street to 90 Morningside Drive, so don't hurry. You may not even be able to do it at first. But keep it up, and you may snap out of it."

Medina agreed to try, but in the beginning the eight miles from his office to his home was too much. At the end of a week, however, he was walking all the way, and within a month he seemed to have recovered, but he did not forget what had happened. He joined the Scarsdale Golf Club, which was fifteen or sixteen miles away in Westchester County, in order that he might regularly get some exercise there.

He was still "Dadoo" to his boys, and despite the pressure of his work, found more than a little time to play with them. The Morningside Drive apartment had a long narrow hall with a door in the middle, a door which served perfectly as a backstop for dart games. Another game called on the contestants to throw rings around a goat's head which was hung on the door. Games were usually played for strange and fascinating "championships", the "championship of the lower half of Mt. McKinley," for instance, or even "the upper half."

A succession of workbenches and toolchests materialized in the apartment, too, and both Harold, junior, and "Dadoo" built elaborate toy boats. Harold, junior, produced a sloop and "Dadoo" a schooner, both of which were sailed in Central Park; and any number of products were created by the use of a jigsaw.

The boys were frequently taken to the movies, usually to the Pershing Theatre on Amsterdam Avenue at 125th Street; and the afternoon before Christmas was certain to see "Dadoo" and his two boys going to movie after movie while Mrs. Medina busied herself at home with Christmas preparations, especially in connection with the Christmas tree, which Santa Claus thoughtfully arranged to deliver at that time.

Long, well-filled stockings appeared at the foot of the boys' beds each Christmas morning, jammed with appropriate contents and always with a coin, or even a dollar bill, in the toe. On one occasion, too, a bill was made a part of Mrs. Medina's present, and she failed to see it, almost throwing it away, which would have been too bad, for it was fresh and crisp and valued at one hundred dollars. The system that "Dadoo" initiated was for each member of the family to open one present in turn, and he himself was always maddeningly slow, untying the bows and knots with greatest care and hanging every bit of string and ribbon about his neck.

Mrs. Medina's health had continued far from good, and in the spring of 1923, a painful and prolonged attack of erysipelas took her to the hospital for a month. Nothing is more disrupting to family life than the illness of a wife and mother, and that is especially true when children are young. Harold, junior was ten and Standish was seven; and, though the apartment continued to function in the hands of a cook and a maid, Harold Medina found it necessary to spend every moment he could spare either with his children or with his wife at the hospital. Fortunately, no bar examination course was in progress at the moment, but there were classes at Columbia and there was work to do at the Nassau Street office. And each evening when the boys had gone to bed, there was time that had somehow to be filled.

Medina's boyhood home in Brooklyn had never been a bookish place. Even such books as are usually available for children had not been present there. As a boy, Harold Medina never read *Alice in Wonderland*. He did not know the *Uncle Remus* stories. He was quite unaware of the *Peterkin Papers*. Strangely enough, he was not acquainted in any detail even with *Mother Goose*, and despite his studious bent and his scholastic record at Princeton, he had never turned to reading for the pleasure there was in it.

Now, however, it was almost inevitable that he should turn to books. His was a mature mind, far above the average in ability and naturally inquisitive, and here was a field that offered endless fascinating possibilities. He had opened a new door and had come upon an exciting region of new interests. It was then that his wide reading and a new enthusiasm for books began, an enthusiasm that he has never since lost.

As Mrs. Medina improved at the hospital, Harold, junior, who was a Cub Scout, announced that the troop of which he was a member had scheduled a hike that would take them across the Hudson River to the Palisades. His father naturally agreed, saw the boy off, and having had no outing for weeks, decided to play a round of golf on that same day. He drove to Scarsdale, and had just about reached the furthest extremity of the golf course when a messenger, hurrying from the club house, called him urgently to the telephone.

The message, which was being relayed by a friend, was that young Harold had fallen over the Palisades and was in a hospital in Englewood, New Jersey.

It is twelve miles from the Scarsdale Golf Club to the Dyckman Street ferry, which then offered the only direct way to Englewood, and as Harold Medina turned into Dyckman Street and headed for the slip, he saw the ferry pull out and knew that the next one would not leave for half an hour. He did not know the extent of his son's injuries. While he waited, there was no way for him to learn more of what had happened. He could only sit there and stare across the river at the Palisades, wondering where along that towering cliff the accident had taken place. When, after the delay, he finally reached the hospital, he learned that, though the boy had fallen sixteen feet, had rolled another sixty feet down a steep slope of sharp, loose stone, had had almost every shred of clothing torn from him, and had been bruised painfully from head to foot, he had carried with him the strange good fortune that seems so often to attend boys, and had suffered no really serious injury.

It is not improbable that Harold Medina had had little time in the preceding years for quiet meditation. But during that month, troubled over his wife's illness, forced to spend evening after evening alone, jarred, as he had been, by the accident that had befallen his son, he must have thought of many things that had been pushed aside during his years of constant, uninterrupted effort. And one of these had to do with a childhood ambition, an ambition of which he had been conscious when, as a boy of eight or nine, he had been taken for the summer to the Apaucuck Point House overlooking Moriches Bay on the south shore of Long Island.

Apaucuck Point (the name is pronounced with the accent on the second syllable) is not a dramatic spot. It is low, level, and lacking in any prominent feature. A portion of it had always been a marsh. But even as a boy Harold Medina had hoped sometime to be able to buy it, to build a house there, and to have it for his own. And now the time had come. He could buy it if he wished—could, that is, if Charley Raynor's sister-in-law, who for a time had run the Apaucuck Point House and who, with her daughters Sarah and Betty, owned the Point, would sell it to him.

Mrs. Medina showed little interest in the idea at first. From her hospital bed she did not view with any enthusiasm the prospect of having such a house to run. By degrees, however, as her health returned and her husband's eagerness to buy the Point became more apparent, she agreed. It was late that year that Apaucuck Point changed hands, and the realization of a boyhood dream began. With the purchase of those acres, the life of the Medina family began to undergo a change—a change that led to something very different from anything Harold Medina had ever known before.

5

LAWYER AND PROFESSOR

HAROLD MEDINA, FOR ALL HIS ENERGY AND CONCENTRATION on his work, is a gay and playful person. He sings in a very good tenor voice in his bath. He whistles while he dresses. He is apt to seize the opportunity to sing in any impromptu chorus, and his notes are true, his repertoire reasonably wide. He regrets his inability to play the piano, and the guitar he had at college hasn't been tuned for years, but he sometimes improvises both the words and the air of songs that are more apt to be nonsensical than solemn.

His sense of humor is easily aroused, and the ludicrous appeals to him especially. "The Keystone Cops" of an earlier day in the movies never threw a custard pie that failed to delight him, and whatever strikes him as funny brings forth not merely smiles of pleasure but great and unrestrained guffaws. When custard pies have been flying at the movies and Harold Medina has been more than usually uninhibited, Mrs. Medina, on more than one occasion, has moved in her seat a little to keep people from thinking that she knew the man.

He approaches his pastimes and his fun with much the same wholehearted enthusiasm with which he throws himself into his work. It was only natural, therefore, once the land he wanted had been purchased, for him to center his attention on its development with all the vigor of his ebullient nature.

The house that was built on the point at Westhampton in the late summer of 1924 was a comfortable structure with four bedrooms and two baths. Its living room and sun porch were large and airy, its dining room was ample. Unpretentious architecturally, it stood only a few feet above the level of Moriches Bay and near enough to be exposed to any gales blowing in from sea.

An important part of the appeal that the vicinity of Westhampton has always made to Harold Medina lies in the waterways that can be reached from there. Even in his boyhood he had been familiar with boats, and an early "luxury" in which he and Mrs. Medina indulged was an antique motorboat that cost one hundred dollars. It had no name and its engine often failed, but throughout one summer which Mrs. Medina and the boys spent at the Apaucuck Point House, that craft, on almost every week-end, gave Harold Medina some new lesson in mechanical unreliability and especially proved that a "weedless" propellor was an important bit of equipment among the eel grass that then grew thick in parts of Moriches Bay.

The following year a new motorboat succeeded this ancient craft, and ultimately the Medinas joined the Huguenot Yacht Club at New Rochelle and purchased a thirty-four-foot Elco Cruisette. In a fit of typical Medinaesque humor this cruiser was named the *Lookey Dook*, and it was she that lay at anchor off Apaucuck Point during the summer of 1924 when the house was being built. She was later succeeded by the *Quest*, a similar cruiser, and later still by larger craft, but from the time the house was built, a comfortable, reliable motor cruiser has always been a part of the Medina establishment.

It is axiomatic that any person building his first house encounters problems for which he is unprepared, and that was true of Harold Medina. The house itself went well enough, but it was clear from the first that the marshy portion of the point was far too close for comfort. Three or four such acres so nearby simply had to be cared for, and the only practical way to correct the situation was to order a dredge that would pump sand from the bottom of the bay and build up those marshy acres until they stood above high water. So the dredge was ordered, at a cost of four thousand dollars, and used to turn the marsh into a slightly more elevated expanse of sand.

Such an operation not unnaturally attracted the attention of the local residents, and one of them, wandering out to inspect the one-time marsh, looked doubtfully about.

"Harold," he began, "when are you going to cover up that sand?"

"Cover it up?" asked Medina. "What do you mean?"

"Why, as soon as the sand dries out," his visitor replied, "it'll begin to blow back into the bay. You have to cover it up with topsoil."

"Don't kid me," objected Medina with his mind on the expense that had already been entailed, but a little investigation proved his informant right. Endless wagonloads of topsoil had to be dug and transferred from some of the more distant sections of his property in order to hold down those acres of untrustworthy sand.

From the first, Medina had decided to pay for this new home as it was built. Already he had paid cash for the land, and as the house and the improvements to the land materialized he paid for them as well. As always seems to happen, the bills exceeded the estimates, but ultimately the house approached completion and the architect mentioned the lawn. It would have to be plowed, he pointed out, and would need to be fertilized—would need perhaps a carload of manure.

Medina was ignorant of such matters and gave little thought to the suggestion.

"Go ahead and order it," he replied, and turned to other matters.

In due course the fertilizer came. It was generously spread about the newly plowed lawn, and later the bill arrived.

Medina opened the envelope casually, glad that this enterprize was approaching its conclusion. He was beginning to feel a bit pressed for funds, though he knew that this new bill was only for manure and wouldn't amount to much. He pulled it from its envelope and unfolded it.

"Manure," he read. "1 carload, $860."

He couldn't believe his eyes, but a phone call to the architect verified the amount. He paid it, but he barely mentioned the matter to his wife; and of all the bills that came to him in connection with the building of that house, the one for the carload of manure seems to have been the hardest to forget.

It was not until 1925 that the house was finally completed. The family continued to live throughout most of the year in New York—apartment dwellers still—but for week-ends, for Christmas, for the Easter holidays, and always for July and August, the Westhampton house was open and the Medinas were there, at home.

The Medinas stayed at the Apaucuck Point House the summer their new home was being built, though they left occasionally for cruises aboard the *Lookey Dook*. Harold Medina, however, had become a golfer, and, as is typical of him, decided really to master that often exasperating game. By now he had been a member of the Scarsdale Golf Club for a couple of years or so, but Scarsdale was the better part of a hundred miles away from Apaucuck Point, so he joined the Westhampton Country Club which lay just across a narrow arm of Moriches Bay.

He had much to learn about golf, for he was not a natural player and still generally failed to break 100, but he had decided that the "pro" at the country club was not an effective teacher. Because of this he undertook to teach himself, and late almost every afternoon he and Harold, junior, who went along to act as caddy, rowed in the *Lookey Dook's* dinghy across to where the golf club's eleventh green lay close beside the water. There the two would land and with a generous supply of golf balls which Harold, junior, somewhat unenthusiastically shepherded, Medina would concentrate for an hour or two on his mashie shots and his putts. Harold, junior, though he was paid for his efforts, found the whole business unexciting at best. He even complained about that daily chore, but his objections had no effect on his father's efforts. Golf required practice, and practice he insisted on giving it. However difficult the game might be, it simply was not necessary for Harold Medina to remain a duffer. Later he actually duplicated the club's thirteenth green on a portion of his own lawn, so as to be able to practice more conveniently. He even prepared a fairway some two hundred fifty yards long and a tee from which to drive.

"I would stand on the tee," he has explained, "and drive fifty balls. Then I would move a few yards ahead and hit fifty brassie shots. Then, moving ahead a bit at a time, fifty midirons and fifty mashies. By this time I would come to a hedge which blocked the green, and here I would pitch fifty balls to the green, putt them all out, go back and pick up what balls I could find, and start all over again. This went on for years."

But it proved effective, for on August 29, 1935, he made a score of 71 on the Westhampton Beach golf course, two strokes under par, and proved to his complete satisfaction that his duffer days were past.

With the completion of the house a wholly new schedule was begun. The family still occupied the apartment on Morningside Drive, and Medina plunged into his work as he had always done. His teaching at Columbia continued. Three times a year his bar examination course was carried on as usual, though with ever larger classes. And his law practice, which had begun so slowly, steadily grew greater.

He made more opportunities for entertainment and for pastimes. He managed occasionally to play golf. On Sundays, after Sunday school and church, he and the boys sometimes busied themselves in the study of the Morningside Drive apartment, building their model yachts or operating a small handprinting press. Dinner parties, both at home and abroad, were a bit more frequent, though otherwise no vital change was evident from September to June.

The heavy pressure of the preceding years had not greatly lessened. Because of his increasing law practice, demands on Harold Medina's time even appeared to be growing greater. It was becoming apparent that he needed some time each year for rest, and he also began to see that such business as came to the offices of Medina & Sherpick during the summer, was very largely "junk."

He made up his mind, therefore, to set aside July and August for himself. He would have nothing whatever to do with the law. He would not even permit a law book in the Westhampton house. He would do no law work—would see no clients.

"I decided to use that period to recharge my batteries," he once told me, and that annual period of rest and relaxation undoubtedly played an important part in his still expanding success.

During Medina's student days at Columbia, Dean Stone

had urged him not merely to join every bar association to which he became eligible, but also to take an active part in their work, and from the time he graduated he took that advice seriously. Being a gregarious person, such memberships appealed to him, and his boundless energy enabled him, whatever other pressure he was under, to find time for such committee work as came to him. Before any bar association had more than recognized his existence, however, he became involved in another task that caught his attention and enthusiasm from the first.

Not long after he graduated from Columbia he attended a meeting of the Columbia Law School Alumni Association and learned from Dean Stone and a handful of others who were present that the association, because of lack of interest, had fallen on evil days. Left to itself, it seemed almost certain to fade from sight, but there were a few who were interested in rebuilding it. It had been with that in mind that the meeting had been called, and at a succeeding meeting Medina was made a member of a committee which was given the responsibility of increasing the association's membership.

Here was a combination of work and relaxation that appealed to him, and he took to it as if it were a challenge. Behind his desk at the Nassau Street law office he installed a metal cabinet and in it he filed the name of every graduate of the law school. The cards he used were arranged three ways: alphabetically, by classes, and geographically. As an occasional relaxation from his work, he would swing his chair about and go over those cards. He telephoned such alumni as he could readily reach by phone. He wrote to others. At every opportunity he worked for more membership. Under his constant urging the association began to come to life.

Ultimately, as the membership grew, a publication was decided upon, a publication to be called *The Columbia Law*

Register, and in it every alumnus was to have a three-way listing as in Medina's own file. As an additional refinement, the name of each member of the alumni association was to be printed in bold-face type.

Here, it seemed to Medina, was an opportunity to build up the association's membership still more. Why not send telegrams, at least to a select group, urging them to join?

He did not think of the differences in time all across the country. He merely drafted the message he wished to send, compiled the list of names, and started those telegrams on their way. He got a lot of acceptances, too, but some of those wires, delivered by telephone during the night, awoke the addressees at all hours, so some replies were sharp and far from satisfactory.

Harold Medina later served for two terms as president of the Columbia Law School Alumni Association, but even before he was chosen for that position he was awarded one of the first Columbia Alumni Federation medals "for conspicuous Columbia alumni service."

These were the years during which the bar examination course was making its most rapid growth. From 1914 to 1923, the first ten years of its existence, it was attended by about six thousand students, and in that time it had firmly established Harold Medina as a person of more than ordinary means. In the next ten years more than twenty-two thousand students registered, and his income from the course grew more or less in proportion.

Because of its growth it had often been forced to move, and just as it had first outgrown his father's private office and then the committee room in the office of Davies, Auerbach & Cornell, so now it often outgrew such larger quarters as he found. Large bare lofts were sometimes rented. For several years the course was held in a huge room in the building occupied by the *Brooklyn Eagle*. For two years arrangements were made to use the auditorium of Town Hall in 43d Street, and even that was crowded. Ultimately, however, ideal quarters were found in the Engineering Societies Building and no further moves were necessary.

But it was not only the bar examination course that was growing; the offices of Medina & Sherpick were coming to be a hive of activity. The three-room suite on Nassau Street was outgrown and larger quarters were taken at 165 Broadway. Here, at the back of the building and on the seventh floor, the new offices looked down upon the Sixth Avenue elevated which, running noisily through Church Street, was forever punctuating the activities of the office. Rufus C. Van Aken and William Gilbert, both of whom had come to the firm as law clerks, had become partners. In 1926 Joseph V. McKee, who was then president of the Board of Aldermen but was to become acting mayor of the city of New York following the resignation of Mayor James J. Walker, became a partner as well, and the firm name was changed to Medina, Sherpick & McKee. Later McKee withdrew from the firm because of the pressure of other duties, but it was to his former partners that he turned when the question of his right to succeed Mayor Walker arose, and he found himself in need of legal help.

Earlier the limited practice that had come to the firm had not necessitated any especial division of duties. Now, the office had to be departmentalized. One partner handled wills, trusts, and related matters. Another handled corporation problems. Mr. Sherpick concerned himself largely with leases and other matters connected with real estate but also tried some of the most important cases for the firm with conspicuous success. Most of the work, indeed, had to do with litigation, and Medina was engaged for all but a fraction of his time in writing briefs and arguing appeals. His reputation had grown, as the firm's had, and though his fees, as yet, were never large, the trifling income of the firm's earlier years had grown until he, personally, was making $25,000 or more annually from the business of the office. That he was a successful lawyer was clearly evident, but he remained naïve and seemingly doubtful about the value of the work he did. He still seemed content to increase his income as a lawyer primarily by piling up large numbers of small fees.

It appears to be essential to Harold Medina that he be busy, and he seems to concentrate on everything he does. Furthermore he went quite consciously about teaching concentration and persistence to his sons. On Sundays, for instance, the family usually walked to church, and at Sunday dinner the boy who succeeded best in paraphrasing that day's sermon won five cents. Then, after the boys had done their best, their father would summarize the sermon for them. Even his pastimes, in order really to satisfy him, must present some sort of challenge. When his boys were small and he decided that they should learn to sail, which he himself had never learned to do, he not only bought them such boats as could be entered in the races held by the Westhampton Yacht Squadron but also eagerly served as "crew" on their boats until both they and he had become adept at handling small craft under sail. Nor are such interests apt to be ephemeral. Because of the football injury he suffered in his freshman year at Princeton he was ultimately forced to give up the active tasks connected with sailing for inability to pull and haul at halyards, sheets, and spinnakers. But every spring the family's three sailboats, the largest a twenty-six-foot sloop named *Ethel* after Mrs. Medina, are rigged and slid into the water to be kept ready for use until late summer.

Even in his teaching, much the same attitude is evident. He

never considered giving his whole time to his classes. From the day he graduated he was determined to be active in the practice of law. Nevertheless, he was as eager to establish his reputation as a teacher as if that were his only aim in life. The income he received from Columbia was a very small part of what he earned. Even when he first joined the Columbia Law School teaching staff his income from other sources was sufficient for his needs and before long he came to be a man of means. But here in the classes at the law school was another challenge he could not resist. Despite the pressure of his other work, his teaching never grew casual, and his interest always remained high. It is difficult to see how he found the time to begin the compilation of the case books he was determined to complete. Nevertheless, he found it and he not only wrote *Pleading and Practice under New Civil Practice Act* in 1922, but also followed that book with others. *Cases in Federal Jurisdiction and Procedure* appeared in 1925, *Cases on New York Pleading and Practice* and *Selected New York Practice Statutes* were both published in 1928; *Cases and Materials on Jurisdiction of Courts* came out in 1931, and *Medina's New York Civil Practice Manual* appeared in 1932. He edited *Medina's Bostwick's Lawyer's Manual* in 1934, and later published both a digest of *New York Statute Law* and a summary of *New York Pleading Practice and Evidence*. Nor was that all. He was a frequent contributor to legal reviews, and with collaborators prepared other volumes still.

This work was well begun by 1925. Two of these volumes had appeared by then, and they must have had their effect on the point of view of the faculty of the law school. Earlier, when Dean Stone had proposed Medina as an associate professor, the other members of the faculty had rejected him, basing their opposition on what they felt to be the lack of dignity of the bar examination "cram course" he was operating. In the time that had passed since that rejection, the course had not changed, except that it had grown. Medina himself had remained the same, though the members of the faculty may have come to know and understand him better. Dean Stone had left Columbia to accept President Coolidge's appointment as Attorney General, but Professor Huger W. Jervey, who succeeded him, chose this time to renew Dean Stone's suggestion, and the faculty approved. After ten years as a teacher in the Columbia Law School, after twelve years as head of the *infra dig* cram course, Harold Medina, to his enormous satisfaction, became Harold Medina, Associate Professor of Law.

The 1920's were successful years for Harold Medina. He had only begun to establish himself when World War I reached its conclusion—as a lawyer he was then very little known—but in the ten or twelve years that followed, his practice grew to impressive proportions. Even without the astonishing growth of his bar examination course he was a very successful man. In fact, he had made *three* successes. First, by his own unaided efforts he had come to be a man of means, and the bar examination course, as the source of his wealth, was his personally owned and personally controlled institution. Second, he had earned the title and position of associate professor of one of the country's greatest graduate schools of law. And, finally, his law practice had grown until it had begun to reach proportions that must have been envied by many another lawyer whose full time had been spent at that profession.

Following Dean Stone's advice, Medina had become a member of the Association of the Bar of the City of New York, as well as of the New York State Bar Association, the American Bar Association, and the New York County Lawyers Association. In 1924, he was elected to the first of three terms he served as director of the New York County Lawyers Association, and in 1926, for the first time, was appointed to a committee by the Association of the Bar of the City of New York.

This committee, of which Medina was chairman, had the responsibility for planning a series of social events at which members of the Association could become acquainted, and the first gathering was to hear the election returns at the Bar Association Building in 44th Street.

A meeting of the committee had been called in order to work out plans for this affair, and while refreshments were being discussed, someone suggested that instead of purchasing merely enough ginger ale and other such supplies for this one evening, enough should be ordered to last throughout the year. The suggestion was casually received and in the absence of any objections Medina gave it his approval and thought nothing more about the matter.

Some weeks later, when the elections were over and the gathering had been more or less forgotten, Medina received word that William D. Guthrie, who was then president of the Bar Association, wanted to see him at his home at 28 Park Avenue. Guthrie was one of New York's outstanding lawyers, and it occurred to Medina that he might be asked to write a brief, or something of that sort, so he was somewhat surprised, when he arrived, to be kept waiting for the better part of an hour before he was taken up to the dignified room in which Mr. Guthrie was seated at his desk.

"Medina," Guthrie began with very little in the way of preliminaries, "don't you know anything about the budget of the Bar Association?"

The question came as a surprise, and what it implied Medina could not guess.

"What do you mean?" he asked.

"You spent $768," Mr. Guthrie explained, "for ginger ale and White Rock, and there was no appropriation for that."

Medina instantly recalled what had happened and just as promptly realized that he and his committee had been wrong. He might have explained, but he decided not to.

"I guess you're right," he admitted. "If you'll let me know what the amount is I'll pay it."

Mr. Guthrie hesitated.

"Well now," he remarked presently. "The Executive Committee told me to talk to you and to call you down. And that is what I've done."

Little more was said before Medina left, and later the committee he headed was dissolved. Whatever became of all that ginger ale and White Rock he never learned, but he was never asked to pay for it. Later, too, he was chosen to serve on many other committees: the Committee on Amendment of the Law (now the Committee on State Legislation), the Committee on Courts of Superior Jurisdiction, the Committee on Post-Admission Education, the Committee on Law Reform, the Committee on Admissions, and the Executive Committee. And these tasks, all of which required time and real attention, were only those of one bar association. In addition he performed comparable tasks on many other committees to which he was appointed by the American Bar Association, the New York State Bar Association, and the New York County Lawyers Association. On one occasion he was even made chairman of the Joint Committee on Public Relations of all the bar associations of the New York metropolitan district, a total of about fifteen.

This committee work was a steady drain upon his time, but it widened his contacts, and because he was more and more called upon to address bar associations throughout the state and elsewhere, his reputation was enhanced. He was recognized as an expert on matters of court procedure, and he was always willing to speak on subjects in this field. He gave dozens of lectures at bar associations, without compensation, to explain the operation of the New Civil Practice Act which had become effective in 1921, and spoke as well on decisions affecting practice and procedure.

Forever willing to perform more than his fair share of these many tasks, he nevertheless clearly understood that in all this work he was increasing his stature as a lawyer, was adding to his reputation as well as to his own learning and experience.

"I was working for the long pull," he has explained.

Following his graduation from Columbia, Harold Medina seems for some years to have given that institution more of his allegiance than he gave to Princeton. His associations at Columbia had from the first been more pleasant and more cordial than they had been at Princeton, and the work he did in building up the membership of the Columbia Law School Alumni Association kept him closely in contact with Columbia, as his teaching also did. Little by little, however, he began once more to interest himself in Princeton, and as he renewed his contacts with former classmates and returned to Princeton for reunions, his enthusiasm grew.

By nature he is companionable, jovial, and convivial, and nowhere do such characteristics show to better advantage than at college reunions. Consequently he more and more often returned to Princeton, driving down from New York with Mrs. Medina or in company with his close friend and classmate, Morton Fry. He is always a moving spirit in any gathering. He enjoys playing poker with his friends. Any "jam session" of which he is a part is certain to be more enthusiastic for his presence, and no gathering is commonplace if Harold Medina is around.

On one occasion a Princeton reunion group of which he was a member did not break up until 5:45 in the morning, and most of those who took part went to bed more or less exhausted. Morton Fry, with whom Medina was rooming, was awakened, after having had only an hour or two of sleep, by Medina who was "bellowing like a walrus" in the shower bath. With no trace whatever of any ill effects from that all night session, he was up for the day and as gay as if he had had a full night's sleep. In his best tenor voice, which, to his sleepy friend, had more than ordinary powers of penetration, he was happily improvising a song which, accompanied by the rush of water in the shower, informed all and sundry that

Old Mort Fry is a so-and-so!
Old Mort Fry is a so-and-so!
Old Mort Fry is a so-and-so!
When he comes back to Princeton!

Such lusty vigor, along with his sincerity, has given Harold Medina a place among his classmates that is unequalled, and though scores of honors of the most impressive kind have come to him, he himself lists high among them his election, in 1949, to the presidency of his class, and since his selection for that position, not a birthday among his classmates has been permitted to pass without his personal greeting.

It was at Princeton that Medina first awakened to an appreciation of literature, though the busy years that followed kept him from developing that interest further. The illness of his wife in 1923, however, had almost forced him to renew his interest in reading, and his later decision to spend July and August in rest and recreation enabled him to find time in which to indulge it. But here again his innate tendency to do thoroughly whatever he attempts led him to approach this new interest in a highly individual and almost unique manner. For several years he purchased such books as interested him—as most of us do—and having read them—or having failed to read them—he placed them on his shelves. But such a comparative lack of method was not typical of Harold Medina. He wanted to read, but he had no interest in pointless reading. He wanted a library, but he wanted one that would be both excellent and complete. Yet what he had in mind was to be a *private* library, and though he was willing to create it on a scale greater than most, he knew that it could never approach any really large proportions. From the first, therefore, he found himself faced with the problem of selection.

As he thought of what he wanted, he decided to divide his library into five sections, each reasonably complete in itself. He wanted a Latin section, a Greek section, and sections devoted to French, Spanish, and English literature. It was French literature that he knew best, for it had been in French that he had specialized at Princeton, so it was with his French section that he began.

It was his idea to collect all the really significant works that were to be found in French literature. He wanted the right editions. He wanted nothing that was expurgated; and he wanted to exclude such volumes as were *not* significant.

As time passed, he began to see that such a collection could not be brought together by a layman—by himself. After the idea had been incubating for several years, he went to "Paddy" Chapman, a Princeton classmate who had married a French girl, and who not only spent every summer in France but also was teaching in the modern languages department at Princeton.

"Paddy," he began, "suppose somebody came to you and asked you to get together everything of significance in French literature including all the necessary dictionaries and reference books. Would you be interested?"

"I'd be delighted," was the reply, "if there weren't any hurry."

Medina himself recognized the necessity for time in such an undertaking, and together the two men agreed that the fee for the work was to be 10 per cent of the cost of the books. It took several years to complete the list, and the two often talked it over as it progressed. Ultimately, however, the actual purchase of the books began, and each summer, when Professor Chapman went to France, he placed orders, mostly in Paris, and attended to such other tasks as were necessary, sending the books to Medina in Westhampton.

It was clear from the first that the library Medina had in mind could not be housed in his Westhampton home; space was not available. It would be necessary either to add a wing or to build a separate structure, and it was the latter that was finally decided upon, though it was not built until 1934. The site Medina selected was in his garden some sixty yards from his house, and it was with much more than ordinary care that the library was planned and erected. It was paneled in pecky cypress, had a mural map of Long Island over the fireplace, and windows looking out upon the garden and upon Moriches Bay. John G. Raynor, a collateral member of the family that had once owned Apaucuck Point, and a great "bayman" in his day, was Medina's superintendent now, and it was he who helped the eager owner unpack and arrange the books as they arrived. There were hundreds of them in the first shipment, and John Raynor grew progressively more impressed as he checked volume after volume against the invoice which, written in French, listed each volume as a *tome*.

He paused finally to mop his brow and to express his astonishment.

"You know," he commented, "this fellow Tome certainly wrote a lot of books."

With the French section of his library developing so well, Medina turned to the English section, and because his arrangement with Paddy Chapman had been so successful he decided to use similar methods. It was to his wife's brother, Robert Hillyer, the poet and Pulitzer prize winner, that he now turned, for Hillyer, in addition to being a poet, is an able teacher of English, and had become Boylston Professor of Rhetoric and Oratory at Harvard. Under an arrangement similar to that which had worked so well with Paddy Chapman, a list of about two thousand volumes was prepared and the books were purchased. They never took their place, however, in the new library, but were kept instead in New York where, in 1929, the Medinas had taken a new apartment at 14 East 75th Street.

It was to Professor Arthur Schiller, who teaches Roman law at Columbia Law School, that Medina turned for help in the selection of his Latin and Greek sections, but the Spanish library, which was a part of the original plan, never materialized. With some twelve thousand carefully selected volumes, over half of which had come from France, Harold Medina found himself the owner of one of the most carefully selected private libraries in the country and one which, in many ways, could hardly be surpassed. And during July and August of each year, as well as on holidays and week-ends, he turned with renewed interest to his reading. He still played golf and looked forward to periodic cruises, but books—good books—had found a place in his life from which they have never again been excluded.

Meanwhile, he continued with his teaching at Columbia.

He understood that so excellent an academic connection was good for his professional reputation and merely on practical grounds wished to maintain it. But more, perhaps, than even he may have realized, teaching appealed to him. He enjoyed it and in all his twenty-five years at Columbia he never rejected any teaching assignment.

"I was afraid that if I said no," he has admitted, "I might have something go wrong."

Nor was he content merely to lecture in a purely academic atmosphere. While teaching a course in code pleading and practice, for instance, he had his students prepare a number of practice papers; summonses, complaints, affidavits, and the like; and as these were handed in, he corrected them and explained such errors as arose. He realized, too, that certain lessons can best be taught outside the classroom, and so he took groups of his students to various courts, and to the offices of the county clerk, the sheriff, and elsewhere.

In 1920, Professor Egbert, of the extension teaching department of Columbia, asked Medina to consider giving a course covering certain practical matters not covered by any law school course: what a lawyer should do, for instance, when a new client comes in; how to keep adequate records; how properly to keep a lawyer's diary; how to send out bills; how to keep a law office running smoothly.

Here was a practical phase of a lawyer's existence that law schools too often overlooked. The idea appealed to Medina and he agreed to give a "Course in Legal Practice." A notice was prepared, the new course was listed, and the fee each student was to pay for the course was set at twelve dollars in addition to the registration fee. Medina, for his part, was to get all the fees up to three hundred and fifty dollars, with anything over that amount going to the university.

As the course was first given in the autumn of 1920, it was

a Monday evening class. When Medina arrived for the first session, which was to be from 8 o'clock until 9:30, he found, to his disappointment, that only five or six students were present. Worse than that, however, the hour was so unpopular that of these few only one lone student, a young woman named Syrena Stackpole, decided to continue with the course.

Medina naturally told Professor Egbert about it, and was immediately told that the course should be discontinued. Egbert admitted that the university could not ask anyone to devote so much time to a course that had attracted only a single student. But Medina disagreed. The course had been announced, and Miss Stackpole had registered for it in all good faith. He would give it, therefore, and give it he did in all the detail that had been originally planned.

Despite this limited beginning the course was announced again for the next year and this time, to Medina's astonishment, fully three hundred fifty students registered, their fees totaling more than four thousand dollars. The arrangement for Medina's reimbursement, however, remained the same, the university taking everything above three hundred and fifty dollars, and he complained to Professor Egbert that this hardly seemed fair in view of the very limited payment he had received the year before. Egbert, however, contended that a deal was a deal. He refused to raise the rate of payment, and Medina, having filed his protest, accepted his defeat and willingly taught that greatly expanded class.

Syrena Stackpole, incidentally, is now a practicing attorney at Riverhead, Long Island, no more than eight or ten miles from Medina's home at Westhampton. She benefited not only from that course but also from Medina's bar examination course which she later took. Along with other former students, she remembers him as a graphic, dramatic teacher; she has even said with more gravity than humor that she learned more from his bar examination course than she learned in law school. Others, too, have said as much, but Medina himself belittles such remarks.

"Of course I know better," he once told me, "though I am sure I taught them how to analyze legal problems, and I dramatized and clarified a good many things their law schools had already taught them."

In his earlier days as a teacher, Medina was apt to give free rein to his quick temper. He kept strict discipline, was angered by inattention, and made no effort to ease the way of his students. His classes at Columbia were much smaller than those of his bar examination course, which was attended by students from many law schools, and discipline at Columbia being easier to keep, put no great strain upon him. In the cram course, however, he was always tense as he lectured, and on one occasion when he was on the platform before a huge class that filled the Town Hall auditorium, he saw a student who had gone to sleep. Angered, he jumped from the platform, ran up the aisle, and without a word, collared the young man who, he thought, had been so inexcusably inattentive. The whole auditorium was utterly silent as he thrust the unlucky fellow before him up the aisle and out the door. Then he returned to the platform and continued his lecture. Twenty years later he met that former student on the street and learned, to his astonishment, that he had thrown out the wrong man!

In the course of time he learned how to control himself better, and learned, too, that sharpness in a teacher is in itself of little value. He still insisted that his students apply themselves and refused to coddle them. They had to work, but his instinct for the dramatic, his clear and realistic presentations, his frequent use of homely telling phrases, aided their understanding and enabled them more easily to remember.

He never neglected humor, and his sharp, inimitable laugh was frequent. If any humorous situation arose he was quick to seize it, and whenever a class began to grow confused in any discussion he would call a halt and lead the way to clearer understanding.

Strong, square-shouldered, and deep of chest, Medina, as he lectured before his classes at Columbia, bore a marked physical resemblance to Professor Ralph W. Gifford under whom he had studied at the law school. It is interesting, too, that Professor Gifford's son, James P. Gifford, later studied under Medina. But this relationship between succeeding generations of students and professors did not end there, for Harold Medina, junior, who was born about the time his father graduated from Columbia, also ultimately attended the law school, and when he did, he in his turn, was a student of James P. Gifford who, by then, had also become a Columbia professor.

Connected as Medina was with Columbia University, and living in upper Manhattan, it was natural that his two sons should be sent to Horace Mann School, which was then being operated as a kind of demonstration school in connection with Teachers College of Columbia University. But Medina, despite the pressure of his many duties, was not one to leave the training of his sons exclusively to others. He evolved a philosophy of his own so far as they were concerned.

Convinced that unsolicited advice is seldom effective, he rarely offered it. Instead, following his own father's example, he was apt to advise his sons only indirectly and often without their knowledge that he even had them in mind. When the boys were present—or, better yet, when they were in the next room listening—he would discuss with others such problems as he had in mind, pointing out the advantages of this or that viewpoint. He tried to influence his boys by example, as he did when Harold, junior, first took up Latin at Horace Mann. Thinking to increase the boy's interest and to give him an incentive, he himself decided to take one of Columbia University's home study courses in Latin, and because he had remembered his own inadequate introduction to the subject at Holbrook Academy he decided to start all over again, and so signed up for an elementary course.

This decision no doubt had its effect upon his son, as he intended, but with typical concentration and determination Medina himself never ceased the study he then began. He has actually continued it until today, and as I write he occasionally turns, in such spare time as he can find, to the perusal and meticulous translation of Horace's Odes and Epodes, to the study of which, after years devoted to other phases of Latin, he turned in 1949.

Now and again, when his boys brought their schoolbooks home, their father picked them up and read them. He made no point of what he was doing, but he hoped that the boys would recognize his interest and come to him for any help he could give them in their studies. Perhaps these methods helped to guide them into efforts of their own which produced such excellent records not only at Horace Mann but also at Hill School where they later went to prepare for college.

As his boys approached the time when they would enter Princeton, and he himself continued to increase his stature as lawyer, teacher, and man of means, the world was moving irresistibly toward the vast economic collapse of 1929. Few were able to foresee it; no one could foretell its outcome. Harold Medina, surrounded by his many tasks, made no serious attempt to do so and, as luck would have it, was to be far less hurt by the debacle than most. His bar examination course did not reach the peak of its success until 1930, and for another ten years was to remain an important source of revenue and influence; his position at Columbia underwent no change; and his growing reputation as a lawyer more than offset such effects as the depression had on the business of his office.

Nevertheless, influences were at work that were to change the whole character of Harold Medina's activities—that were ultimately to give him access to new opportunities beside which those he had so far known were lacking both in color and in consequence. He did not see them coming. He had no inkling of the developments that lay ahead. But by degrees, as the 1920's came to a close, a new phase began in the career of Harold Medina.

6

STORMS—ECONOMIC, LEGAL, AND ATMOSPHERIC

THOROUGHNESS IS A CHARACTERISTIC OF HAROLD MEDINA. Endowed with so much more than ordinary energy, he also has the ability to direct his efforts so narrowly and effectively toward the end he has in view as almost to exclude all other matters from his mind. This is apt to be true whenever his interest has been really aroused, and is evident whether he be studying Latin or French, learning to play golf, or preparing a case for trial. It is to this intensity of application, in fact, that much of his success in appellate work can be traced.

The task that faces a lawyer when a case is on appeal differs enormously from that of the trial lawyer. The case has already been decided. A notice of appeal has been served. Every word spoken during the trial by witnesses, lawyers, and judge has been printed in an appeal book or record on appeal. This record has then been filed in the appellate court, and the lawyer for the appellant—the person who lost in the court below—offers a printed brief in which are set down the arguments and points upon which, it is hoped, the appellate court will reverse the original judgment. Another brief has been prepared by the opposing lawyer, and the case ultimately comes up for argument.

The trial itself may have covered almost any length of time —days or even weeks. A carefully drawn brief, too, may take weeks to prepare. But such is the pressure on our courts that judges cannot be expected to read all this detailed record. It is there for them to refer to as they wish, but the oral arguments, which are usually restricted to an hour or less, are vital. The effective preparation of a brief is in itself an important matter, for here is the concise statement of the client's case. But the oral argument may be no less important, for in it the skillful lawyer is able to develop the proper sequences and facts, calling to the attention of the judges the essence of his case which may be less apparent, and far less human, in the cold print of either brief or written record.

A good brief differs widely from an effective oral argument, but Medina learned early in his career that great accuracy is essential to them both. He noticed, too, that the appellate arguments he heard were often dull, that they lacked color and even clarity, and often failed to dramatize even such points as lent themselves to dramatization. Yet judges are human; they are normally subject not only to boredom on the one hand but also to alert interest and concentrated attention on the other.

In the preparation of briefs his training had been good. His five years with Davies, Auerbach & Cornell had given him much practice, and Mr. Tuttle, himself a master of brief-writing and appellate argument, had been a constructive critic. In this matter of oral argument, however, Medina developed his own ideas, and he did it in typical Medina fashion. He decided that the best oral argument was one that made the most effective presentation of the facts, and in preparing his arguments he began to experiment. He would try out what he had to say on his wife, perhaps, or on his friends, watching carefully to see what caught or failed to catch their interest.

He studied the record in detail until, with no thought whatever of turning to notes or other references, he could present every phase of the subject under discussion and could answer clearly and concisely any question that was likely to arise. Depending upon an unusually retentive memory, he refused to clutter himself up with notes or reminders, and even made it a point to be so intimately acquainted with his technical references as to be able not only to give their meaning but also their actual phraseology, not only the volume in which they were to be found but even their exact location in that volume.

In preparing for his oral arguments, he often strode up and down in his living room at home or, less often, paced in his office, rehearsing his presentation. He never committed such arguments to memory, for he had an innate distrust of any memorized version, but he carefully rehearsed the sequence of his points as well as effective phrases and the logical development of his facts. Seldom content with the first form that occurred to him, he often tried out other arrangements, sometimes half a dozen or even more if the argument was involved or more than usually difficult. Having arrived at what he felt was the most effective arrangement, he did his utmost to put life into his presentation, to put expression into his voice, to speak with enthusiasm, with sincerity, and, above all, with accuracy.

Perhaps, in a way, it was fortunate that among Medina's earliest cases there were a number that he lost. Such defeats troubled him and forced him to realize that defeat is not only always possible but also that it can be highly unpleasant. One early client committed suicide after an adverse decision. and this tragically brought home to the young attorney the depth of feeling that may lie behind the problem which it is an attorney's duty to attempt to solve. His successes, however, far outnumbered his defeats, and his reputation was well established when, in 1927, Earl Carroll, the theatrical producer, was tried for perjury and convicted in his widely publicized "bathtub case."

The Carroll case had been the result of an especially extravagant display of bad taste in the Prohibition Era—a party that was given by Earl Carroll on the stage of the theater in which his *Earl Carroll's Vanities* was then playing. During this affair a girl who was said to be nude, and who certainly gave every impression of being so, appeared on the stage in a bathtub that was filled with liquor, or with what was supposed to be liquor. Much gossip naturally followed, and a grand jury, having decided to inquire into the affair, called Carroll himself.

The curious part of the matter was that, if he had told the whole unvarnished truth, he could not have been prosecuted, for the law would have granted him immunity; but either because he did not know this, or because he was ill advised, he told a story that was wide of the truth, and as a result he was not only charged with perjury but also was tried and convicted.

Until after Carroll's conviction, Medina had no connection with the case, but now, with certain legal points in mind upon which an appeal could be based, Herbert C. Smyth, who was Carroll's lawyer, asked Medina to write the brief that had to be prepared in connection with the appeal to the Circuit Court of Appeals, the very court on which Medina today sits as a judge. Convinced that the points were sound, Medina agreed, with the understanding that Smyth was to argue the appeal.

Having prepared what he thought was an especially effective brief, Medina was naturally interested in the result of Smyth's argument, but Judge Charles M. Hough, who was then a member of the Circuit Court of Appeals, made short work not only of Smyth's argument but also of the legal points that appeared in Medina's brief, and Carroll's conviction was affirmed.

Carroll, of course, was just as eager as ever to stay out of jail, and now decided to carry the case to the Supreme Court to which, by this time, Harlan Fiske Stone, formerly Attorney General and, earlier still, Dean of Columbia Law School—and Medina's good friend—had been appointed a justice. It so happened, too, that Stone had been assigned to the Second Circuit, and was consequently the person to whom application had to be made for a stay of execution pending determination of the petition for a writ of certiorari—that is, an order in writing bringing the case before the Supreme Court for review. In order to keep out of jail while the justices were deciding whether or not to hear the case, Carroll asked Medina to see Stone and try to get a stay.

The task would not have been difficult, for it was necessary merely to make the request orally, and it would have been worthwhile, for Carroll offered Medina a fee of twenty-five hundred dollars. But Medina refused. Not only had Judge Hough's pointed questioning weakened his belief in the legal arguments he had made in the brief he had written, but Justice Stone was his friend, and there was the subtle matter of professional ethics.

"There wouldn't have been anything actually wrong in my going," he once explained to me, "but I'm glad I didn't. The difference between right and wrong is not all down in the books."

Medina's success in oral arguments appears to have been largely due to the great care he took in their preparation. On one occasion he was congratulated by an opponent whom he knew well and from whom he had just won a case that had had to do with nothing more spectacular than a flock of ducks owned by a duck farmer and the duck food that had killed most of them. The argument Medina had made had appeared to be utterly simple and unprepared—had given the impression of being just such a conversational explanation as might have been made casually by one friend to another.

"I wish I had the nerve," his opponent told him after the case had been decided, "to walk into court and talk to the judges in that happy, carefree way of yours."

What had not been apparent even to this other lawyer was that that argument had been most carefully and thoughtfully prepared. Medina had spent a whole day at home, pacing up and down the living-room floor until, after having tried that argument out in thirteen different forms, he had finally hit upon the "carefree" presentation, which, because of its apparent artlessness, had proved so effective and convincing.

As his experience widened and he formulated the rules that guided him, other matters also proved to be important. Probably the rules he came to accept were evolved rather than formulated, and came into sharp focus only by degrees. Ultimately, however, he actually wrote them out. Having been invited to speak before the Cleveland Bar Association on "How Law Suits are Won and Lost", he listed them as follows:

1. Prepare your case with thoroughness.
2. Never take a chance in the courtroom.
3. Never try to take unfair advantage of your opponent, no matter how tempting the opportunity may appear.
4. Always try your case like a gentleman.
5. Don't lose your temper. Nothing befogs the mind so quickly as anger.
6. Be considerate and thoughtful of others in the courtroom. The amenities of life pay big dividends at all times.

7. Never take yourself too seriously. It might conflict with the ideas the judge or members of the jury may have of you.

8. Never tell a half-truth or a near-truth. Too many cases have been lost as the result of misstatements on minor matters.

9. Concentrate at all times on the human materials in the case. This means the judge, your adversary, the jurors, the witnesses, and yourself.

10. Never cease trying to improve the technique of your art. This includes enunciation, diction, and voice inflection.

11. Your personal appearance in the courtroom is an element of no mean importance. Don't be slovenly or dress loudly.

12. Keep yourself fit in mind and body.

He seems to have followed these rules consistently, but much of his success can be traced to other causes less capable of being included in any set of rules: to his astonishing memory, for instance, which he had developed by industry and mental discipline; to the ability he developed in presenting his facts and arguments without recourse to notes or other references, an ability that made it possible for him to carry in mind even page numbers and the location of specific words and phrases in exhibits; to his natural interest in people; and to the easy friendliness he so readily displayed. But in addition he became an expert in trial strategy.

It is not too much to say that trial strategy somewhat resembles military strategy. There is always the over-all picture, always the possibility of surprise by the maneuvers of a resourceful adversary; there is always just the right time to bring out certain evidence in order to get the most out of it. Every case has its imponderables. Largely assisted by his training, Medina had enough imagination and creative ability to develop trial strategy to a greater degree than most lawyers, and this played an important part in earning him his enviable reputation at the New York bar.

A woman, who later came to be a client of Medina's, had once established a trust fund of over half a million dollars. Under the terms of the trust she was to receive the income, but at her death the greater part of the principal was to go to relatives, among whom were the wife and daughter of the lawyer who drew up the trust instrument. After the instrument had been drawn and signed, however, the woman learned to her dismay that the lawyer-relative had so worded it as to give himself far more authority than she had intended him to have. By the terms of the trust as he had drawn it, his wife and daughter and the daughter's children would ultimately, in all probability, inherit a large part of the principal, and in the meantime the lawyer had given himself control of the investment of the funds so that the income on which the woman depended could be greatly reduced by investing in securities which favored the conservation of the principal for the "remaindermen."

Because of this, the woman decided to bring suit to set aside the instrument, contending that it had been procured by fraud, and Medina was retained to represent her at the trial. The lawyer-relative, in turn, was represented by an eminent attorney who was widely known as an especially skillful cross-examiner.

Almost as soon as Medina and his assistants started to work on the case it became apparent that the woman had very little recollection of the various conversations which led up to the preparation and execution of the deed of trust. Her husband, on the other hand, had some recollection, but he was nervous and excitable and there was much doubt as to how he would stand up under a well-planned and shrewd cross-examination. The woman, as the plaintiff, would normally be put on the witness stand first, and Medina felt sure that his opponent expected him to do just that. When the trial began, however, Medina called as his first witness the defendant—the lawyer-relative who was sitting in the back of the courtroom apparently looking forward to seeing his former client torn to pieces on cross-examination. Caught unawares, the defendant was soon floundering. He could not remember this; he could not remember that.

"Where are your records?" asked Medina.

"Down at my office," the man replied.

"Very well. Send for them," Medina suggested. "I have plenty of other questions to ask you while we are waiting for them."

Applications for delay were unavailing. Medina was adamant and the court upheld him. The questioning went on until the records arrived, and then every step in the sorry business was brought out. The effect was not merely to show how the man had overreached his client; it also brought the whole story back to the mind of the plaintiff who up to that time had truthfully said she could not recall the details. It was an application in trial strategy of his knowledge of people and the ways of humanity that Medina had built up over the years. Because of it, this case was promptly settled, the original deed of trust was canceled, and a new one was made.

During these years Medina was inclined to keep away from publicity, and largely on that account the public did not know him. It was not that he had any aversion to public notice. From his college days on he has been an avid keeper of scrapbooks in which an astonishing number of clippings have been collected. Nevertheless, there are very few that appeared about him during the years between his graduation from Columbia and the early 1920's. As he himself has said, the really important clients do not want a lawyer whose very association with the case will get their names in the newspapers. However, it was only his popular reputation that was limited. Professionally he was well known, and lawyers widely recognized his ability. Thousands of lawyers practicing in the state of New York and elsewhere had studied under him, both at Columbia and in his bar examination course. Many others knew him through books he had written and through his law practice, and many of his retainers came from those who had listened to him in the courtroom. His activities seldom made the headlines, though now, with a dozen years of independent practice behind him, that was about to undergo a change.

On October 29, 1929, the greatest stock exchange panic in history ushered in the first phases of the Great Depression. The prosperity of the Coolidge years came abruptly to an end, and a little over a year later, as the depression deepened and bankruptcies grew in number, a bank in New York City—the Bank of United States—was closed by the bank examiners, never to reopen.

By the time the Bank of United States closed its doors the country had fallen into a kind of economic chaos. Everywhere business had suffered. Fortunes had been wiped out or were shrinking rapidly as values continued to decline; unemployment had enormously increased; mortgages were being foreclosed; loans were being called. Many, even of those who had no debts and had never thought of speculation or even of investment, awakened to find that their family savings were being swept away, wholly or partially, as savings banks and building and loan institutions collapsed. Fear for the future and fear even of the present swept across the country, and everywhere, as frightened people tried to understand what had befallen them, there was a cry for help and even for a scapegoat.

The failure of the Bank of United States, bringing disaster

as it did upon so many thousands of small depositors, naturally increased the public clamor, and when several of the bank's officers were indicted and charged with felony in the handling of the bank's funds, there was a furious and widespread demand not only for their immediate trial but also for their conviction and swift punishment.

Harold Medina was conscious of this only as any other person might have been. He was personally untouched by the failure of the bank. He knew little of the matter except as the whole affair was a part of the news of the day. Even when Bernard K. Marcus, the bank's president, and Saul Singer, its executive vice-president, were indicted along with Singer's twenty-four-year-old son Herbert, Medina was interested only as he realized that Herbert Singer had been one of his students a year or so earlier at Columbia.

It so happened that Meier Steinbrink, a judge of the New York Supreme Court who knew Medina well, was a friend of the Singer family. Naturally concerned over the charges that had been brought against Saul Singer and his son, Steinbrink began to see that the legal problem that faced the one differed sharply from that which faced the other. The elder Singer was an important official of the bank; the son was not even an employee. It was true that the young man was connected with the events that had resulted in the indictment, but only as a youthful member of the bar, and an employee, at fifty dollars a week, of Isador J. Kresel, a lawyer who was counsel for the bank. Nevertheless, Herbert was charged with "aiding and abetting" in the irregularities for which the others were to be tried. Arrangements had been made to have the son represented, as the father was to be, by Emory R. Buckner, a lawyer of exceptional ability who had formerly been United States Attorney for the Southern District of New York.

In thinking over this situation, Steinbrink became certain

that the defense that might be most effective for Saul Singer would in all probability be less effective for Herbert, and having reached this conclusion he strongly urged that the son be separately represented. He even suggested that Harold Medina, for whose ability he had much respect, be chosen for the task, and, shortly before the trial opened and the selection of the jury began, Medina entered the case. For the first time in his career he was about to begin the defense of a client in an important criminal case.

The defendants were to be tried for misapplication of the funds of a safe deposit company which was one of the subsidiaries of the Bank of United States. All the stock of these subsidiaries was owned by the bank, and there were several affiliated companies which had borrowed large sums from the bank. These loans had been criticized by the New York State Superintendent of Banks, and the suggestion had been made that they be paid off or reduced. Unfortunately there were no funds available for the purpose, and in their efforts to remedy the situation the officers of the bank, working with their counsel, finally evolved the so-called "Bolivar transaction," which was an extremely involved series of corporate transfers as a result of which the loans to the affiliated companies were marked "paid" and were transferred, on the books, to the safe deposit companies which were owned by the bank.

Intricate, involved, and filled with skulduggery though the transaction was, it consisted, for the most part, merely of bookkeeping entries. No money changed hands. No one lost anything by it. No one claimed that it caused the ultimate closing of the bank, or that it directly or indirectly caused any loss to anyone. Nevertheless, following the closing of the bank, the defendants were indicted and brought to trial at the very moment when a wave of bitter feeling against banks and bankers was sweeping the country.

In the action in which Medina had now been called to play a part, four men were to be tried: Bernard K. Marcus, the bank's president; Saul Singer, its executive vice-president; Henry W. Pollock, vice-president and head of the bank's law department; and Herbert Singer, the son of Saul Singer and a law clerk in the employ of Isador J. Kresel, counsel for the bank. Kresel was also indicted, but he had obtained a severance of his case and so was not to be tried at the time the others came before the Court of General Sessions.

It was Herbert Singer whom Medina had been asked to defend, and in that defense he found himself closely associated with three famous trial lawyers: Charles H. Tuttle, counsel for Marcus; Emory R. Buckner, counsel for Saul Singer; and David Podell, counsel for Pollock. Both Tuttle and Buckner were very widely known, each having served as United States Attorney for the Southern District of New York and it had been Tuttle who, as a member of the firm of Davies, Auerbach & Cornell, had brought Harold Medina to that firm as a law clerk when he had graduated from Columbia Law School.

The trial, which came before Judge George L. Donnellan of the Court of General Sessions, was held in the huge courtroom on the ground floor of the old Criminal Courts Building in Lafayette Street. The special prosecutor was Max D. Steuer, whose ability was widely respected and who had at his disposal all the personnel and facilities of the District Attorney's office. When the prosecution opened its case, on April 8, 1931, after nine days spent in selecting the jurors and in other preliminaries, the courtroom was crowded to the doors. Every seat was occupied. Hundreds of people who had been unable to gain admittance still stood in a long double line outside the door, and the very air of the courtroom, as Harold Medina entered, seemed to him to be heavy with prejudice.

The special prosecutor and his assistants were seated at a large table beside the jury box. The defendants with their chief counsel and various assistants were crowded into a little pen immediately before the judge's rostrum, but as the judge entered, and everyone in the crowded courtroom rose, the lawyers representing the defendants were unfortunately not in agreement as to the strategy to be employed.

Conscious that prejudice was so great as to make any favorable outcome almost hopeless, Mr. Tuttle wished to play the game most carefully, picking up every possible exception so long as it offered any possible legal error for appeal. Mr. Buckner, on the other hand, insisted on making every effort to convince the jury of his client's innocence, and, in order to do so, was anxious to develop the case as fully and completely as possible. He insisted on putting his client on the stand, which forced the others to do the same with theirs. Medina, who had hoped to keep his client in the background, feeling that his youth would go far to show that he was an innocent agent of the others, found himself in a very difficult position.

The decisions that had resulted in the complicated and improper "Bolivar transaction" had been made by the officials of the bank, but Herbert Singer, as a law clerk in the office of the bank's counsel, had handled practically all the complex details. He had even been made the sole stockholder of the Bolivar Development Corporation, which had been used as one of the instrumentalities of the transaction and, though he acted under the instructions of the others, he had drawn up the hundreds of bookkeeping entries as well as the other intricate records, contracts, and waivers that were a part of the record. In fact, it was he who was most intimately acquainted with the endless details. Guided and directed by his father and the lawyer who employed him, however, he had never doubted the essential honesty of what he had been called upon to do, and now, though he, too, was on trial, his every impulse was directed toward saving his father, in whose honesty he resolutely believed. In fact, his intimate knowledge of the whole transaction and his desire to save his father caused him, under the skillful cross-examination of Mr. Steuer, to give the impression that perhaps he had been, not a minor, but a major figure, in the affair, and one who had taken a full and equal part in all its complicated development.

The trial lasted for twelve weeks, and filled more than seventy-five hundred typewritten pages of testimony. From first to last more than ten thousand spectators were said to have crowded into the courtroom; no case in a score of years had attracted such attention or consumed so much time. The task of the defense was difficult, for prejudice continued to run high, and Max Steuer, the special prosecutor, was a formidable opponent. But in a way it was Harold Medina whose problem was most difficult, for the very honesty that guided his youthful client as he testified in such detail day after day played into the hands of the prosecution. Nevertheless, when Medina gave his summation, following that of Mr. Tuttle, his force and sincerity were clearly evident.

"An eloquent appeal," read the report in the *New York Sun*, "was made in behalf of Herbert Singer," and the *Herald Tribune* referred to "the summation by Harold R. Medina, counsel for Herbert Singer, whose eloquent plea in defense of the young law clerk brought tears to his father's eyes."

It was a little after noon a week later when Judge Donnellan began his charge to the jury, but it was long past midnight before any sign suggested that a verdict had been reached. As 4 o'clock approached on that June morning, the jury solemnly re-entered the courtroom. As to Pollock they had disagreed; as to the other three—guilty.

The formalities that followed were short. Bail was not continued, and Harold Medina still remembers the depression that he felt as he saw young Herbert Singer marched with his convicted father and Bernard Marcus out of the courtroom on his way to a cell in the "Tombs."

The convictions were appealed, but the court known in New York as the Appellate Division upheld the verdict, and it was not until 1933 that the case reached the next higher court, the Court of Appeals. By that time, the wave of prejudice against banks and bankers had begun to subside. Even Mr. Tuttle, and former Governor Nathan Miller who by now had come to represent Saul Singer, felt some optimism for their clients. But Harold Medina, as he studied the problem that confronted him, reached a surprising conclusion and chose to offer an argument that may have had no precedent and that differed radically from the one he had presented before the Appellate Division.

It must be remembered that Herbert Singer, when he had been put on the witness stand, had testified in great detail about every phase of the transaction upon which the indictment had been based. Many who heard him during the several full court days he spent on the witness stand gained the impression that, despite his youth, he had played an important part, even a guiding part, in the whole affair. But Medina, offering his new argument, called the court's attention to a well-known characteristic common to young men just out of college: to the conceit they so often develop, to the exaggerated ego that is so often apparent at that time of life. He insisted that despite the young man's testimony it was incredible that he, an inexperienced boy less than a year out of law school, could have directed the actions of such mature and experienced men as his father and the president of the bank. He pointed out that it was perfectly evident that the young man had neither instigated the idea nor abetted his seniors in the transaction, that he was nothing more than their agent, guilty of no crime, guilty of nothing greater than a weakness that is common to youth—a natural conceit that had led him to magnify his own importance and the importance of the work he did.

This argument was clearly based on sound understanding of the psychology of youth. On the other hand, the Court of Appeals has no jurisdiction to reverse the action of a lower court on the facts. It is only on errors in the law that a reversal can be based, and this argument was more closely related to the facts than to the law.

It was on January 16, 1933, nearly two years after the trial, that the Court of Appeals heard this argument which differed so widely from the traditional appeal of lawyers, and the case was not decided until the fourteenth of March. In the meantime, President Roosevelt, having been inaugurated, had issued a series of proclamations having to do with banks and banking. For days every bank in the country had remained closed and a new wave of bitter feeling against banks and bankers swept the country.

It is impossible to say whether or not this had any effect on the seven judges of the Court of Appeals, but when their decision was announced it affirmed the conviction of Bernard Marcus and Saul Singer. At the end of that long decision, however, it had this to say about Medina's client:

> Not so regarding Herbert Singer. As to him our view is different. . . . It is difficult to believe that he intentionally aided or assisted his father and Marcus in wilfully misappropriating the funds of corporations of which they were directors. . . . We

are not unfamiliar with the importance frequently assumed by the young practitioner who is apt to magnify his work and worth. It is inconceivable that Saul Singer who, in thirty-two years after landing in this country, had passed from the crockery, steam laundry, and garment business to a position of one of the leading financiers of New York City, could be influenced or directed by the young son he had brought up in the soft places of life. . . .

The judgment as to Saul Singer and Bernard K. Marcus should be affirmed. The judgment as to Herbert Singer should be reversed, and the indictment dismissed.

As I write, nearly twenty years have passed since Herbert Singer's case was won and the young man was reinstated as a member of the bar, but Judge Medina still recalls it vividly.

"It is the one thing in my life as a lawyer," he once told me, "of which I feel most proud."

Though the Singer case had been lost before a jury and won only on appeal, the new and added reputation Medina had earned because of it, and the widespread attention he had attracted, now began to bring him other jury cases. For the first time in his highly active career he had been widely publicized, and it had become apparent not only that he was warm and human as a person but also that he could be both appealing and eloquent as an advocate. Throughout the long-drawn trial it had been clear that chicanery was foreign to his nature—that he would not stoop to cheap or underhanded practices. He had shown himself capable in handling complicated subject matter and had demonstrated his ability to simplify and clarify involved complexities. He had also shown that he was entirely willing to fight with everything that was in him even so vigorous an opponent as Max D. Steuer.

Formerly the income from Medina's law practice had been the result of large numbers of comparatively small fees, and though, on occasion, he was paid as much as seventy-five hundred dollars for cases he handled on appeal, there were very few in his whole career, hardly half a dozen, that paid that well. Ultimately his customary minimum for such cases rose to twenty-five hundred dollars, but even then, when cases interested him especially, he handled them for fees that were often far less. Following the Singer trial, however, cases of an entirely different nature from any he had theretofore been asked to consider began to come to him—commercial cases, for the most part, in which large sums and important interests were involved, and which brought him fees of ten or twenty thousand dollars or even more. These differed widely from the cases in which he had specialized for so long. Among them were no one-day trials, no arguments to be completed in less than the full time allowed to counsel. Each of these new and greater cases might be a matter of weeks or even months, and where, theretofore, he had thought nothing of handling a dozen or more cases on appeal each month, he found himself fully engaged in this new field when he had no more than two or three cases a year.

His background for this work was excellent. He knew the law as few lawyers knew it. His technical knowledge was wide and detailed. The mental discipline that had made it possible for him to prepare his earlier cases with such care served him as well with these new and greater ones. Now, however, his unwillingness to resort to trickery or chicanery was even more important. He had seen that kind of thing at work in court and it revolted him, but, realizing that jurors are apt to be much wiser than many people think, he began more clearly to realize that they also disliked it. Jurors, he knew, were apt to be little acquainted with the technicalities and complexities of the law, but he never questioned their practicality or their essential wisdom, and because he was inclined to acknowledge their sincerity and honesty of purpose as he appeared before them, they, in turn, seemed willing to accept him in much the same spirit.

With this new type of practice taking more and more of his time and with much appellate work still continuing, he began to see that his teaching would be apt to suffer. The Appellate Division and the Court of Appeals, before which so many of his cases had always come, usually sit from 2 until 6 P.M., and no more than an hour is ordinarily allotted to each side for argument. Jury cases, however, usually begin at 10 or 10:30 A.M. and, with only time out for lunch, continue until 4 or 4:30. But even then the day's work is never over. Many tasks are likely to require attention at the office. There may be conferences. Law clerks may be ready with references that are needed for the next day. Reports of investigators and those of assistants who have interviewed possible new witnesses must be considered. The court stenographer's minutes may not be ready before 8 or 9 in the evening, and yet they must be read.

With schedules such as this repeated day after day for weeks at a time, Harold Medina found it difficult to arrange for the lectures at Columbia or for those that filled the high-pressure periods of the bar examination course. Ultimately, his teaching was forced to give way in order to make it possible for him to devote his full time to his practice, but that was far in the future. Meanwhile, as he had always done before when new tasks had come upon him, he merely worked the harder, always somehow finding the time that was required.

Late in 1937, Medina was called upon to defend the Trans-Lux Corporation, which operated a number of motion picture theaters, in a suit that had been brought by a real estate broker named Abraham Felt, who claimed that under an arrangement to which he and the president of the corporation had agreed, he had earned a commission of about forty-five thousand dollars. The corporation, in turn, claimed not only that no such commission had been earned, but that there had never been any such agreement as Felt alleged. As the agreement, according to Felt, had been oral, with no one present at the time it was entered into but the corporation president and himself, the case revolved not only about Felt's testimony and that of the corporation executive but also about all the correspondence that passed between the corporation and the man who now had brought suit. Much additional evidence ultimately played a part, and during the course of the trial many witnesses were called to the stand, with the result that the trial lasted more than two weeks, and fully a thousand pages of testimony were taken, most of which, to any outsider, was repetitious and unexciting, but in which, because of his attention to detail, Medina was able to establish facts that seemed, at first, to be almost impossible of satisfactory demonstration.

When the problem was first brought to him, Medina was naturally uninformed as to its details. But as soon as his client's contentions had been outlined, he asked for all the letters and other documents that bore on the matter, however indirectly, and had his assistants correlate them so that he could begin his study of the material.

What he found was not entirely to his satisfaction. What was missing he did not know. He could not even be entirely certain that there were any actual documents or letters that had not been included. Nevertheless, he vaguely felt that something, though he did not know what, was missing—that somewhere there was something else that would add to his understanding of the picture.

Many of the witnesses he would have to call were connected in various capacities with the theatrical profession. There were managers, producers, and others, in addition to the officers of the Trans-Lux Corporation, and it was hard to get them to give the time and the thought necessary to help him prepare for the trial as he wished. Even in checking the contents of their files and in refreshing their memories, he found them lax or unable to find the time, and while each was interviewed separately, less progress was made than Medina wished. They insisted that he had everything, but he could not get away from the feeling that something—he could be no more accurate than that—was missing. In fact, he was so confident that there must be more that he finally told his clients that unless every one of those who was connected with the transaction on which the suit was based agreed to meet at his office in order to help in locating what he believed to be missing, he would refuse to go ahead with his preparations for the trial.

There was a tremendous howl. Almost without exception the men he wanted to see insisted that they were too busy, that they had already told everything they knew of the matter, that they could not spare the time, that they had endless duties to perform. And no doubt some of them asked what a lawyer was for anyway, if not to get together his own information without intruding so far on the invaluable time of those who were paying his fee. But Medina stood his ground and ultimately a dozen or fifteen of these busy and occasionally temperamental people came to his office, still grumbling but compelled, for the moment, to do as he asked. And the result was what he had imagined it might be. One of them began to recall some additional correspondence, some letters and a few telegrams which were ultimately located—in the wrong file!

Until that moment Medina had felt that the task he had

been called upon to face was all but hopeless. Even yet he knew that it would not be easy. Nevertheless, he began to see that there was a chance, though little more than that. In fact, even without knowing in any detail the evidence his opponent planned to offer he began to see that there simply could not have been any such oral agreement as Felt claimed he had made. When the trial opened Medina made that statement even before a word of testimony had been taken.

But it was one matter to *say* that it did not exist, and quite another to *prove* it to the satisfaction of the jury, especially in view of the complicated and often conflicting testimony that was offered. Nevertheless, the theory on which he based his case led him to say in his opening statement that "we think this case has no foundation in fact," and the strategy he followed led him to fill in every detail of his case so accurately and completely as to leave no opening upon which serious doubts could convincingly arise.

His opponent, on the other hand—Alexander Pfeiffer of the firm of Pfeiffer & Crames—had already announced that he would prove "the bad faith of these defendants." He had even said that he would prove it by documentary evidence, and for two weeks the intricate, involved and conflicting testimony of the many witnesses bore on these two contentions.

It was on the morning of December 28, 1937, that Medina began his summation, and it took him most of the day. In more than twenty thousand words he bound scores of seemingly conflicting facts into a unified and integrated whole. He listed in the utmost detail all the statements which served to complete the picture. He clarified by letters, telegrams, and other documents, every single contention that was susceptible to such proof and stressed again and again the facts which, he contended, proved the absence of any such agreement as the one on which his opponent's claim was based.

Pfeiffer followed in a summation of even greater length, a summation that occupied parts of two days. The judge's charge to the jury occupied an hour. It was 3:20 in the afternoon when the jury retired, and it was not until 10:37 that evening that they returned.

"Mr. Foreman and Members of the Jury," intoned the clerk, "have you agreed upon a verdict?"

"We have."

"And how say you?"

"We find a verdict for the defendant."

I once asked Harold Medina how he won that technical and highly intricate case—a case that attracted no public interest at the time.

"The additional letters," he told me, "that had been filed in the wrong cabinet were not, in themselves, especially important, and at first glance certainly did not appear vital. But they completed the picture I was able to present. They also helped to keep my witnesses from making any inadvertent errors in their statements, and that is often a very important matter. I won that case because of the care I took in its preparation—perhaps actually because of those lost letters and telegrams that were turned up. Many a case is lost because erroneous statements inadvertently made on the witness stand are blown up by the other side as deliberate falsifications, and I had guarded against that."

Years had passed by now since the house at Westhampton had been built. During most of the time the Medinas lived in their 75th Street apartment and were busy throughout the larger part of the year in New York. They regularly had Monday night seats at the Opera, the same seats year after year. They attended the theater, went now and again to the movies, and gave or attended small dinner parties. Every winter they got away for two or three weeks at Pinehurst or Bermuda. In the summer of 1933 they took a car to Europe and toured France, but at every opportunity the Westhampton house was opened—and in a very special sense it was "home."

Both boys, after attending Hill School, had entered Princeton where, in 1934, Harold, junior, won his Phi Beta Kappa key and graduated "with highest honors" in philosophy. Standish, in his turn, became intercollegiate pole-vault champion in 1936 and 1937, and as I write, still holds the Princeton record of 13 feet, 10¼ inches. He also was elected to Phi Beta Kappa, and graduated in 1937 "with high honors" in English.

From the time both boys entered college they were given reasonable allowances, but their father had not forgotten those few boys he himself had known at college who had been given too much money. The effects, in some instances, had been bad, and he was determined not to give his sons enough "to let them get into trouble." Neither of them was asked to work on a budget until his junior year, but then each one was told to estimate his expenses for a year, including tuition, clothes, amusements, and such additional expenses as could be justified.

"Get it together," Medina told Harold, junior, on whom this idea was first tried, "and I'll see if I can let you have it."

In due course the budget was submitted and approved.

"Now look here, Harold," Medina explained. "You must remember that this is to cover a year—twelve months—and it's all you're going to get. So don't forget."

The fiscal year that had been decided upon was from September 1 to August 31, but before that time was up the boy began to develop financial difficulties.

"By the next June," the Judge once said, "his tongue was

hanging out, but I didn't give him any more until time for the new budget came. And he didn't ask for any, either. I wasn't niggardly, and they never took advantage of me, but they learned that they had to figure it out right."

Nor was this training in judgment and self-reliance confined merely to the matter of budgets. Later, when Harold, junior, was a student at Columbia Law School and wanted to work in his father's law office during the summer he was permitted to try it—for a time.

"It wasn't long before some of the others in the office were telling me how 'wonderful' he was," Medina once explained. "But I knew better. He was doing well enough, but there was lots he didn't know, and I didn't like the praise he was getting; it might ruin him. So I decided it wasn't good to have him there. I formulated the policy of throwing both boys to the lions. I made up my mind to let them go on their own. I wouldn't even help them to get jobs."

In the years that followed the building of the house in Westhampton, Medina's first cruiser gave way to another, and later to a 42-footer named *Spindrift*. And this cruiser was replaced, in 1930, by the 46-foot *Spindrift II*. The house underwent no changes unless it was to grow more homelike as it was lived in. Ultimately the library, too, wore off its newness and settled down comfortably among the shrubs and trees and flowers of the garden.

By 1938, both boys had married—Harold, junior, to Janet Williams of New York, and Standish to Hope Kiesewetter of South Orange, New Jersey—and as usual the Westhampton house was the center of the Medina family's activities during July and August of that year. About the middle of September, when Medina himself was busy in New York representing Julian L. Reynolds, called the "tobacco heir" by the *New York Journal-American*, in a much publicized suit for separation,

Standish's wife, Hope, was taken to the hospital for an appendectomy. All summer the Westhampton home had been occupied and busy, but now Mrs. Medina found herself alone there with the family's two servants, and on September 18 she closed the house and left with the servants for New York.

For several days there had been warnings of a hurricane in the Caribbean, but few people in the vicinity of Westhampton gave the reports much thought. Usually such hurricanes expend themselves in areas far removed from Long Island. This time, however, the storm, which was greater than most, swept to the north. It missed Florida, touched Cape Hatteras, kept well out to sea as it passed up the coasts of Maryland, Delaware, and New Jersey, but presently struck Long Island with astounding fury.

Westhampton, guarded by nothing except the narrow expanse of the dunes, lay directly in its path, and the succession of tidal waves that were driven across this low-lying area swept almost everything before them. All the way from New York City to Massachusetts the damage was widespread, but where the center of the hurricane passed—Westhampton, Saybrook Point, New London—the storm was unparalleled in its intensity. There were hundreds of deaths. Thousands of people were left homeless. For miles the Long Island shore was swept almost clear of houses, bridges, boats—everything—and the house Mrs. Medina had so fortunately left three days before was torn to bits by the storm-driven tidal waves and scattered with the remains of scores of others that had once stood in that shattered area.

The house was so utterly demolished that even some of its cast-iron radiators were later found a mile or more away, and not even a portion of the structure remained standing above the wrecked foundation. The outer walls and roof of the library still stood, but its thousands of volumes, swept from the shelves by the storm-driven water, were either lost amid the debris that covered the countryside or, still recognizable in the sand and mud that covered everything, were ruined.

A thousand personal belongings were gone. *Spindrift II*, swept from her mooring by the storm, was seen by a frightened observer as she shouldered her way in a smother of foam across the Medina lawn, and later, when the storm had spent its force, was found with a hole in her bottom, lying on the twelfth green of the Westhampton Country Club a mile away. And except for three cars that had been left in the garage, for the cruiser, and for one lone silver fox wrap, there was no insurance! Insurance on damage done by wind—yes. But not on damage done by water pushed by the wind.

Almost everything the Medinas had owned there at Westhampton was swept away. The losses they suffered in that wave of wind and water reached $125,000, and the home they had occupied for fourteen years was gone. But no member of the family had been hurt.

"We had much to be thankful for," said the Judge. "It showed us the futility of material things."

7

CASES IN BLACKMAIL AND TREASON

THE HURRICANE OF SEPTEMBER, 1938, DESTROYED THE HOME around which the Medina family life had been centered for fourteen years, but what was not yet apparent was that another hurricane—one infinitely more vast and of a different kind—was about to sweep the world. In one, the damage had been confined to a narrow path extending across parts of three states. In the other, there were no limits to the storm, which was felt in every corner of the world. In one, Medina lost a home that he could build again. In the other, his whole career was changed.

It took a year to clear Apaucuck Point of the debris of the hurricane. Wreckage was everywhere, and endless personal belongings lay buried or half buried in the sand and mud. Sightseers came by scores in the weeks following the storm, and, wandering wherever their curiosity led them, picked up and carried off whatever caught their fancy. Personal belongings, silverware—anything—appealed to them as nothing more than mementoes of the storm, and on one occasion when Medina objected and pointed out to such a group wandering about his property that what they were picking up was his, he was astonished at their reply.

"Why, a catastrophe like this," he was told, "belongs to everybody!"

Long before the wreckage of the Medina home had been cleared away, plans for a new house had been completed, and in the spring following the storm a contract for its construction was let. While the work of reconstruction went on, *Spindrift II*, repaired and refinished during the winter, lay at her mooring once more and, along with the partially rebuilt library, served as headquarters.

For the most part the losses had been complete, though now and again belongings that were still usable came to light. A ruined buffet that had been in the Medina dining room was found on the golf course and in it some of the family's silver was still intact. The two poles with which Standish had won his intercollegiate pole-vault championships reappeared when their loss was advertised. A neighbor had found them and now returned them, refusing the reward. The library was the greatest single loss, for though the structure that had housed the books remained more or less intact, the books were gone, or, found here and there in the mud and decaying vegetation, were ruined. Of all the thousands of volumes that had once filled the library's shelves only thirty remained, and even these were damaged beyond repair.

Aside from trying to re-establish some kind of order in the chaos, little could be done at Apaucuck Point that autumn. Men were at work clearing the debris, and from time to time the Medinas joined them and searched the ruins. Medina himself was busy in New York, where his classes at Columbia demanded his attention, where the October bar examination course followed closely on the heels of the hurricane, and where the offices of Medina & Sherpick were busy with a variety of legal matters.

In the years that had passed since the Herbert Singer case the firm had grown, and Medina himself, assisted on most of his cases by William Gilbert, a partner in the firm, and

Richard T. Davis, who later became a partner, was mainly handling litigation very different in nature from that which had earlier occupied much of his time. More and more he found himself engaged in complicated, protracted cases on which he spent months in preparation and weeks on trial. The reputation he had earned in appellate work still brought him many cases, but the nature of his practice was changing. He was now engaged chiefly with commercial problems, though now and again he was called upon to represent clients in much-publicized marital tangles; and one such case—it was the result of a unique mixture of bigamy and blackmail—had reached its unsavory end the better part of a year before the hurricane.

The client had the courage, which few men possess, to resist a claim which Medina felt was blackmail pure and simple. Although married and the father of a family, this man had been led into a clandestine and bigamous marriage in the concealment of which he had been weak enough to sign a document in which he promised to pay one million dollars in certain contingencies, which were bound to happen—and did, in due course. He had made a settlement by the payment of a large amount of cash and had destroyed the document only to find that his wily "friend" had preserved a photostatic copy and was ready with a story which explained everything. She was so confident that he would capitulate that she brought suit, although in the meantime she had married a respectable man in a distant state. The defense was blackmail, and a counterclaim to recover the amounts already paid.

In deference to a number of innocent people involved no names will be mentioned, although the newspapers were full of the case at the time.

Basically it was a question of veracity between the two.

The woman denied that she had known that the man was married at the time he bigamously married her. On the other hand, the attendant circumstances backed up the story of Medina's client, but he had been such a rotter in the whole affair that he was unlikely to receive the slightest sympathy. The general reaction was sure to be that he who dances should pay the piper.

That the defendant had gone through a marriage ceremony in which fictitious names had been used, was admitted. That the woman had lured him into it for purposes of blackmail could never be established on his mere say-so, and his wealth and social position were actually a handicap. These were some of the problems that faced Medina when he went to work on the case.

A careful search into the woman's background ultimately turned up the fact that she had been married and divorced prior to her marriage to Medina's client, and in connection with this earlier marriage an odd fact appeared. In having the records checked it was found that this first man she had married had signed his name "Sanford J. Clarke" in one place on the marriage license while in another he had signed it "Sanford H. Clarke."

Here was something strange. Errors of many kinds creep into such records, but this kind of error is clearly outside the realm of the probable. Even a drunk who is incapable of logical thought or sensible action is not apt to make a mistake in setting down his middle initial. Yet here was just such a mistake, and Medina wanted to know how it had occured. Was it possible that this woman who, according to Medina's client, had been the one to suggest that bigamous marriage, had previously engaged in a similar enterprise? It sounded farfetched, but the search was continued.

The woman in the case had later been divorced from this

man "Clarke," as an Illinois court record showed, but search as they would, Medina and his assistants were utterly unable to find the slightest trace of the man during any period before the marriage license had been obtained or after the divorce had been granted. In fact, except for these two documents, there was no record whatever of his existence.

Medina still had that middle initial in mind. It seemed to him to be a kind of riddle that needed to be solved, and he found a clue to the answer in the records of the Illinois divorce court. A witness in that court had testified to acquaintance with both the woman and the man from whom she had obtained the divorce, and had related the acts of cruelty upon which the divorce decree was based.

After some difficulty and the use of detectives this man was found. He turned out to be a banker of some reputation, and he finally admitted not only that he had been the witness in the divorce suit but also, fantastically enough, that he had been the husband against whom he had testified—the man who, in those marriage papers, had used the fictitious name Sanford J. Clarke in one place and Sanford H. Clarke in another.

Not unnaturally he was very evasive, but it was easy to put two and two together. Clearly, the woman who was trying the blackmail game against Medina's client had used it before. The trouble was that the story was almost unbelievably extravagant, and no one could predict what "Sanford Clarke" would say under oath. Furthermore, the woman was a cool customer.

But the preparation of the case was now complete and the trial was about to start. The problem of strategy was how best to use the surprising material that had been turned up. Medina decided to spring his mine when the woman, full of confidence under the guidance of her own counsel, was in the midst of her direct examination. As she completed telling the court how, as an innocent girl, she had been led by the defendant into this marriage, Medina casually asked the judge and the woman's lawyer if he might interrupt for a moment to have the plaintiff identify someone. They readily agreed and "Sanford Clarke" was brought in.

"Have you ever seen this man before?" asked Medina.

"No," said the woman.

"Is it not a fact," Medina asked, "that you were once married to him?"

"No," she replied. "I never saw him before in my life."

Medina pressed her no further and the case went on, but the damage was done. She knew that she had committed perjury, and after court had adjourned she admitted it to her counsel. Shocked by this revelation, the attorney withdrew from the case, after putting her back on the stand the next day to recant and thus avoid prosecution for perjury. While new counsel was brought in, the outcome of the case was a foregone conclusion. But the judge, in a brief but scathing opinion, dismissed not only the woman's complaint but the counterclaim as well—a just but not very logical conclusion. Nevertheless, the result might well have been very much worse for Medina's client had it not been that those marriage papers were studied with enough care to detect that the signature was "Sanford H. Clarke" in one place and "Sanford J. Clarke" in another.

It was in June, 1939, that Harold Medina's class at Princeton assembled for its thirtieth reunion, and few who returned did so more eagerly than Harold Medina himself. While he had missed some of the early reunions because of his bar examination classes, and over the years had been more active in the alumni affairs of Columbia Law School, he had been on hand for all of the dinners and other meetings of the Class of 1909. It was in large part owing to the influence of his classmate Josh Brush that Medina's enthusiasm for Princeton and for his class had grown. He had been made a member of the executive committee that arranged that thirtieth reunion. He was responsible, along with another classmate, Frank L. Cunningham, for the class dinner. He was a member of the committee that was responsible for the "Nought Nine Art Exposition," and no one was a more eager participant in the card games, the impromptu entertainments, the "bicker sessions," or the sports programs. He had come to be a member of his class in a different and a far more enthusiastic sense than he had ever been as an undergraduate. Thirty years before, he had sometimes felt ill at ease among his classmates, but now no one was more comfortable or confident among his fellows. Formerly he had held no class office, had been a member of no class committee; now he was busy on several committees, was to be chosen vice-president at the next important reunion and later was to be made president. And this development was taking place for no other reason than because he was Harold Medina, an increasingly popular member of the class in which—so he had felt, at least—he had once had so little popularity.

It has been the custom at Princeton, as at other colleges and universities, to elect alumni trustees, and many years ago Harold Medina, urged by Mort Fry, permitted his classmates to submit his name to the nominating committee of the Graduate Council. He was nominated, together with several others, and the alumni voted in due course, but Medina was defeated.

There is little doubt that he was hurt, though it would be surprising if he ever mentioned the matter to a soul. It may be that he never quite admitted it to himself, and were he to be questioned, would no doubt find some way to rationalize whatever feeling he may have had. But when it was later suggested to him that he run again for the same trusteeship, he refused. His bluster, his heartiness, his lusty geniality—what the late Dean Christian Gauss once called "the excessively generous and exuberant nature of the man"—may seem, at first glance, to be the outward and visible signs of a nature proof against small hurts, but that is far from true. Under an exterior that may sometimes appear impervious there is still much of the sensitiveness of the undergraduate.

By the spring of 1940, Medina found himself confronted by a problem that necessitated one of the great decisions of his life. It was not a situation that had arisen suddenly. It had been developing ever since he had taken part in the Singer case nine years earlier and was due to the growth, and the change in character, of his law practice. During the 1920's, the hundreds of cases he had argued before the appellate courts had still permitted him to carry on his bar examination course and his teaching at Columbia. He had even continued to do so throughout the 1930's, as his cases in the appellate courts grew more complicated and important and the jury cases he was called upon to handle grew more numerous and time-consuming. But ultimately, despite his energy, despite his application and concentration, he began to see that he could no longer spare the time his teaching required.

The fact that he was completing his twenty-fifth year at Columbia University Law School may, in his own belief, have had something to do with bringing about the decision he reached at that time, though he would have been forced before long to reach the same conclusion even had this anniversary not been in the offing. The part that he had played at the law school meant much to him. In twenty-five years he had never missed a Columbia class for which he was responsible. He had never asked for a leave of absence or even for any momentary relief from duty in all that time. He had never refused any request the school of law had made so far as teaching was concerned. But now, because of the pressure of other duties, he could no longer continue to carry on this work, or knew that he would shortly be unable to.

By now, too, he had completed the twenty-seventh year of his bar examination course, had given his eighty-eighth uninterrupted series of lectures, had brought the total of prospective lawyers who had come to him for instruction to the astonishing figure of 39,258, and had seen nearly a million and a quarter dollars paid in for this one long-sustained activity. But this, too, he decided to discontinue.

So it was in June, 1940, that he taught his last class at Columbia and ended the bar examination course. At the request of Dean Young B. Smith he retained—and still retains—his membership on the faculty of the Columbia Law School. A year later he once more gave his bar examination course, and in March, 1942, delivered a portion of those lectures to a limited group. Essentially, however, his teaching career had been brought to an end. An activity that had played a controlling part in his life—in his philosophy—in his mental and professional development—came to an end, and with the conclusion of the bar examination course he voluntarily turned off a source of revenue such as few men are ever given an opportunity to tap.

There were two reasons behind these two decisions: the one practical, the other philosophical. The practical reason was his expanding law practice, which by now so clearly encroached upon the time he had always before given to his teaching. The decision was not easy. Nevertheless, the choice had to be made, and it was his interest in the active practice of law that won.

In the matter of the bar examination course the decision may, in a way, have been less difficult than that which concerned Columbia University. He was proud of what he had accomplished with the course and the reputation he had created for it, but from the first he had recognized that activity as a practical one—practical from his own point of view as a welcome source of revenue—practical from the viewpoint of his students as an effective and relatively inexpensive aid in reviewing what they had studied and in passing New York's difficult bar examinations. By 1940 Medina's one-time need for the income from the bar examination course no longer existed. In a way he even felt it to be a kind of handicap, for he had decided many years before to forego any thought of continuing actively to accumulate wealth after he was fifty. It was not that he had any objection to wealth in itself, but he felt that his sons would be likely to develop more initiative and independence if he discontinued any further thought of accumulating additional wealth to leave them when he died.

Except for a very few years when Harold and Ethel Medina were first married, money had never been a problem in their lives. Mrs. Medina has never thought much about it, and Medina himself has never been inclined to discuss such matters with her or with anyone else. The money that was involved in the bar examination course had very little to do with their decision now. Momentarily Medina considered turning the course over to his sons, but Mrs. Medina knew what she had undergone during the endless lonely evenings of the bar examination lectures, and now she was opposed to the very idea of permitting her sons' wives to face a similar problem. The sons may have felt that they did not have their father's ability to carry on so specialized and so demanding an activity. At any rate, they showed little interest in it, and so it was that Medina decided to bring the course to a conclusion about the time his law school teaching ended.

The new home the Medinas had built on the site of the old one at Westhampton was ready for occupancy that summer. *Spindrift II*, in commission since the year before, lay at her mooring, and even the library was beginning to take shape once more, though the war had started in Europe the preceding autumn and hardly more than a third of the books that were to form the replaced French section had been shipped from Paris before the city fell to the invading Germans.

Once the summer had passed and Medina had returned to New York, he found himself engaged in many activities in addition to his increasing practice. He spoke in a dozen places on "New York Practice." He was made a member of the American Bar Association's New York State Committee on Improvement in Judicial Procedure. Under the auspices of a committee of the Association of the Bar of the City of New York he lectured on "Recent Cases and New Developments in Pleading, Practice, and Procedure in State Courts," and the *New York Law Journal*, recognizing the value of what he had said, reprinted that lecture "in the longest serial which had appeared in the *Law Journal* within recent years," giving as its reasons "the exceptional interest of the subject and the exceptional clarity and thoroughness with which the subject has been discussed."

He was made a member of the Joint Committee of New York Bar Associations. He lectured before the Binghamton Bar Association on "Trial Evidence" and before a bar association on Staten Island on "Cross-examination." He spoke most thoughtfully to the students of the Garden City (Long Island) High School on the subject "Why Study Latin?" and received a letter of congratulation on his treatment of the subject from his old friend Harlan Fiske Stone who, a few days later, was elevated to the position of Chief Justice of the United States. He was made chairman of the Executive Committee of the City Bar Association and later its vice-president. As chairman of a committee of the New York Law Society he directed a study of Federal Deposition and Discovery Procedures. He was made chairman of the Advisory Council of Princeton University's department of modern languages and literatures, was elected to succeed United States District Judge John C. Knox as president of the Lawyers Club in New York City, was one of the organizers of the War Committee of the Association of the Bar of the City of New York and a member of the executive committee. And these activities formed only a part of what he did, in addition to carrying on a practice that was growing in size and importance with every passing month.

The energy and widespread interests that made these activities possible are beyond most men, but Medina still found time for other things. At Westhampton, for instance, he was troubled by a pest of tent caterpillars that had regularly for years disfigured the trees of that portion of Long Island. He was not alone in being annoyed, but he was apparently alone—or almost so—in believing that something should be done about it. The most effective way of dealing with the caterpillars was to destroy the egg clusters which, deposited on the twigs of the affected trees in late June and early July, hatch out the following spring; and so, singlehanded, he started the collection and destruction of egg clusters. During autumn and winter week-ends for a couple of years he succeeded reasonably well in eliminating the pest within half a mile or so of his Westhampton home. He realized that he alone was not equal to the task he had begun, and so he enlisted the cooperation of the children of the school closest to his home, agreeing to pay them at a modest rate for such unhatched clusters as they brought in.

This campaign soon began to produce results, and in an effort to widen the good work, he wrote a letter to the local paper, the Hampton *Chronicle*, suggesting that the children of other nearby schools join in the hunt—at his expense. In that letter, incidentally, he made a report of what had already been accomplished, and pointed out that within a period of a few weeks he and the children of the school district in which he lived had collected and destroyed no fewer than 3,897 egg clusters.

A difficulty arose when the children somehow got the impression that the caterpillars were poisonous or otherwise harmful, but Medina spiked that rumor by giving a talk at one of the schools and actually swallowing a caterpillar before his audience. He even repeated that surprising performance—once—for the benefit of a girl who, having failed to see him do it the first time, expressed some doubt that he had ever done it at all. When, a little later, some question arose as to what he was doing with those egg clusters he was paying the children to collect, and, particularly, what he got for them "when he sold them," he arranged to have them brought to him at his library where, having paid for them, he destroyed them in the fireplace in full view of those who had brought them in.

That caterpillar campaign, from beginning to end, covered several years, and ultimately, aided by a providentially cold spring, reached a very successful conclusion. For years tent caterpillars have been few in the vicinity of Westhampton.

Throughout these years Medina was constantly busy with his practice, but few of the cases he handled during the period that immediately followed his departure from Columbia were dramatic to the layman, or entertaining. Instead, for the most part, they were long and often difficult struggles that dealt with problems and complexities concerning which the public had little interest. On one occasion, for instance, he defended the Manufacturers and Traders Trust Company of Buffalo in a case having to do with the sale of stock in which an estate claimed an interest, and which the newspapers called "the longest trial in the history of the United States District Court for the Western District of New York"—a case in which some six thousand pages of testimony were taken and nearly seven hundred exhibits were presented. Other cases were hardly less involved or technical. Each summer, however, he escaped for a time from the duties connected with his practice in order to "recharge his batteries" at Westhampton. *Spindrift II*, unable to operate because of shortages brought on by the war, was not at her mooring off Apaucuck Point for several years after 1941, but lay, instead, high and dry in a boatyard. Still, Medina had his golf clubs and his books, and except as wartime duties now and again called him away, he was apt to be at Westhampton during July and August.

He was there on an afternoon late in August, 1942, and was as concerned as most other Americans were about the discouraging war reports that had come at intervals for months. Japan had struck at Pearl Harbor only eight months before. Rommel had pushed the British back to El Alamein in Egypt.

Our forces on Bataan had surrendered in April. Corregidor had fallen in May. The Japanese had been defeated at the Battle of Midway in June, but a week later they landed in the Aleutians. And now the Marines had landed on Guadalcanal, a remote, unheard-of island, and no one knew whether or not they could hold their beachhead. Little good news had recently come from there or from anywhere else.

It was peaceful on Long Island, or it seemed to be. But even such peace as appeared to exist there was apparently being threatened. There had been a story in the papers not long before about German saboteurs who had landed at Amagansett, thirty miles or so east of Westhampton. Still, the war seemed remote from those quiet shores, and on that August afternoon Medina had just finished a round of golf, was on the terrace at his home, ready for a cocktail, when the phone rang. It was John C. Knox, Chief Judge of the Southern District of New York, who was calling.

"Harold," he began when Medina had answered. "I've got something I want you to do."

"I don't know what it is, John," Medina replied, "but the answer's yes."

"You'd better not say that," warned the judge, "until you know what it's about."

A man named Cramer, he explained—Anthony Cramer, German-born but an American citizen—had been arrested by the Federal Bureau of Investigation and charged with treason. He had no money—worked in a New York factory, shoveling coal for forty-five dollars a week. And he had had some dealings with a group of German saboteurs.

"The man is poor," Judge Knox continued, "and he's charged with a hated crime. But it's important to demonstrate both to our people and to the world that such a man can have as good a defense under our system as if he were rich. Will you defend him—as assigned counsel—without compensation and as a patriotic duty?"

Medina did not hesitate.

"Yes," he replied. "I'll do it."

"I went into it with my eyes open," he once told me. "I knew there would be public feeling. I expected criticism. My friends—or many of them—wouldn't like it. Some people would be sure that I must be getting something for it. I was sure to take a beating. But according to my idea of a lawyer's obligations to his profession and to the community, he is duty-bound to accept such a call. Nobody could have made me do it, but if I refused I couldn't have held up my head before my friends or my associates at the bar."

He went to New York to talk the matter over with Judge Knox, and arrange to see Cramer in the towering Federal Court House that looks out on Foley Square. It was a little room in which he first met Cramer, a bare little room containing only a few chairs and a wash basin. Though Cramer was being closely guarded and the door may have been barred, their conversation was private.

Cramer was convinced that he was not guilty of treason, but he was frank enough—or seemed to be—as to what had happened. For years, he explained, he and a German named Werner Thiel had been friends. For ten or twelve years after he had come to America following World War I, the two had gone through a good many vicissitudes together. They had worked in auto factories and elsewhere, and Thiel, after Adolf Hitler came into power, had somehow interested himself in the Nazi business, though Cramer had not. Cramer, perhaps, was the steadier of the two. At any rate, he had loaned small sums to Thiel from time to time until Thiel owed him about two hundred dollars. Then, sometime before Pearl Harbor, Thiel, who had never become an American citizen as Cramer had, said he was going back to Germany by way of Tokyo. Cramer saw him off, and later got a postcard that had been mailed in Tokyo. After that Cramer heard no more.

The United States was drawn into the war, and in June, 1942, Cramer was living in a rooming house in 86th Street, working nights and sleeping in the daytime. He had had no further word from Thiel and knew nothing of his whereabouts or of his activities. But awakening late one afternoon he found a note that had been shoved under his door. It was signed by a name he did not know and was written in a hand he did not recognize.

"Meet me," it read, "at the information desk at Grand Central Station at 8 o'clock tonight."

His first impulse was not to go, but his curiosity got the best of him, and exactly at 8, as he waited beside the circular Grand Central information desk, he was astonished to see Werner Thiel approach, accompanied by a man named Kerling. They greeted each other and, going to a bar nearby, Cramer asked Thiel over their beer how he had managed to return, but the answer was evasive. What he wanted, Thiel said, was to have Cramer help him get in touch with Norma Kopp, a laundress and kitchen maid to whom Thiel had been engaged. And in addition he said he would give Cramer back his two hundred dollars if he would take care of a money belt—a money belt that contained the better part of four thousand dollars.

Cramer agreed, and wrote a letter to the girl, who was employed at Westport, Connecticut, asking her to meet him in New York. He met her two days later, just after putting Thiel's money in the smallest safe deposit box he had been able to rent; but they failed to meet Thiel. The FBI had already arrested him, and before Cramer and the girl parted that evening, they arrested Cramer as well.

It was this story that Cramer first told Medina there in the bare little Court House room. It was this story, too—or so he said—that he had already told the FBI, though he admitted telling them a lie or two which he had then corrected.

"Now Mr. Medina," he said at last, "that can't be treason, can it?"

It was implicit in Cramer's story that he did not know that Thiel was a saboteur or that he had returned to America aboard a submarine, but there were many things Medina did not know—many things having to do with Cramer's story as well as with the law—and he found it difficult to answer.

"Well," he said at last, his manner thoughtful and serious, "I don't know."

Judge Medina remembers that Cramer's face turned white at that reply, though the man said nothing. He merely went to the wash basin, turned on the water, and stood there for several minutes lifting his wet hands to his face time after time. Nearly three years were to pass before that case was finally decided, and in that time Medina came to know Anthony Cramer more than ordinarily well, but that was the only sign of distress he ever saw in the man whose defense he was about to begin.

The task that faced Medina was far more difficult than might at first appear. Prejudice was running high and at every turn was inclined to have its effect on Cramer's case. But to make the problem even more difficult, the case was exceedingly technical, and the work that was required was stupendous. Medina himself knew little—almost nothing—about the law governing treason. Few lawyers did, for treason, providentially, has rarely troubled the security of the United States. Never in our history, for instance, had any such case ever been carried to the Supreme Court, and much of the applicable law had never been clearly and positively interpreted.

The work that was required was much more than Medina himself could adequately perform. Help was essential, so he put his own staff to work, with John W. Jordan especially helping him. He then enlisted the help of John McKim Minton, because of his wide experience in criminal trial work. And all of them began to study in detail the whole legal history of treason in England and in America.

It was on September 4, 1942, that Anthony Cramer, indicted on ten counts for aiding Werner Thiel and Edward John Kerling, two of eight German saboteurs who had landed from submarines in June, pleaded not guilty. Bail was set at fifty thousand dollars, and trial was later set to open on November 9. Cramer had learned that in the event of his conviction the minimum penalty would be five years' imprisonment and a fine of ten thousand dollars—the maximum would be death.

Medina had decided long before the trial began not to explain to the jury that he had been assigned to the case. It was his belief that it would not be to Cramer's best interest to make any point of it. The papers were constantly referring to him as assigned counsel, but so far as the jury was concerned he was determined to play his part in exactly the same manner as if he were being paid an excellent fee.

Ten "overt acts" had been listed in Cramer's indictment, but from the first Medina began to develop all the points that could be raised under the treason section of the Constitution. With the greatest care he raised questions as to the sufficiency of the overt acts that were charged, and especially stressed the "two witness rule."

> Treason against the United States [reads Section 3 of Article III of the Constitution] shall consist only in levying war against them, or in adhering to their enemies, giving them aid and com-

fort. No person shall be convicted of treason unless on the testimony of two witnesses to the same overt act, or on confession in open court.

The Congress shall have power to declare the punishment of treason, but no attainder of treason shall work corruption of blood, or forfeiture except during the life of the person attainted.

As the case progressed, Medina, for the first time in the history of American jurisprudence, developed all the points that could be raised under this section. He raised questions on points of evidence. He developed the proper motions and exceptions. He raised all the questions possible as to the sufficiency of the overt acts that were charged, especially in the light of the curious two-witness rule—a rule which applies, under our Constitution, to no other crime than that of treason.

Neither Judge Henry W. Goddard, before whom Cramer was being tried, nor United States Attorney Mathias F. Correa, who was prosecuting the case against him, at first appeared to believe that the points for which Medina was contending were of any great importance. Nevertheless, because of his contentions—particularly in connection with the two-witness rule—seven of the ten overt acts were later withdrawn by the prosecution, leaving only three for the jury to consider.

From the first, Medina was faced with a problem connected with putting Cramer on the witness stand. Evidence concerning each of several charges, except his mere presence in the company of Thiel and Kerling, had been offered by only one witness. But if, in an attempt to reply to these charges, Cramer himself were to be put on the stand, would that make "two witnesses" under any reasonable interpretation of Section 3, Article III? Medina could not know, for the matter had never been decided. Then, too, were Cramer to take the stand, the prosecution might possibly bring out facts concerning which Medina knew nothing, and as a result Cramer might be given the death penalty.

It was a difficult decision to make, and being unwilling to make it without explaining the situation most carefully to Cramer, Medina asked Judge Goddard for permission to take the prisoner from the courtroom in order to be able to speak privately with him. Permission was granted and Cramer listened carefully, but when the problem had been made clear to him he said he wanted to be put on the stand, that he was confident of the outcome, that he knew he was innocent.

From the time the trial opened prejudice ran strong against Cramer. Day after day, the courtroom was crowded. Misconceptions were common, and the very atmosphere seemed heavy with bitterness. On one occasion, when Mrs. Minton, the wife of Medina's associate in Cramer's defense, was in court she overheard a conversation between two men who sat near her.

"Who's that fellow with the black mustache?" asked one, tilting his head toward Medina.

"Oh," replied the other, "he represents the German government."

Throughout the trial people sometimes shrank from contact with Medina as he entered court, as if they feared contamination, and once, as he made his way through the crowded courtroom toward the counsel table, a man leaned toward him and deliberately spat in his face.

What passed through Medina's mind at that moment no one can know. Perhaps even he did not have an opportunity fully to understand his own feelings at the time. He bitterly resented that foul, unnecessary insult, and would have been more than human had he not felt the urge to drive his fist into the fellow's face. For days he had been working under tension. No one knew better than he how utterly unfair that crowded courtroom was—unfair not only to his client but also to himself. But with that man's cold spittle on his face, and a shudder of anger and disgust running through his system, he continued down the aisle. He did not even turn his head, but merely reached in his pocket for his handkerchief and silently wiped his face, taking his seat at the counsel table without a word and without a sign that anything out of the ordinary had happened. Few in the courtroom were aware of what had occurred. No more than a handful had seen it, and fewer still—perhaps no one—realized what sudden powers of restraint had controlled his normally impatient and combative nature.

Nor was it only those who came to the courtroom who so greatly misunderstood the part he played. Even his own mother never understood it or sympathized with it, despite his explanations.

It was on the tenth day of the trial that Cramer took the stand, and he told the same story he had originally told Medina. Even under heavy cross-examination no new facts came out, no inconsistencies developed.

"He was the only person I ever saw in so dreadful a jam," Medina once told me, "who constantly told the truth."

As the trial approached its end, Medina used almost twenty thousand words in his summation, covering every detail of the case, and finally both defense and prosecution rested. Judge Goddard charged the jury. Then he turned toward the counsel table.

"Mr. Medina," he continued. "Will you please rise?"

Surprised, Medina did as he was told and stood there frowning thoughtfully as Judge Goddard praised him for the part he had taken in the trial, praised him for his willingness to assume so unpopular but so important a responsibility, for his willingness to perform so heavy a task at the court's request and without pay. And when the judge had finished his generous commendation, Medina felt forced to do what he has called "the hardest thing" he ever did.

"Judge Goddard," he replied. "I do not wish to appear ungracious, but I must respectfully except to what you have said. I do not believe that you had any right to tell the jury that I have been defending this man as assigned counsel."

He sat down and the jury withdrew. An hour passed—two hours. The government attorneys began to appear perturbed. The jury asked to have some of the testimony reread. Clearly they were doubtful, or some among them were. But finally they returned.

Their verdict—Guilty!

It is natural, at such a time in any trial, for the defendant to feel discouraged, but Cramer gave no sign that he was depressed. He sat listening as motions were made and denied, and before he was led out he thanked Medina for his summation.

"It was wonderful," he said. "I'll never forget it. And I want to tell you—I've got forty-five dollars coming to me for the last week's work I did. I haven't anything else, but I want you to be sure to get that."

"Thanks, Tony," Medina replied, "but I think you'd better keep that for yourself. You'll need it to buy tobacco while you're up there in jail."

It was two weeks before Cramer was brought into court to hear his sentence, and it was clear that even Judge Goddard was under a heavy strain. United States Attorney Correa was demanding the death penalty.

"We are still at war," he said. "Attempts to send men

here by submarine can be made again. We cannot be sure that they have not been made already. And when they are made, their success will be dependent on people like Cramer. All people of his kind should be made to realize that swift retribution awaits them."

But Medina still fought hard, and he deeply felt what, in his last words at the trial, he told the judge.

"Your Honor," he concluded, "it rests on your own conscience. I do not see how, on this record, you can sentence this man to death. But that, now, is your problem."

Cramer was sentenced to forty-five years in prison and, in addition, was fined ten thousand dollars. The man was forty-two years of age, and the sentence, in effect, was for life, but as he was led away he gave no sign of emotion except for the flush that had spread across his face.

Medina appealed at once, and began the preparation of a brief which, when it was typewritten, ran to 123 pages. There is a rule that such briefs, unless special permission has been granted, should never exceed fifty pages, and Medina went to Judge Learned Hand of the United States Circuit Court of Appeals, in order to get permission to file a typewritten, instead of a printed, brief. Because no funds were available for Cramer's defense, the judge approved the request, and an order was entered permitting the presentation of the appeal *in forma pauperis*. But when Medina asked for permission to submit a brief of 123 pages, Judge Hand objected.

"No," he replied, not realizing the trouble and expense he was making Medina. "A hundred pages will be enough."

The 123-page brief was edited and shortened. Every point was studied again, and finally it was submitted in its shortened and retyped version. But when the case was argued before the United States Circuit Court of Appeals, Cramer's situation remained unchanged. The verdict of the District Court was unanimously affirmed.

Now Medina applied to the Supreme Court of the United States for certiorari—for an order bringing the case before the Supreme Court for review—and the writ was granted.

Everywhere the details of the Cramer case had been widely reported, and by now Medina's part in this difficult affair was beginning to be more adequately understood. Even before Cramer had been sentenced, Judge Knox, who had assigned Medina to the case, had written a letter of appreciation.

In my judgment [he said at the conclusion of that letter] your action was not only commendable from a professional standpoint, but it was, in addition, of a highly patriotic nature. You brought to Cramer's defense the great ability that is yours, and it was no whit less than it would have been had you been retained for one hundred thousand dollars. Judge Goddard has told me of the splendid way in which you conducted this case, and I want you, Mr. Minton, and Mr. Jordan to know that the court fully realizes the faithful and competent services you rendered.

J. Edgar Hoover, director of the Federal Bureau of Investigation, wrote to express his appreciation of Medina's methods during the trial, especially where the special agents of the department were concerned. Lawyers widely expressed their admiration. Even laymen commended him. But the case was not yet over.

It was not until November 8, 1943, that Cramer was promised a review of his case by the Supreme Court, and in that time Medina made an even more extensive study of the background of the treason clause in the Constitution. He studied colonial and early state constitutions, and when the time for the argument had been set he went to Washington a week ahead of time in order to work intensively in the Supreme Court library.

Ordinarily the Supreme Court sets aside no more than an hour for any single argument, but in this case a whole day was reserved, and Medina, convinced of the rightness of his cause and the soundness of his contentions, was ready. He spoke as he almost always speaks—after meticulously careful preparation but without notes, and he knew, as he developed his argument, that he was presenting it effectively.

In the Supreme Court of the United States there is a long space in front of the counsel table, and as Medina spoke he saw a man there, a court reporter, it seemed, for he had a stenographer's pad and seemed to be taking notes. Beyond that space in which the supposed court reporter was sitting, sat the nine justices of the Supreme Court, with Medina's friend, Harlan Fiske Stone, now the Chief Justice, occupying the center chair, with Justices Roberts, Reed, Douglas, and Jackson on his right, and Justices Black, Frankfurter, Murphy, and Rutledge on his left. It was before these men that Medina made what he believes to have been "the best argument I ever made before any appellate court."

Again and again the justices leaned forward to interrupt—asked questions—were given replies. Again and again Medina returned to his detailed argument, to the reasons for the two-witness rule, to the concepts upon which Section 3, Article III of the Constitution was based, to the meaning of terms used by the framers of the Constitution, and to their application to Cramer's particular case. Finally he came to the end, thanked the Court, and left for New York, wondering what decision the justices would reach and when it might be announced.

The next day George Sokolsky, the newspaper columnist, called Medina on the phone. He was interested in Medina's argument, and in the questions the justices had asked. Medina tried to answer, but he had made no notes, and had no written record.

"But you don't have to take my word," he told Sokolsky. "I saw a man taking down the argument. I'll get a copy of it. I'd like to have it anyway."

A letter to the clerk of the Supreme Court brought a reply saying that there had been no stenographic record made. Medina, however, was unconvinced. He had seen the man with the notebook. Surely he could be located.

He boarded a train for Washington and found the man in the Department of Justice. But the clerk of the Supreme Court had been right after all. The man had made no record of what Medina had had to say. He had been there merely to take down what the solicitor general had said. For the rest, he had been "doodling." There was no record whatever of "the best argument I ever made before any appellate court."

It was six months later—in May, 1944—when the Supreme Court, instead of deciding Cramer's case, ordered it reargued. Already serving in Atlanta Penitentiary, Cramer was not to learn for still more months the ultimate outcome of his appeal, and Medina, having already given endless time to the case, had now once more to argue it before the Supreme Court, and this time, as the order pointed out, he had need especially to have in mind the definition of "treason" and of the term "overt acts."

It was on November 6, 1944, that that reargument was heard, but Lewis Wood, of the Washington office of *The New York Times*, wrote Medina a week before then:

Kind words are few indeed in these hectic days . . . and . . . I feel I should like to pass on a spontaneous compliment I heard for you today.

Happening to be down at the Supreme Court press room I mentioned that the Cramer case would be reargued next week, whereupon the AP man broke in with:

"Did you hear that man Medina argue that case originally? I think he's the finest lawyer I ever heard. I hope I can hear him next week—just to hear him."

This tribute was so utterly out of the clear sky that it was valuable. Later, I heard Mr. Dilli, one of the Court clerks, also praise your ability highly.

Medina had been hopeful of getting a new trial for Cramer, but now he knew his client had a chance for the dismissal of the case. He began at the beginning and prepared all over again, and when he rose beside the Supreme Court counsel table and began to speak, the courtroom was jammed. Wives of justices, members of the diplomatic corps, lawyers, newspaper men, legislators—all were present as he once more presented his argument and answered the penetrating questions of the justices.

The brief that had been submitted covered hundreds of pages, and delved deeply into the history of treason in England, in the colonies, and in the United States. It especially took notice of developments in the interval between the time of the writing of the Declaration of Independence and the debates that took place during the drafting of the Constitution. It was Medina's contention that, despite their abhorrence of the crime of treason, the founders had used highly restrictive language to define it and had adopted the two-witness rule in order to make the clearest possible proof necessary. He argued that in Cramer's case such proof as the Constitution itself required had not been forthcoming, that the man should have been prosecuted under the Espionage Act and not for treason which the prosecution had failed to prove.

It was not until April 23, 1945, that the Supreme Court finally announced its decision in the first test of the law of treason ever to reach that tribunal. By a vote of 5 to 4 it reversed the conviction of Anthony Cramer.

The majority opinion was written by Justice Robert H. Jackson, who was joined by Justices Roberts, Frankfurter, Murphy, and Rutledge, but a dissent which called the majority conclusion "ridiculous" was written by Justice William O. Douglas, who was joined by Medina's old friend Chief Justice Harlan F. Stone and by Justices Black and Reed.

Admitting in the majority opinion that agents of the FBI had seen Cramer meet and talk with Thiel and Kerling, Jusice Jackson wrote that

> This is the sum of the overt acts as established by the testimony of the two witnesses. There is no two-witness proof of what they said nor in what language they conversed. There is no showing that Cramer gave them any information whatever of value to their mission or indeed that he had any to give. No effort at secrecy is shown, for they met in public places. Cramer furnished them no shelter, nothing that can be called sustenance or supplies.

It was a victory that had taken Medina nearly three years to obtain. Never before had he spent so much time and effort on any single case, and he had contributed not only this time and this effort, but in addition, had paid his own expenses. He had been joined in the work by John McKim Minton, by John W. Jordan, and, in the Supreme Court, by Richard T. Davis. But even yet, though Cramer's conviction had been reversed, there was work to do. The man, though not guilty of treason, was plainly guilty of something, and punishment of some sort should be meted out.

In New York, John F. X. McGohey was now United States Attorney, and Medina urged him to reindict Cramer, charging him no longer with treason, but with "trading with the enemy." To this lesser charge Cramer pleaded guilty, as Medina advised him to do, and was sentenced to a term of six years which, with time off for good behavior, was completed in four.

Medina has often heard from Cramer since that long-drawn-out case was completed, but of all the letters he has received perhaps the most touching reached him from Atlanta Penitentiary just before Christmas, 1943, long before anyone could guess what the ultimate outcome of the case would be. Neatly hand-lettered on a ruled sheet of prison stationery, it read as follows:

FROM Anthony Cramer 35647 DATE December 15th 1943
TO Mr. Harold Medina ADDRESS 165 Broadway, New York.

My dear Mr. Medina:

It is a great pleasure to send you my greetings of the season; and at the same time wish you a prosperous and happy "New Year."

But these lines are really meant to be a bit more than customary, seasonal greetings. Therefore, dear Mr. Medina, permit me to add a few inadequate words of gratitude and appreciation for your endeavors and troubles you submitted yourself to help and assist me during the blackest days of my life. You were my champion in those days and as such you shall remain with me. Always I had an abstract conception of what a man should be and this abstraction has become reality through you; by your noble efforts to help an underling, in whom you believed and of whose innocence you were convinced. I still marvel about your abilities as a lawyer; about your enchanting eloquence, your undaunted courage and your fighting spirit with which you defended a hopeless case against prejudice, calumny and lies. Let me assure you, dear sir, your manliness, your excellency of character, of spirit and soul have deeply impressed me and have my highest esteem. Unfortunately my situation is such that I have nothing to offer but words as a requital for your splendid assistance. But in turn I assure you, with all my sincerity, that your name is honored in my personal hall of fame, in my memory, as a great man and a great lawyer.

Wishing you once more for the coming year all the good which Heaven and earth can bestow I am forever gratefully yours,

ANTHONY CRAMER *35647*

More than a year had to pass after this letter was written before the case was finally won. Once the decision of the Supreme Court had been announced scores of letters came to Medina, two of which, from the Chief Justice of the United States, came in the same envelope.

The first of these was short and formal:

Supreme Court of the United States
Washington, D.C.

Chamber of the Chief Justice,
1929 Twenty-Fourth Street, N.W.

June 20, 1945

Harold R. Medina, Esq.,
165 Broadway,
New York, N. Y.

Re: No. 13, Cramer v. United States

Dear Mr. Medina:

In behalf of the Court, and at its request, I write to express the appreciation of the Court, and my own personally, for the fine service which you rendered as voluntary counsel for the petitioner in the above entitled case.

Yours sincerely,
HARLAN F. STONE
Chief Justice

The second was much longer and far more personal. It began as follows:

Dear Medina:

May I add my personal congratulations to the word of appreciation which is enclosed. It was a great victory for you and your client. . . .

[And it ended]

Yours, as ever,
HARLAN F. STONE

8

UNITED STATES DISTRICT JUDGE

EARLY IN 1945, JOSEPH S. FAY, A VICE-PRESIDENT OF THE International Operating Engineers' Union of the American Federation of Labor, and James Bove, a leader of a hod carriers' union, were tried in New York and convicted of extorting large sums from contractors who were engaged on the Delaware Aqueduct project. The case was widely publicized and when the two were sentenced to identical terms of eight and one half to sixteen years in prison, the action of the court was widely approved. A few months later the Appellate Division, First Department, upheld the sentence, and in July, 1946, the Court of Appeals did the same.

Medina had been retained to argue the case in the Court of Appeals and to lay the necessary technical foundation for getting it before the Supreme Court in case the conviction was affirmed. Accordingly, upon the issuance of the mandate of the Court of Appeals, Medina was again faced with precisely the same step he had many years before refused to take on behalf of Earl Carroll. Unless a stay could be obtained, Joe Fay would soon be on his way to prison.

On this occasion Medina was unhesitating and even enthusiastic. Despite the unpopularity of the case for which he pleaded, he was—and still is—a believer in the jury system as one of the safeguards of the citizen against the possible tyranny and oppression of government. He firmly believes in the decency, fairness, intelligence, and competency of "the little guy," and he was ready to fight the New York "blue ribbon" jury system whether the men of means and the corporate clients, who now were coming to him in increasing numbers, liked it or not. He filed the application for certiorari, asking the Supreme Court to take the case, and argued the motion for a stay before Justice Stanley Reed at his summer home in New City, New York. The stay was granted, and the Supreme Court took the case.

In New York State a statute had been in effect for some fifty years providing for special blue-ribbon juries in certain cases, the jurors to be chosen from a specially selected panel. It was Medina's contention that this special panel was not truly representative of a cross section of the population, but was for the most part chosen from the upper strata of economic and social life. The theory back of the blue-ribbon jury was that superior jurors would be selected under the methods that had been devised to control it, and that the ends of justice would thereby be furthered. It was Medina's belief, however, that by ingenious devices, workers and others who occupied the lower positions in the economic and social scale were systematically excluded—that because of this the jurors selected were more inclined to convict—that they were apt to have natural though perhaps unconscious prejudices—that justice, consequently, was handicapped. His application for the writ of certiorari was based on the alleged unconstitutionality of the blue-ribbon jury system under which Fay and Bove had been tried, and he charged particularly that the system violated two provisions of Section 1 of the Fourteenth Amendment to the Constitution—the due process clause and the equal protection clause.

The case came up for argument before the United States Supreme Court on April 3, 1947, two years to the day from the time Fay and Bove had been convicted.

About sixty thousand persons were on the general jury list in New York County, where Fay and Bove had originally been tried. The special list, however, from which the jurors in this case had been selected, included only about three thousand names, and as he argued the case before the United States Supreme Court, Medina contended that all laborers, as well as all factory workers, all service workers, practically all craftsmen, and practically all women had been excluded from this special list. He pointed out, for instance, that though there were about seven thousand women among the sixty thousand "general" jurors, there were only twenty-five to thirty among the three thousand "special" jurors, and workers had been excluded in most ingenious ways.

"For what cases are blue-ribbon panels used?" asked Justice Frankfurter.

"Generally for murder cases," Medina replied, "but here [in the Fay-Bove case] the set-up was made to order for them in a case involving union leaders."

He went on to describe the blue-ribbon panel as "a permanent set-up," pointing out that one person whose name was on the list had claimed to have served in fifty trials, while others claimed to have been members of the special panel for fifteen or twenty years. He pointed out that the jury in the Fay-Bove case had been drawn from a list "composed primarily of bankers, manufacturers, executives, stockbrokers and the like. Not a single laborer or factory worker or service employee" had been on the panel.

"Is the evidence to which you refer," asked Justice Black, "sufficient to show that the whole system is invalid or merely the administration in this case?"

"I must admit," replied Medina, "that the strongest part of our argument is the way the law was administered in this particular case. It may be that Your Honors will find sufficient evidence to show the whole system unconstitutional."

Medina was opposed by Whitman Knapp, assistant district attorney of New York County, who upheld the system and pointed out that since Revolutionary times New York State has had various kinds of qualifications for jury service. Originally there was a property requirement, and even yet a woman cannot be forced to serve. Furthermore, the law that was under attack did not apply evenly throughout the state but authorized these special panels only in counties in which the population exceeded one million. The purpose of the law, he contended, was to facilitate the administration of justice in criminal cases by providing a readily available list of competent, impartial jurors.

It seemed evident, as the argument was concluded, that Medina's charge of discrimination had impressed the justices, or at least some among them, and when, two months later—the date was June 23, 1947—the Court announced its opinion, it upheld the conviction of Fay and Bove by the narrow margin of 5 to 4.

Justice Robert H. Jackson wrote that the majority "failed to perceive" any constitutional offense in the standards used for setting up special panels of jurors in New York State. Justice Murphy, however, who with Justices Black, Rutledge, and Douglas, dissented, wrote that "The constitutional vice inherent in the type of blue-ribbon jury panel here involved is that it rests upon intentional and systematic exclusion of certain classes of people who are admittedly qualified to serve on the general jury panel."

When the Anthony Cramer treason case had been fought before the Supreme Court, Medina had won by a 5 to 4 decision. Now he had lost by the same close vote. But during the months he spent on this case a new and vitally important development had taken place, and Harold Medina, whose growing law practice had compelled him to bring his career as a teacher to an end a few years earlier, was now about to bring his law practice to an end as well.

From the days of his earliest experience in court Medina had always looked upon the judges before whom he appeared as men especially fortunate in the positions they had attained. There was about them, or so it seemed to him, an appealing aura which came less, perhaps, from the men themselves than from the posts they held. He had this feeling in every court in which he argued his cases, but nowhere, it seems, did he feel it more definitely than when he appeared before the Appellate Division of the Supreme Court of the State of New York, First Department.

This court is housed in a dignified structure at the corner of Madison Avenue and 25th Street in Manhattan, a building that appears smaller than it actually is because of towering nearby office buildings. The courtroom itself is especially handsome, with dark and intricately carved woodwork and furniture, polished marble walls, and dignified murals. It is lighted by a beautiful dome-shaped skylight of glass in which, halfway up the curve, and as a part of the pattern, are set the names of great figures in the history of American jurisprudence—Marshall, Taney, and others. Many times, as a young lawyer called to argue cases in that courtroom, Medina's attention was attracted to the delicate beauty of that dome and to the names that are inscribed there. From the first, he seems to have been impressed by it and by the names that are a part of the pattern, but his interest seems to have been caught less by the somewhat remote greatness of the names that are placed high up the curve than by a group of lesser names that are set modestly in the glass all about the lower edge of the glass dome—the names of the judges who, as the years have passed, have occupied the five carved and handsome chairs that form the bench in that courtroom—chairs that stand before the dark and intricately decorated wooden screen that is their background.

So greatly did these names—and the idea behind them—appeal to Medina that the thought of becoming a judge made its appeal as well. He had made a detailed study of New York pleading and practice, a subject to which his teaching was largely confined, and the idea of becoming a judge on the New York Supreme Court especially attracted him. He had no thought of anything more than that. The idea of becoming a judge on the federal bench did not enter his mind. He was so interested in the state bench, however, that he went to see Judge Frederick Evan Crane about it.

Judge Crane, at the time, was Chief Judge of the New York State Court of Appeals, and thus occupied the highest judicial position in the State of New York. He was a good friend of Medina's, who often saw him at Westhampton, and his son, Frederick Ralph Crane, had been one of Medina's students. The judge heartily approved of Medina's interest in obtaining a position on the bench, but despite his enthusiasm he made no specific suggestion, and Medina hesitated to push the matter further. Following Judge Crane's death, however, Medina had a talk with Chief Judge Irving Lehman, who succeeded Crane. Judge Lehman, a brother of Herbert Lehman who had been elected governor of New York in 1932, seemed as enthusiastic over the idea as Crane had been, and advised Medina to get in touch with the Democratic leaders in Manhattan, but the idea of ingratiating himself with the Democratic district leaders in order to further his aspirations jarred on Medina's sensibilities. To do so, he saw clearly, would be to put himself under some obligation, and the suggestion repelled him even to the point at which he shrugged the whole idea aside.

Late in 1946, quite without Medina's knowledge, a series of events began to play an important part in his life, though for fully three months he had no inkling whatever of what was going on. In November, 1946, Judge Samuel Mandelbaum, a United States district judge for the Southern District of New York, died, and an appointment had to be made by the President in order to fill this post. The judges of the Southern District of New York are called upon to handle a much heavier load of litigation than are the judges of any other federal district, and it was important not only that the vacant post be filled promptly, but also that the person to be appointed be especially well qualified. This was apparent to leaders of the legal fraternity, and the Judiciary Committee of the Association of the Bar of the City of New York was quick to tackle the problem. On November 26, 1946, a meeting was called by its chairman, Bethuel M. Webster, and a subcommittee made up of F. W. H. Adams, Edward S. Greenbaum, and William C. Chanler, was instructed to discuss the appointment with Attorney General Tom C. Clark, and to offer the assistance of the Judiciary Committee.

It was on December 11 that the subcommittee saw Mr. Clark, and on December 16 that it made its report, explaining that the Attorney General had requested the committee to report on the qualifications of certain candidates who had already been suggested. But in addition, the Attorney General had clearly indicated that he would welcome other suggestions.

In response to this, the committee, in a letter written on January 6, 1947, suggested several names, among which was that of Harold R. Medina, saying that in the committee's belief any one of those named was qualified "to an outstanding degree." No single person was especially recommended, for it was the purpose of the committee to urge the appointment of no particular candidate, but rather to suggest several highly qualified lawyers any one of whom President Truman might choose with complete assurance as to his character and fitness.

No one had mentioned this possible appointment to Medina who, in February, went to Bermuda with Mrs. Medina for a winter vacation. But on February 18 Bethuel M. Webster, chairman of the Judiciary Committee of the Association of the Bar of the City of New York, was called on by Judge Samuel I. Rosenman, who had formerly been a close adviser of President Roosevelt and since his death had been close to President Truman.

Judge Rosenman explained that the President was not satisfied with the names that had been suggested to him, and that he was anxious to make a popular appointment. The two then discussed the names the Bar Association committee had suggested to the Attorney General including Medina's, but in response to a question by Judge Rosenman, Mr. Webster was unable to say whether or not any of the men on the list would accept the appointment if it were offered. This applied to Medina as well as to the others, for the committee had spoken to none of them. Judge Rosenman, consequently, offered to make some inquiries of his own.

In making these inquiries he went to see Eugene A. Sherpick, Medina's law partner, and Sherpick, who was as unable as Webster had been to say whether or not Medina would accept, promptly phoned his partner in Bermuda to ask.

The question was no sooner asked than Medina knew

what he was inclined to do, but he could not guess how his partner felt about it, and did not want to appear to be running out on his law firm.

"What do you think about it?" he asked.

"I think you ought to take it," Sherpick replied.

"O.K., Gene," Medina agreed. "Tell them all right."

He hung up the phone and returned to his wife.

"I've just had a call," he told her, "that may completely change our lives."

It was on February 26 that Judge Rosenman told Mr. Webster of Medina's response, and added that his name had been "submitted"—to the White House, Mr. Webster assumed.

During the weeks that followed, nothing much happened except that reports now and again suggested that other candidates were being considered. On March 11, however, the *New York Daily Mirror* appeared with a news item under a Washington date line which said that Medina had definitely been selected, and ended by saying that "A White House statement announcing the appointment is expected shortly."

This was news to Medina, as well as to those who had suggested his name, but the report was so specific that Medina accepted it as true. Others did, too, for letters of congratulation followed and any number of friends warmly shook his hand. Nevertheless, the report was definitely premature, and presently began to appear untrue. Reports from other sources suggested other names and also plainly suggested the political influences that were at work, with the result that a number of bar associations went into action. On April 21 a telegram was sent to the Attorney General in the names of President Carl Rix of the American Bar Association and John G. Buchanan, chairman of that Association's Judiciary Committee; Robert E. Lee and Jackson A. Dykman, representing the

New York State Bar Association; Joseph M. Proskauer and Theodore Kiendl, representing the New York County Lawyers Association; and Harrison Tweed and Bethuel M. Webster, representing the Association of the Bar of the City of New York. Signed by Mr. Webster, this telegram asked for a conference on April 23—a request that was promptly granted.

Those who went to Washington for that conference were Carl Rix, John G. Buchanan, Robert E. Lee, William D. Embree, Louis M. Loeb, L. R. Mason, William C. Chanler, Terrence McManus, and Bethuel M. Webster, and following that meeting with the Attorney General, Mr. Tweed and Mr. Webster saw Senator Robert Wagner at the Gramercy Park Hotel in New York. About this time, too, both *The New York Times* and *New York Herald Tribune* published editorials calling for the appointment, as the *Times* suggested, of "someone whose essential qualifications are knowledge, experience, and character."

Throughout all these weeks Medina did nothing. He had never met the President, and not only made no effort to see him now but made no effort to see anyone. He had never thought of being appointed to the federal bench and consequently never had had occasion even to think of obtaining any support that would further such an appointment. Friends and acquaintances urged him to see this person and that, particularly to see political figures whose influence, they thought, might play a part in the appointment, but he refused. He saw no one in connection with the appointment except members of judiciary committees of bar associations who sought him out, and the support of these men was as disinterested as it ultimately proved to be effective.

"I felt at that time," he once told me, "that it was not only the dignified and proper thing to do, but that it was good judgment, too. In any event I wouldn't beg or be put under any obligation."

Many names seem to have been offered. Edward J. Flynn, Mayor William O'Dwyer, and other politicians eagerly furthered the claims of those whom they suggested, and before long the complicated developments surrounding the appointment began to be apparent. On March 15, for instance, only a few days after Medina's appointment had so prematurely been announced by the *Daily Mirror*, the *North Side News*, a neighborhood paper published in the Bronx, Boss Flynn's stronghold, referred to "the sensational fight being waged for the Federal Judgeship," and on April 1 the same publication went into more detail.

The detailed story [it said] of how Ed Flynn scotched the plan to name Professor Medina to the Federal Court was told by ace columnist Drew Pearson. . . . He states that "Last week Ed Flynn . . . could not even get Truman on the phone. Reason for Flynn's call was that it leaked out that Truman was planning to appoint to the Federal Judgeship . . . Harold Medina, a former Jew [sic] and now an Episcopalian, whose reported selection pleased no one. After Flynn tried to get Truman on the telephone, he called Bob Hannegan in Boston. 'This one you had better stop,' Flynn exploded. 'I can't get Truman to answer the phone. Maybe he will take your call.' "

Other political observers say [the column then explained] that Mr. Flynn went so far as to threaten to resign from his party posts if Medina were named.

On April 17, Ed Sullivan, in his column in the *New York Daily News*, apparently having obtained his information from partisan sources, wrote that "Ed Flynn, Frank Sampson, and Paul Fitzpatrick won over Senator Robert Wagner;

Federal Judgeship made vacant by Judge Mandelbaum's death goes to Ben Rabin. . . ."

But others beside the politicians were at work, and among those who were now actively furthering Medina's appointment were many outstanding members of the bar.

"More distinguished lawyers joined in this proposal," George Sokolsky later wrote in his syndicated column, "than had favored a candidate for a judicial office in a generation."

On May 13, the Association of the Bar of the City of New York received a report from its Judiciary Committee in which it was stated that "it is known that certain political leaders have actively resisted his appointment and have sought the nomination by the President of a candidate preferred by them on political grounds."

The American Bar Association was active in Medina's support. John G. Buchanan, chairman of its judiciary Committee and a Princeton classmate of Medina, and Jackson A. Dykman, a member of the committee, both urged favorable action. C. C. Burlingham and George W. Alger, Nestors of the profession, actively supported his appointment. Whitney North Seymour, Harrison Tweed, and Bethuel M. Webster, of the Association of the Bar of the City of New York continued their activities, and many others were busy. And on May 15, to the surprise and disappointment of more than one Democratic political leader in New York, the President sent Medina's name to the Senate.

As soon as news of the appointment had been confirmed, Mr. Webster sent the City Bar Association's long-prepared release to the papers. *The New York Times* published an editorial entitled "A Judge Worth Waiting For." The *New York Herald Tribune* expressed its belief in Medina in an editorial headed "Superb Selection." Other papers were similarly enthusiastic, and Walter Winchell very accurately explained that "The White House gave the appointment of Federal Judge to Harold R. Medina, not because it didn't recognize any New York political leaders but because it recognized them all. The New York politicos fought to a fierce draw—so a political outsider (and a fine man) got the White House nod."

But perhaps Harrison Tweed, president of the Association of the Bar of the City of New York, commented as clearly and as pointedly as anyone. "Appointed on the merits," he was quoted as saying, "at a time when he is at the peak of his intellectual and professional powers, Mr. Medina will strengthen the court and render valuable assistance to the overworked and able judges now serving there."

Viewed after the passage of five years, this comment appears to have had a touch of prophecy about it.

On June 18, 1947, the United States Senate unanimously confirmed the appointment of Harold R. Medina to the Federal District bench, and ten days later the *New York Law Journal* announced that he would be inducted into office at 10 o'clock on the morning of July 1.

His career as a teacher had ended seven years before. Now his active career as a practicing attorney was about to be concluded. His father had not lived to see this change in Harold Medina's life—had died in 1932—but his mother eagerly followed these new developments. Still a resident of Brooklyn, as she had been from the time of her marriage, she was eighty-nine when her son was appointed to the bench, and that very year he built a summer cottage for her on his Westhampton property. Apaucuck Point was to continue to be Harold Medina's home, though in accepting the appointment to the bench he would be forced to give up a law practice that paid him something like one hundred thousand dollars a year, and in return would be paid a salary of fifteen thousand. But a new career awaited him—a new career that was soon to make his name familiar not only throughout the United States but also beyond its boundaries.

There is a sentimental side to Harold Medina's character and this was illustrated on the morning of his induction. Judge John M. Woolsey had formerly been a judge of the court to which Medina had now been appointed, but in addition he had been a graduate of the Columbia University Law School and a member of its alumni association. It was this association, it will be remembered, in which Medina had been so active; and Judge Woolsey, having been elected to its presidency when Medina was chosen as its first vice-president, came to have a high regard for the younger man—so high a regard, in fact, that he resigned from the presidency, as he later explained, in order to permit Medina to assume that office and thereby be assured of re-election to it. Medina had no inkling of this until Judge Woolsey later told him of it.

Judge Woolsey, having retired as a United States District Judge for the Southern District of New York, died on March 4, 1945, and Medina, about to become a judge of the same court Judge Woolsey had formerly served, went to Mrs. Woolsey and asked the privilege of using Judge Woolsey's robe for the coming induction. Furthermore, Medina was so fortunate as to find the chambers formerly occupied by Judge Woolsey vacant and asked to be assigned to them himself.

At 10 o'clock on the morning of July 1, 1947, Judge Henry W. Goddard, in the absence of Judge Knox, who had been called to Washington unexpectedly, rose in Room 506 of the United States Court House in Manhattan and in the presence of the other judges of the court and of a large gathering of Medina's friends, ordered the clerk to read the President's commission appointing Harold R. Medina a United States district judge. Then followed the administration of the oath, and Judge Medina, invested by the marshal with Judge Woolsey's robe, was escorted to the bench.

A new phase in his career had begun.

The first twelve months the new judge spent on the bench gave him an opportunity to view the world from a new and interesting angle, and to try—though not always successfully—to live up to certain ideas and ideals he had set for himself. For one thing, he wanted to guard against developing any exaggerated idea of his own importance. He objected, to use his own expression, to "getting stuffy," and Mrs. Medina, too, even before the Judge was sworn in, gave him a bit of advice that was all her own.

"Now, Harold," she warned, "don't be judgey. Don't be judgey."

"One of the things I am worried about," the Judge remarked a little over a year after he went on the bench, "is that I don't get rid of a great big lot of cases. I am not accustomed to snap at a thing and pass it out in half an hour or so. I really like to go into it and get to the bottom of it. That takes time. I don't seem able to rush through cases in a hurry."

He found, too, that he had little tendency "to blackjack people into settlements." As a lawyer he had not been inclined to settle cases at any time after they reached court, and now that he was a judge, he was hesitant to propose such settlements. But perhaps the most appealing incident of his first year on the bench had to do with a settlement that came about because he himself urged it. The case presented no particularly difficult legal problem, but in it a son was suing his mother, and as Judge Medina listened to the son's testimony on the first day of that trial it bothered him.

"I said to myself," he later explained, "'I cannot sit around and let this thing go on, because if it does, this family will be disrupted forever.' So I did the very thing I said I would never do. I shooed the lawyers out and started working on the family."

Those involved were a mother, a stepfather, a son, and a daughter-in-law, and as the problem was discussed in the judge's anteroom just behind the bench, to which Judge Medina took them, there appeared to be little interest on anyone's part in arriving at a settlement. The judge made no effort to hurry them. He brought the lawyers in and sent them out again, and even on the next morning continued to talk to the family.

"You know," he told them, "if we get this case settled I might get up some sort of paper that you could each sign and have a copy of, that might do some good for the future."

None of them seemed impressed by that suggestion, but the discussion began to go a little more smoothly. By noon they had all modified their points of view considerably, and Judge Medina took the group to lunch as his guests.

Then they called the lawyers in again, and by 4 o'clock it was all settled. They returned to the courtroom where the judge dictated the terms of the settlement, and as he was about to leave for his chambers the daughter-in-law turned to him.

"Judge," she asked, "you remember that paper you were going to get up?"

"Yes," he replied, "but I thought we decided to forget about it."

"Well, we felt," she explained, "that if you got that paper

up, we could each have a copy, and if we felt like scrapping again we could read it and say to ourselves 'Judge Medina wouldn't like that.' "

The Judge agreed to draft the paper he had had in mind and when each of them had signed, they asked him to add his name as well. This is what he had written:

> With mutual forgiveness of all that is past and with a sincere resolve not to look back but ahead, in the spirit of the Golden Rule, we and each of us, now happily in affectionate accord, and earnestly desirous of remaining so, do solemnly promise that we will avoid all mention or discussion of matters large and small connected in any way with the proceedings which have just been terminated in a manner so satisfactory to all concerned.

The general administrative part of the criminal branch of the court to which Judge Medina had been appointed is referred to as "Crime 1." The various judges of the Southern District of New York, as well as such visiting judges as are now and again assigned to the district, rotate in Crime 1, and the judge who is temporarily assigned attends to many routine matters. He hears all pleas and imposes sentence on those who have pleaded guilty. He handles the criminal calendar. He sometimes fixes bail and hears arguments on motions. He assigns cases to the various judges of the court, though when any matter of exceptional consequence arises, the judge in Crime 1 is certain to discuss it with the Chief Judge of the Southern District.

On July 20, 1948, a federal grand jury, which had been at work studying charges against twelve members of the national board of the Communist party of the United States, returned an indictment against them. A few weeks later Judge Medina was sitting in Crime 1, and at the end of the calendar, counsel arose to argue a motion for an extension of ninety days within which to make any motion with respect to the indictment against the Communist leaders. Medina knew little or nothing about the defendants or the indictment, but extensions, though frequently granted, are usually for only ten days or so. A demand for ninety days is most unusual, and Medina, wondering what it was all about, asked the clerk for the indictment. It was somewhat involved and legalistic, but its essential features were evident almost at once.

"Why," he remarked, "these men are charged with conspiring to teach and advocate the overthrow of the Government of the United States by force and violence."

Discussion followed in which it was made amply clear that in case of a charge so serious an extension for such a lengthy period was absurd.

No sooner had Medina disposed of the application than the lawyers for the defendants filed an affidavit of "bias and prejudice" based upon the remarks made by Judge Medina during the argument. Within an hour he struck the affidavit from the record as insufficient in law on its face, writing a short opinion explaining the applicable law. The defendants promptly appealed to the United States Court of Appeals, which affirmed Medina's action.

In the meantime the Communist leaders made various motions—to dismiss the indictment and for a bill of particulars. These were argued before Judge Murray Hulbert and denied. It was then the duty of Chief Judge John C. Knox to assign the case to one of the district judges for trial.

Here, obviously, was something that was anything but routine. Judge Knox, busy with his administrative duties, had no thought of taking the case himself, and it seemed perfectly obvious to him that the trial would be both long and difficult. Only a few years earlier, a judge in Washington before whom a sedition case was being tried, had actually died of heart failure in the midst of just such a trial as this one promised to be, and that alone suggested that the judge to be assigned had need of more than ordinary physical strength and endurance to carry the matter through. It was also necessary to keep certain judges free for regular duties as they arose, and, in the circumstances, it might prove unwise to assign to the case any judge who was a Roman Catholic. The Catholic Church had taken a strong stand against communism, for which these defendants stood, and the attorneys for the defense would be sure to claim that their clients were being "railroaded," if a judge who was a Catholic were called upon to preside.

All these considerations entered Judge Knox's mind, but it also seemed clear to him that the judge to be assigned to the case should, if possible, know at least a little about the preliminaries that were already a matter of record, and there were only two who did—Judge Hulbert and Judge Medina. Judge Hulbert was far from well and on that account could not be asked to assume so arduous a task, but Judge Medina was sturdy, enthusiastic, and willing to work. Furthermore, his experience was wide, even though he had been on the bench for only a year, and his knowledge of the law was exceptional.

It was as a result of some such reasoning as this, as Judge Knox himself has explained to me, that Judge Medina came to be selected. The two talked the matter over. Judge Knox made his suggestion, and Judge Medina agreed almost without comment. The indictment had been the first important step, and this was the second in the longest and one of the most widely publicized jury cases in the history of American jurisprudence.

On August 23, 1948, Judge Medina, over the heated objections of counsel for the defense, set October 15 as the date for the opening of the trial. But delays intervened, and on November 1, the judge set November 15 as "the actual date of commencement." The lawyers for the defense, however, had only begun their delaying tactics, and they made much of the fact that William Z. Foster, one of the defendants, was ill and unable to appear. On November 15, Judge Medina granted another postponement. Two days later, the defense was ordered to face trial on January 17, 1949, and United States Attorney John F. X. McGohey, who was to represent the government, announced, in referring to Foster's illness, that "We will go to trial with or without Mr. Foster."

The campaign of delay, however, was hardly more than well begun. On January 7 counsel for the defense announced a petition to the Supreme Court to void the indictments, giving as their reason the "illegal exclusion" of Jews, Negroes, workers, and low-rent families by the federal jury system in the Southern District of New York. They also asked the Supreme Court to entertain an appeal from the Circuit Court decision that had refused to disqualify Judge Medina on grounds of "bias and prejudice." But three days later both petitions were denied. On January 14, Judge Medina denied another defense motion for a ninety-day postponement, and at 10:43 A. M. on January 17, with William Z. Foster absent because of his illness, the trial actually opened in high-ceiled, dark-paneled Room 110 on the first floor of the towering United States Court House that faces Foley Square in lower Manhattan.

Judge Medina now denied still another defense motion for a postponement and ruled adversely on a dozen more. The government prosecutor moved for severance of the trial of Foster from that of the other eleven defendants, and at 4:30

P.M. court was adjourned. The Communist trial had begun, and already it was clear that it would be both prolonged and difficult.

There were eleven men on trial—eleven strangely different and yet strangely similar individuals with widely diverse origins and backgrounds, but with identical points of view so far as communism was concerned. In the absence of Foster, the most important was Eugene Dennis. An American, forty-four years of age, and born Francis Xavier Waldron, Jr., he was known to have used at least six different aliases. A burly, florid person, with a small and hesitant voice, he had become general secretary of the Communist party in the United States, and was out on bail, having been recently convicted for contempt of Congress.

Jacob Stachel was forty-nine and was chairman of agitation, publication, and education of the American Communist National Board. To use their own jargon, he was "Agitprop of the American Politburo." Born in that portion of Poland which has now been made a part of the U.S.S.R., he had once actually been permitted to meet Stalin in person. He had entered the United States illegally, and at the time he was arrested with the others of this group he was facing deportation proceedings.

John Gates, thirty-five years of age, was the "wonder boy" editor of the *Daily Worker*, the official publication of the Communist party in the United States. Born Sol Regenstreif, he had attended the College of the City of New York, had become head of the Young Communist League, and had earned a reputation as an inflammatory propagandist for the party.

Gus Hall, thirty-seven, was the son of Finnish parents who had settled in Minnesota and had themselves become members of the American Communist party. He had changed his name which was originally Arno Gust Halberg, and had attended the Lenin Institute in Moscow. Tried for rioting in Minneapolis in the early 1930's, he admitted that he was ready to overthrow the American government by force of arms in order to establish a Soviet government here. Later he became chairman of the Ohio Communist party, and, in 1937, pleaded guilty and was fined five thousand dollars on charges of possessing explosives during a steel strike.

Robert Thompson, who was thirty-four, was the New York State Communist party chairman, a thick-necked person with a somewhat contradictory record who was much given to talking. He had fought in Spain as a member of the Communist-controlled Abraham Lincoln Brigade. He had become an official of an American Federation of Labor machinists' union, and as a staff sergeant in the American Army had earned a Distinguished Service Cross in the Pacific.

John Beattie Williamson, a small, forty-five-year-old Scotsman who was already facing deportation proceedings, was national labor secretary of the Communist party. The government claimed he had sworn falsely that he was born in San Francisco, and it was reported that the Communist attempt to infiltrate and destroy the American Federation of Labor had been made under his leadership.

Carl Winter, forty-one years old, born Philip Carl Weisberg, had become chairman of the Communist state committee of Michigan. He was said to have visited Russia eight times between 1933 and 1935, and for twenty years was educational director of the Ohio Communist party. Physically a soft, unimpressive, almost flabby person with a pronounced lisp, he had come to be one of America's top Communists.

Henry Winston, thirty-eight, was the organizational secretary of the Communist party in the United States. Formerly he had been the head of the Young Communist League, and at one time had been a Communist organizer in Kansas City. A Negro, born in Hattiesburg, Mississippi, he had attended the Lenin Institute in Moscow, had obtained a passport by fraud, and helped others to do so.

Gilbert Green, who was forty-three, was born Gilbert Greenberg and had come to be New York State chairman of the Communist party prior to being made district chairman for the Communist party in Illinois. He had often visited the U.S.S.R., once as a delegate to the Communist International—the Comintern—and admitted giving untruthful information in applying for passports. At one time he was secretary of the Young Communist League, and in 1935, while in Moscow, he was awarded a medal for his work in building up such "united fronts" as the American Youth Congress.

Benjamin Jefferson Davis, Jr., forty-three, was a tall, broad-shouldered, Alabama-born, Negro attorney. An alumnus of Amherst and of Harvard Law School, he joined the Communist party not long after he graduated, and became chairman of the Communist party's legislative committee, as well as secretary of the *Daily Worker*. Twice he was elected as a Communist member of the City Council in New York, and at one time he was charged by the *Pittsburgh Courier*, one of the finest Negro publications in the United States, with having written a Communist plan to form a Negro republic in the South.

Irving Potash, forty-six, born in Russia, never became an American citizen, though he was elected vice president of the Fur and Leather Workers Union, C.I.O., and manager of the leftish C.I.O. Furriers Joint Council. In 1920, he was convicted in Brooklyn and sentenced to three years for criminal anarchy, and was later convicted of conspiracy to obstruct justice. At the time the trial before Judge Medina began, he was out on bail in a deportation case.

These were the men who had been indicted and brought together for trial, and the crime with which they were charged was, to state it simply, that they had conspired to teach and actively advocate the overthrow of the Government of the United States of America by force and violence.

The five principal attorneys for these eleven defendants were themselves a strangely assorted group. Harry Sacher, of New York, a small, slender man active as chief counsel for the defense, had often represented Communists before—most frequently, perhaps, in deportation proceedings. Richard Gladstein, of Los Angeles, had formerly represented Harry Bridges, the Australian-born, West Coast labor leader who has so often been said to be a Communist. It was apparently because of this connection that Gladstein had become a member of the defense counsel in an important Communist case that was tried in Honolulu. Louis F. McCabe, of Philadelphia, who wore a Phi Beta Kappa key, had been counsel for Eugene Dennis at the time Dennis was convicted of contempt of Congress. Tall, spectacled Abraham J. Isserman at one time represented Gerhart Eisler, the admitted Communist who later jumped bail and fled the country aboard the Polish steamship *Batory*. George W. Crockett, Jr., was a Negro lawyer of Detroit about whom little was popularly known, and there were others, notably Mrs. Yetta Land, a somewhat dowdy, past-middle-age labor lawyer of Cleveland, and pipe-smoking Maurice Sugar, a lawyer who had been disbarred in Michigan and who, it was said, was to be "over-all adviser" for the defense.

The prosecution was in the hands of United States District Attorney John F. X. McGohey, a slender man, smooth-shaven and spectacled, with slightly graying hair brushed back from his high forehead. He had at his disposal the entire personnel of the United States Attorney's office, but was especially aided by Assistant United States Attorneys Frank H. Gordon, Edward C. Wallace, Irving Shapiro, and Lawrence K. Bailey.

As the trial began Judge Medina had much the same point of view toward the defendants that the average citizen had. He was conscious of a lot of talk about Communists, but he had no intimate knowledge of them. Actually he was inclined to be a bit skeptical of much that he heard. He believed that those Communists who existed in this country were rough and willing to make trouble. He felt sure that they were interested in dividing up other people's property, but he never accepted what seemed to him to be the exaggerated stories of their purposes and methods. An article in the *New York World-Telegram* had predicted that the defendants in this case would be tumultuous and excessively difficult to control; and Paul Gallico, in a syndicated column published the day the trial opened, warned of the danger they presented and wrote that "the Commies will be kicking up all the dust, yelling, screaming, picketing, parading, getting into the papers, bringing pressure to bear, holding meetings, and spending money. . . . If the boys lose this trial they will be badly crippled in their designs to destroy the United States as you know it. And they do not mean to lose it." Such accounts gave the judge a little warning of what was coming, but he still thought of the defendants and their supporters as "hell-raisers" rather than as dangerous, well-organized revolutionaries.

Judge Medina knew that Judge Eicher who, in 1944, had been assigned to preside over a mass sedition trial in Washington, D. C., had died as a result of strain put on him by the excesses of which the defendants and some of their lawyers had been guilty in court. Medina had asked a friend in Washington to get together all the information that was available about that abortive trial, and this material arrived about a month before the Communist trial opened. He studied it carefully—studied especially the gavel-pounding and the angry rulings into which Judge Eicher had been goaded. It would not do, he saw, to permit himself to be irritated to any such degree. Perhaps it was because of this—in part, at least—that he never once used a gavel throughout the whole length of the trial. In fact, he never even brought one with him into court.

The day before the trial began, a deputy police commissioner spoke to the Judge about assigning police protection to him, but he objected. He felt sure that there would be pickets, and realized that he might have a little trouble now and then, but the idea that he would be in any actual danger seemed ridiculous. He so heartily disliked the very idea of protection that the police commissioner left. A week later, however, he was back.

"Judge," he began. "You know your business, don't you?"

Medina was puzzled.

"Why, I suppose I do," he replied. "What are you driving at?"

"Well, we know ours, too," the visitor replied, "and we want you to do what we tell you. From now on you're going to have a guard."

That was language the Judge understood, and he bowed to the authority of the police. Even yet he was not entirely conscious of the dangers that surrounded him, though he began to think that the police might be right when a friend whom he had invited to lunch phoned and called off the engagement.

"Oh, Bob," Medina objected. "Why can't you come?"

"I could if I wanted to," his friend replied bluntly, "but they might take a shot at you and hit me. I'm staying away."

It was on the second day of the trial that Judge Medina issued the order severing the case of William Z. Foster from that of the others. Almost at once Harry Sacher, physically the smallest but soon to prove the most irritating of the defense attorneys, asked to have the trial recessed for ninety days, insisting that the four hundred policemen who had been assigned to the vicinity of Foley Square influenced prospective jurors—that the defendants were being subjected to a "police trial." Then, one after another, McCabe, Isserman, Crockett, and Gladstein sprang up and insisted that their clients could not be tried fairly and without prejudice because of the wide publicity that was being given the trial by newspapers and the radio. Sacher even insisted that Medina disqualify himself because of "prejudice," but the Judge maintained his calm and denied those motions as they were made.

There was much talk on the part of counsel for the defense of "fear" and "terror," of "intimidation" and "mob rule." Frequent references were made to the Scottsboro trial, to Tom Mooney, to the Sacco-Vanzetti case, and even to the Reichstag fire and the Nuremberg trials. The attorneys for the defense attacked the entire jury system that had long been in use in the Southern District of New York. They had asked Judge John C. Knox to supersede Judge Medina, and when, in response, Judge Knox referred them to Judge Medina, they demanded not only that Judge Medina disqualify himself but also that he disqualify all the other judges of the district.

Objections of a score of kinds were overruled; almost as many motions were denied; and Richard Gladstein, when Judge Medina refused to grant delays for which he asked, began another attack on the jury system—an attack which, with its many ramifications, was to last for weeks.

As this attack went on from day to day, and then from week to week, Judge Medina's "leniency" began to be criticized by those who wished to see the case handled with more "firmness." The lawyers for the Communists were little concerned with clarifying the subject they were discussing. Instead, it seemed to be their purpose to keep it as involved and unclear as possible, with the result that the public had little understanding of what the argument was all about. Men on the street grew critical of the leeway they thought Medina was granting the defense. Editorials called upon him to use a heavier hand. Criticism grew in Congress, and almost the friendliest comments were those which held that Medina was giving the Communists "plenty of rope with which to hang themselves."

"The fact is," the Judge told me long after the trial was over, "I didn't know how I was going to stop the argument. I wasn't leaning over backward; I was doing my best not to lean in any direction. My whole purpose was to do only what was right. But the lawyers for the defense were calling grand jurors—petit jurors—everybody. It began to look as if there wasn't any end to it."

Early in this involved campaign of delay Judge Medina was almost led into committing an error that would have ended the trial then and there, and was saved only because some sixth sense seems to have guarded him from it. On the fifth day of the trial, Gladstein, one of the defense lawyers, stated that he might call as witnesses all the judges of the Southern District, including Medina. In reply to this, District Attorney McGohey suggested that the court should be informed then and there whether or not Judge Medina himself was to be called. He pointed out that there was a question of law, which he could not immediately answer, and which bore upon whether or not a judge would disqualify himself by serving as a witness in a case over which he had been assigned to preside. Judge Medina himself was doubtful and remarked that it "would be an extraordinary thing if a maneuver of this kind could delay the case." He then polled each of the defense attorneys, asking them whether they planned to call him, and if so, what they expected to ask.

Each of the lawyers refused to answer, though it began to appear that it was their belief that even after being sworn the Judge might still determine whether or not to reply to such questions as might be asked. The Judge declined to rule at once, and decided to think the matter over, holding it in abeyance until the following morning.

It was fortunate, too, that he did so. He had known that were he to give evidence in the case he would thereby disqualify himself, but what he had *not* known was that even though he had replied to no questions whatever, but had merely taken the oath as a witness, he would have been just as effectively disqualified and the case would have been brought to an abrupt end, to the delight and advantage of the defendants and their lawyers.

The following morning session began briskly as Judge Medina entered the courtroom with an armful of books. A little research, he announced as he set the books down before him, had clarified his views. "It is plain," he added, "that I may not testify as a witness in a case over which I preside, and I shall not."

From the time the trial began, Judge Medina had expected to be confronted with every difficulty counsel for the defense could think up. He was prepared for a certain amount of hellraising. But he was not prepared for what he soon began to detect.

Because of his long experience at the bar he was quick to see that the five most active lawyers for the defense—undersized Harry Sacher, bald Abraham Isserman, mustached Richard Gladstein, gray-haired Louis McCabe, and spectacled George Crockett—were men of more than ordinary ability. There was no lack of legal training among them. They were all at home among the complexities of the law. They were competent and even forceful advocates. But for some time their strange technique, their unexpected moves, and their surprising mental attitudes were more than Medina could understand. He had seen many surprising developments in court, and knew that lawyers of ability are sometimes unpredictable. But here was something he had never seen before: though these lawyers were supposedly before him in order to represent the interests of the defendants, they showed little concern in that phase of the case. Time and again—and apparently by design—they passed up opportunities to benefit their clients—passed them up, sometimes, as if they were more interested in spreading Communist propaganda than in furthering their clients' case, or sometimes passed them up merely in order to throw legal monkey wrenches into the proceedings.

In all his thirty-five years of legal experience he had never seen such a thing before, and for ten days or two weeks could not quite believe what was so constantly apparent. Little by little, however, he became convinced—and no later evidence caused him to change his mind—that everything done by the defense in that seemingly endless trial —literally everything—was intended to accomplish one of only two purposes:

First, it was their intention and desire to spread Communist propaganda at every possible opportunity.

Second, they intended to break up that trial by any possible method that was open to them.

Nor should it be imagined that the activities of the defendants and their sympathizers were confined merely to the courtroom. The case had no sooner begun than numbers of delegations asked to see Judge Medina: delegations of workers, of housewives, of veterans, of Purple Heart veterans, of Negroes, of union members, and of all sorts of unexpected groups. When he reached his chambers at 8:30 in the morning they were waiting for him. Others were waiting to see him when he went to lunch, and others still when court was adjourned for the day. They said they came not only from New York but also from the Middle West, the South, the Far West—everywhere—and without exception they presented the warped and one-sided viewpoint of the Communists. At no time during the entire course of the trial did any delegation approach him in order to express its *opposition* to the defendants. Invariably the groups that came *favored* the eleven who were on trial, and they never stopped coming for a moment. Twice in the first two weeks of the trial Medina missed his lunch in order to talk with such delegations, and almost every morning they interfered with work he needed to complete. But here, too, he was slow to realize the purpose behind these interruptions. Only when he began to see that he was working too hard—that in addition to his other work he was giving more thought and attention to these delegations than he should—that this added effort, combined with the strain of his court duties, was beginning to wear him down—did he begin to see that that was the purpose behind these impositions.

He recalled the 1944 sedition trial in Washington—the trial over which Judge Eicher had presided, until his death, amid just such mad conditions as now were daily taking place in New York. And suddenly he understood that these defendants and their supporters were doing their utmost, both in court and outside, to wear him out—even, perhaps, to shorten his life or to break him down mentally or physically.

It was when he began to understand their plan that he made his decision:

No more delegations;

No more casual use of any portion of his time;

No more irregular hours.

He decided to schedule everything and laid out a program that covered every minute of the day—a program that revolutionized his habits and even controlled the least detail of his private life. Gregarious and friendly though he is inclined to be, he closed the door on every social and personal contact save only with his wife. The opera, the theater, the late, convivial hours with friends, were all eliminated. No more dinners. No more parties. No more pastimes. Once he reached home each evening he saw no one but Mrs. Medina.

The trial had hardly more than started when he found it difficult to sleep or, when he did fall asleep, sometimes awoke in the middle of the night. He disliked the idea of sleeping potions of any kind, but Dr. Donald Keller of Westhampton prescribed a mild liquid sedative, and throughout the remainder of the trial the judge took it every evening before retiring and took it again if he awoke at night.

He set 9:30 as the time to go to bed. He arose at 6:30 and after breakfast he read the morning papers. At 8:30 he was in his chambers on the twenty-second floor of the Court House, where he studied and read the endless material with which he had to familiarize himself. And regularly at 10:30 he appeared in court. He lunched alone in his chambers in the Court House, after which, for half an hour, he took a nap before returning to the courtroom.

At 4:30 court was adjourned, and at 5:15 he drove his car from the Court House to the Woolworth Building where, in a "health club," he went through a mildly strenuous series of exercises. Next he went to the "dry-hot" room for several minutes, then to the shower, hot and cold, and finally to the massage table. At home each evening, dinner was carefully designed by Mrs. Medina to place the least possible strain on his digestion.

The trial had been under way only a little while when his back began to trouble him. It was the old football injury showing up again because of the long hours he was spending day after day in the high-backed, leather-upholstered chair he was forced to occupy in court. The seat, he decided, was too deep, and the back failed to give him the support he needed. So he ordered the chair rebuilt, bringing the back forward several inches. It helped, but still his back troubled him, and he found it necessary to wear a broad, uncomfortable, stiffly-stayed brace throughout all the long-drawn months of the trial.

The delegations, by now, had quit coming. Until he decided to see no more of them, they were forever waiting to take his time, but he had no sooner let it be known that he would not receive them than their visits ended abruptly. But now a new campaign began—a campaign of letters, postcards, telegrams.

The phrases they contained were often repeated. Many times he was called "a degenerate from the bowels of hell," a "tyrant," a "fiend incarnate," a "travesty on justice." He was often referred to as an "S.O.B." or, more openly, a "son-of-a-bitch."

He did not have the time to read *all* this mail, but he kept himself informed as to its contents, and now and again was even amused by it. "You know," he once remarked, "if you're called a son-of-a-bitch often enough you actually begin to wonder!"

Within three or four weeks he had begun to realize that the task that faced him was infinitely more difficult—and infinitely more vital to the welfare of the country—than he had imagined it could be when he first faced his assignment. But now he was seeing it clearly, and knew that day by day for an indefinite period he had need to watch his every move—to guard constantly against any reversible error as he considered the endless points and motions and objections that were raised in court.

He was being guarded wherever he went. Police were on duty every night in the lobby of the apartment house at 14 East 75th Street. They rode to and from the Court House with him—went with him to the "health club." There was no hour, whether he was awake or asleep, during which he was not guarded. And yet he was alone. All day in the crowded courtroom he still seemed to be alone. Going and coming he was alone, despite the friendly, watchful guards who accompanied him. It was only when he reached home that he was not alone, for there he found Mrs. Medina waiting—Mrs. Medina without whose help his task would have been far greater than it was—Mrs. Medina who, from the time of their marriage in 1911, has played a much greater part in Harold Medina's career than this account has been able to suggest.

9

THE TRIAL OF THE COMMUNIST LEADERS

BY THE END OF THE FIRST FIVE WEEKS OF THE COMMUNIST trial, three thousand three hundred and thirty-seven typewritten pages of testimony had gone into the court record, and the jurors had not even been selected. This phase of the trial, as *The New York Times* pointed out, "was a kind of trial within a trial—a challenge to the grand jury which had indicted the men and the petit jury panel which was to try them."

Twenty-three grand and petit jurors and a statistician were called to the witness stand, and the defense attempted to prove that Jews and Negroes, as well as poor people and residents of certain sections, were excluded from the jury lists or, at least, were discriminated against. For four weeks counsel for the defense did its best to prove that the whole system was based on discrimination, but after four additional days during which the government presented its side of the argument, Judge Medina told the Communists that they had "proved nothing." Less than two years earlier Medina himself, in the Fay-Bove case, had attacked the blue-ribbon juries of New York State because of the way certain sections of the population were excluded from the "special" jury panel. It had been made clear by now, however, that no comparable situation existed in connection with the federal jury lists that were now being attacked.

"I kept thinking all the time," he remarked, "that you had something. But the last four days have pretty well convinced me to the contrary." And on the final day of the fifth week of the trial he commented again.

"I very much dislike," he said, "to curtail any proof of the actual working of the jury system, but I'm beginning to get the impression that we're getting back to the same old endless chain. . . . I'm getting so bewildered here by the constant change of subject I can hardly follow it any more. It is a perfect mass of confusion. Now they want to subpoena all these little people around the Court House and keep this thing going, but I intend to find a way to stop it."

On Friday, February 25, 1949, he ruled that the actual trial of the eleven would start on March 7, and told the defense attorneys that they had proved nothing.

"The evidence the defense has presented in support of the jury challenge," he said, "has been based on speculation, surmise, and perhaps suspicion. . . . Now it is my duty to terminate the proceedings. I direct the defendants to conclude their evidence next Thursday. . . . Then my purpose is to adjourn for the balance of the week and use the interval to write a short opinion."

With the time at their disposal now definitely limited, so far as this phase of the trial was concerned, the defense subpoenaed Judge Knox, the senior federal judge of the district, who, more than any other person, had worked to develop the system under which jury panels in the Southern District of New York are selected. But they were no more able to demonstrate the truth of their contentions through his testimony than they had earlier been through the testimony of others.

"If, in making up our jury lists," Judge Knox had once

told a Congressional committee, "my court were to follow suggestions that have been made to me, the result would be that our panels would be filled not only with the halt, the lame, and the blind, but also with the venal and corrupt."

And he made this point effectively as he was questioned by Harry Sacher, insisting that a careful method of selection was necessary, but that it was the purpose of his plan to have "every economic and social group in the community" on the juries. The newspapers were almost unanimous in saying that the lawyers for the defense had been set back by Judge Knox's testimony, especially when he made it perfectly clear that the jury selection system "is not based on race, religion, color, political affiliation, or economic status."

The termination of this phase of the trial came on the twenty-seventh court day in the seventh week of the trial. Judge Medina gave the defense thirty-two minutes beyond the usual adjournment hour of 4:30, but then crisply remarked "Well, the time's up."

Richard Gladstein immediately denounced "this system of so-called justice," and said that if he were allowed sufficient time he could prove all his charges.

"If you and your colleagues had your way," Judge Medina replied, "we would never be through with this challenge. I gave you all the time I felt reasonable, and you've proved nothing more of significance as I see it. At the beginning of this trial I took the statements of defense counsel about what they would prove just as I would take the statements of any counsel, but I have had bitter experience here, and now it is the end."

"In the last analysis," he stated in the opinion he read on March 4, "the challenge comes down to the assertion, contrary to all precedent, that those who administer the jury system must by some means produce a jury list which shall have proportional representation of Negroes, manual workers, poor people, and members of various racial and religious groups.

"Any attempt to secure such representation would not only result in chaos and confusion but, in my opinion, inevitably breed the very intolerance which every right-minded person should be vigilant to avoid."

Elsewhere in his opinion he pointed out that "There is affirmative evidence showing that Jews and Negroes serve in this district and that special effort has been made to secure qualified jurors of the Negro race." And he concluded by saying that "had any such iniquitous system as that alleged by defendants been in force for such a long period . . . its existence would necessarily have been widely known, and it is hard to believe that a storm of protest would not have arisen to uproot such intolerance and discrimination. Of all places in the United States it seems to me that New York City would be the one least likely to permit such a system to flourish in its midst.

"The challenge is overruled; the motion in all respects denied."

The selection of the jury began on Monday, March 7, but not before additional time-consuming arguments had been advanced by the defense. Five days earlier, William Z. Foster and Eugene Dennis had issued a statement that many people felt was treasonable, and President Truman, when asked to comment about it, authorized the use of a direct quotation in which he said "I have no comment to make on such a statement by traitors."

Counsel for the defense were quick to use this remark as a basis for a series of motions, contending that the President's comment would make a fair trial impossible. Most of the day was wasted in listening to these contentions, but Judge

Medina denied most of the motions, taking only a few under advisement. After hearing the sixteenth of the day's twenty-two motions he remarked that "This must be almost the world's record for motions," and a little later he postponed further argument in order to have the first group of prospective jurors brought into the courtroom.

Under the rules, the judges of federal courts are permitted to question jurors, and Judge Medina had long since decided that he would keep that task tightly in his own hands. He would not permit the lawyers for either the defense or the prosecution to ask any questions directly. Nevertheless, he carefully considered their points of view, and in preparing for this difficult task he asked both sides to submit such questions as they wished to have asked. He was guided by these to a marked degree, but throughout the week that was spent in the selection of the jury he adhered closely to his original plan.

Both sides presented lists of organizations to which they objected, asking that members of these be rejected. Catholic and veterans' organizations, among others, were listed by the defense, and almost a hundred subversive groups were listed by the prosecution. Lists of Communists, former Communists, and prominent anti-Communists were compiled in order to make certain that no juror was personally acquainted with any of them. The prospective jurors were even asked if they had read any of a number of books: *The Road to Serfdom*, *I Chose Freedom*, *Out of the Night*, and others.

The defense was permitted fifteen peremptory challenges, the prosecution six, and Judge Medina himself rejected several individuals for reasons that seemed good to him. On March 16, the jury, as it was completed, proved to be a dramatic denial of the exaggerated criticisms of the jury system that had been advanced by the defense.

The foreman of the jury was Mrs. Thelma Dial, a Negro housewife and a part-time dressmaker, whose husband was a musician.

Russell Janney was a writer and theatrical producer.

Mrs. Ida F. Howell was a Negro housewife and a worker in a beauty parlor, whose husband was a taxi driver.

Miss Kathryn E. Dunn, a former clerical worker, was temporarily unemployed.

George L. Smith, a Negro, had formerly been a receptionist for the Delaware & Hudson Railroad, but at the moment was selling fur coats and real estate on commission.

Mrs. Lillian Berliner was a housewife and former stenographer whose husband was a salesman of woolens.

Patrick S. Reynolds was a retired salesman for a brewery.

Henry E. Allen was an industrial engineer who was temporarily unassigned.

Mrs. Lillian Schlesinger, a widow, was a clerk in a department store.

James F. Smyth was a wireman and assembler for the Bell Telephone Laboratories.

Mrs. Carrie L. Robinson, a widow, was employed as a clerical worker.

Mrs. Gertrude Corwin was a housewife whose husband was a salesman of women's wear.

In reply to protests by the lawyers for the defense that his rulings made it impossible for them to determine whether or not those who had been selected were biased against the defendants as Communists, Judge Medina made one final explanation.

"I have made a most serious and conscientious effort," he said, "to ascertain any bias that may exist, and to make sure that no juror sits in this case who has any bias or partiality.

I have done my best and I do not believe a single member of this jury is laboring under any bias or partiality whatsoever. I can do no more."

The jury was called into the courtroom and sworn in by William J. Borman, the clerk of the court. The Judge explained that four alternate jurors would be selected, and then turned to speak to the twelve who had been chosen, explaining that an indictment, in itself, is no evidence of guilt, and that the defendants were "clothed in the presumption of innocence" throughout the trial.

"You have been so carefully selected here," he concluded, "because your minds are free and open and you are fair and impartial. I want you to stay that way to the end."

It was on the following day that the alternates were selected, but before that had been accomplished, Eugene Dennis, in an unexpected move, announced his intention to dismiss his lawyer, Louis McCabe, and asked permission to represent himself.

Judge Medina pointed out that a layman, struggling with the technicalities of the law, without the aid of counsel, might easily sacrifice some of his rights, and asked Dennis if he had considered that risk.

"I certainly have considered it," Dennis replied in a voice that seemed very small coming from so large a man.

Judge Medina further explained the difficulties and asked if Dennis still wished to represent himself.

"I do, Your Honor," he replied.

United States Attorney McGohey suggested that this move might be a "device" to enable Dennis to inject unsworn statements into the proceedings and in this way add testimony that might appear "in the guise of argument." Nevertheless, the request was granted, and Dennis left his place in the line of defendants and took a seat at the counsel table beside McCabe who still remained to represent Henry Winston.

The following day, Friday, March 18, the Judge gave the jurors his instructions, telling them especially to keep their minds "right on the ball" in following the evidence.

"I do beg of you, as we go through this trial," he continued, "to be patient. There are few qualities in life that are so important. If you once get yourself in the frame of mind where you know you have a task to be done, and it has to be done carefully, and you don't let little things disturb you at all, why then you get a certain calm and peace of mind about it. That is the sort of thing that is of the essence in the administration of justice. Now, do that."

Nine weeks had passed since the trial had originally opened, and only now was a jury ready to hear testimony upon which the fate of the eleven defendants would depend.

As the tenth week of the trial began, United States Attorney McGohey, in his opening statement to the jury, said that he would prove "through their own documents and by witnesses" that the defendants had established "leadership training schools" in which "the Russian revolution is studied in detail as a blueprint for revolution." He pointed out that the issues in the trial were whether the defendants were guilty, as charged, of violating federal law in "wilfully and knowingly organizing the Communist party of the United States to teach and advocate the overthrow and destruction of the United States Government by force and violence," and "having created the organization through which to operate, conspiring to carry out their program."

He said he would establish it as fundamental to their philosophy that "Socialism cannot be established by peaceful evolution, but . . . only by violent revolution, by smashing the machinery of government, and by setting up in its stead a dictatorship of the proletariat."

He pointed out that in the belief of the defendants this could be accomplished only "by the violent and forceful seizure of power by the proletariat under the leadership of the Communist party." He explained that their local clubs, beginners classes, other classes, and "leadership training schools" were all established with this end in view, and added that "it is reiterated constantly that the students are being trained as professional revolutionaries," and that "Marxism is not merely 'dogma' but a 'guide to action'."

"It is pointed out," he added, "that fifty thousand trained revolutionaries succeeded in establishing the dictatorship of the proletariat in Russia. This is the model for the revolution in this country. At the proper time, they are taught—the proper time being a time of national crisis, unrest, disorder brought about by severe depression or war—at such a time, the party members will be in positions of influence in the key trades in the basic industries and, when the national board decides that the revolutionary situation is at hand, the party will lead the proletariat in violent revolution. They teach that this revolution cannot be without violence, for to be successful the entire apparatus of the Government must be smashed."

Louis F. McCabe, attorney for Henry Winston, and George W. Crockett, Jr., attorney for Jacob Stachel and Carl Winter, followed with their opening statements. Winston, according to McCabe, was "guilty only of devotion to the American people," and Crockett contended that the case was unusual because "we're not trying facts, we're not trying men, but ideas."

Eugene Dennis, having been given permission to conduct his own defense, spoke for an hour or more, but frequently wandered away from the points to which he should have confined himself, in order to enlarge upon the virtues of the Communist party. Judge Medina stopped him several times in an effort to keep him within bounds, and grew firm when Dennis started talking about "the economic depression which has already begun in this country" and endeavored to explain what Communists proposed to do about it.

"Now, Mr. Dennis," interrupted the Judge. "That's the end. I'm not going to allow any more of that. I've tried to be patient, but I don't know what I'm going to do with you without taking some action I don't want to take. You apparently understand what I say, but you look me in the eye and go right ahead, regardless. If you were running this court it would be all right, but you're not."

At this point Dennis omitted several pages of his prepared speech and in his conclusion denied that Marxism-Leninism taught force and violence. Admitting that the Communists hoped to bring about fundamental changes, he insisted that he and his associates would establish "that throughout history such far-reaching social change has been accompanied by force and violence. But we will bring evidence to show that Marx and Lenin did not advocate force and violence, but that it results when reactionary groups, representing powerful vested interests, try to stop the march of social progress."

After nine weeks of bewildering delay, the trial had finally begun, and Judge Medina, who had earlier remarked that he was going to perform the tasks that faced him "as best I can with the light God gave me," had still to face seven uninterrupted months of concentrated effort before the newly selected jury could retire and reach its verdict.

The second day of the trial was devoted to the opening statements of other lawyers for the defense, and to various attempts at delay. Gladstein moved for a mistrial, accusing

Judge Medina of "improper" remarks which "constituted prejudice."

"I have sat here," added Harry Sacher as he came to Gladstein's support, "and watched Your Honor scratch his head, pull his ears, smile, and do other things which have had the effect of negating what we say."

"I want you gentlemen to know," the Judge replied, "that when I'm scratching my head I'm just scratching my head."

Crockett joined the demand for a mistrial, and called attention to "the emphasis of the tone of your voice."

"I used no unusual tone of voice," the Judge replied. "Motion denied."

The government called its first witness, Louis F. Budenz, on the third day. Formerly a Communist and managing editor of the *Daily Worker*, Budenz had quit the party, rejoined the Catholic Church, and become a member of the faculty of Fordham University. Called to the witness stand by United States Attorney McGohey, he admitted that as editor of the *Daily Worker* he had followed orders based on a program for world revolution that had been adopted by the Communist International in 1935, and identified a copy of the program. He admitted changing his editorial "line" after the Stalin-Hitler pact was signed in 1939, told of interviews he had had with several of the defendants, in one of which Eugene Dennis and William Z. Foster had told him he had been named managing editor of the Communist publication.

"I object," Dennis faltered, rising from his chair. "This is entirely hearsay."

"Why, he says you told him," said the Judge. "You see, Mr. Dennis, this is a result of your being your own lawyer. You don't understand this hearsay business. This isn't hearsay at all."

In the days that followed, Budenz told of the loyalty pledge to Stalin that some of the defendants had taken in Moscow, of Communist plans to seize arsenals, naval vessels, aircraft, poison gas, and weapons in the United States, and gave definitions of words and phrases as they are used in "Aesopian" Communistic statements. He even told of how American Communists began plotting to start civil war in this country in the event of war with Russia. Then, having completed his testimony on direct examination, he successfully withstood the combined attacks of the lawyers for the defense.

The government's second witness, Herbert A. Philbrick, was called on the afternoon of April 6. Mr. Philbrick was a Boston advertising man who had spent the preceding nine years in the Communist party as an undercover "contact" of the Federal Bureau of Investigation. As part of his testimony he explained that the Communists had been taught that there were ideal times for "violent revolution by bands of armed workers." These were during any period of depression in the United States or during war. Three days of cross-examination by the lawyers for the defense failed to shake Mr. Philbrick on any of his direct testimony, and his appearance as a government witness so startled the Communists that, according to *The New York Times*, they promptly instituted "a loyalty investigation in reverse," in order, if possible, to rout out any other undercover agents who might have become members of the party.

William O'Dell Nowell, another former Communist official, was the next witness to be called. A Negro, who had been sent to the Lenin Institute in Moscow for more than a year, Mr. Nowell testified that Jacob Stachel, one of the defendants, had told him of the party's plans for a separate Negro nation in the South. Charles W. Nicodemus, also a former Communist official, followed and explained how party members were told to compile information about the plants in which they worked and of a Russian plan for the invasion of the United States by way of Alaska and Canada.

On Monday, April 25, Garfield Herron, an Arkansas carpenter, took the stand and testified that he had joined the Communist party as an undercover agent for the FBI. He told of the secret party school he had attended and explained that he had been taught to use certain Marxist-Leninist books as a "guide to action" in violent revolution in the United States. When Herron was being cross-examined, Richard Gladstein, of defense counsel, tried to introduce in evidence the full texts of the books that had been mentioned by the witness, and as a test offered a pamphlet entitled "Value, Price, and Profit," by Karl Marx.

The prosecution objected that the pamphlet was irrelevant, but Judge Medina ruled that though Gladstein might not read the whole pamphlet, he might read such portions as would bring out the points he wished to make. It was his desire, the Judge explained, to give the defendants an opportunity to explain "what they say they really were doing," but he was fearful that the trial might get off onto things that were not at issue. At this point Harry Sacher rose and insisted that it was "essential" to bring in the books "in their entirety."

Several weeks earlier, because of "wilful, deliberate, and concerted" delay, Judge Medina had ruled against either side arguing on the admissibility of evidence without his permission, and with that in mind he attempted to put a stop to the argument.

"This is not a trial of books," he explained, "because the question is whether these individual defendants entered into a conspiracy. If they used these books as paraphernalia and apparatus to serve their purpose —"

Sacher leaped to his feet and interrupted:

"To call these books paraphernalia and apparatus," he shouted, "is to reduce books to the level of the tools of thieves. I tell you the culture of the world will not long survive with that approach to books."

The Judge told Sacher to say no more, and he sat down, but Eugene Dennis rose at once. He, too, was told that the Judge did not desire any further argument, but he refused to stop.

"I don't think," remarked the Judge, "that you are helping yourself by doing that, but that is your lookout."

Apparently unimpressed, Dennis argued that the indictment against the defendants was much the same as charging them "with exercising our inalienable rights to free speech, free press, and free assembly."

"I suppose," Judge Medina replied, "that you are just daring me to do something. You gentlemen can be just as disorderly, just as unruly as you choose, but you will not goad me into taking any hasty action which may create a prejudicial atmosphere. Now I tell you again to stop."

"We defendants," Dennis began again, "intend to show—"

"I will take an adjournment for five minutes," announced the Judge, getting up and leaving the courtroom.

Five minutes later, when he returned, Dennis made no effort to continue his remarks, and the pamphlet was ruled inadmissible.

It was not only within the courtroom that the defendants and their supporters were at work. Day after day pickets were marching before the Court House—carrying placards—singing—shouting insults, many of which were aimed at Judge Medina himself. This had been almost continuous since the day the trial began, but the Judge made no move to stop it.

"Can you imagine anything more stupid for me to have done?" he asked long after the trial was over. "Would it have been smart for me to do that, and thus embroil myself in further proceedings, appeals, and repercussions in the courtroom?"

He was careful to make no comment at the time. He did his best to give the impression that he was little more than barely conscious of the pickets, but the public was conscious of them and so were a good many members of Congress. Senator Eastland, of Mississippi, for instance, though agreeing that Medina was making it clear that the trial was a fair one, was nevertheless critical.

"What's wrong," he was quoted as saying, "with a United States judge who doesn't see that they are stopped from parading?"

And Senator Ferguson of Michigan, agreeing that Medina had "tried hard to control the trial," felt that it sometimes appeared to be "out of control."

Medina's patience, however, was also being praised. Editorials commended him. Cartoons did the same, and one, which appeared in the *Daily News* and was entitled "Only Known Precedent," showed the Judge in his robes, holding a copy of the Book of Job.

On April 26, the government surprised the defense by calling Angela Calomiris as its ninth witness. A small, slender person, she had engaged in Communist activities for seven years, had become financial secretary of the group of which she was a member, and had reported regularly to the FBI.

"I have reported to the FBI," she explained, "from the day I joined."

Being a photographer, she had ultimately become financial secretary of the Photo League, a party-front organization, and had photographed Communist individuals and groups.

Such photographs, she explained, as well as her reports, had regularly been turned over to the FBI which not only paid all her Communist expenses, but had even given her fifty dollars so that she could contribute that amount to the "defense fund" of the eleven defendants against whom she was testifying.

The trial had been under way for almost four months by now, and the strain under which Judge Medina had been laboring from the first was beginning to tell. The lawyers for the defense had long since developed a method of leaping to their feet one after another—voicing objections—charging the Judge with prejudice—asking insinuating questions—changing the subject under discussion—arguing—demanding—denying—repeating—until the trial sometimes seemed utterly aimless and almost without point. From the first, Judge Medina had been surprisingly patient—far too patient, according to his critics, but now and again he grew sharp—vehement—almost explosive.

"You are incapable of showing respect," he once snapped at Harry Sacher in the absence of the jury. "Your whole violent temper is such that it is impossible."

"You are not only putting the defendants on trial in this case," retorted Sacher, "but the lawyers, too."

"Mr. Sacher," threatened the Judge, "you will never try another case before me, I'll tell you that."

"You can't intimidate me," shouted Sacher.

"And you're not going to intimidate me, either," countered the Judge.

The interchange ended when the jury returned to the courtroom, but, as other witnesses were called and other situations developed, it threatened to be renewed.

Other undercover men who had posed as Communists took the stand—Thomas A. Younglove, a St. Louis contractor, and

William Cummings, a Negro automobile worker of Toledo—and the lawyers for the defense branded them "stool pigeons," "informers," and "squealers" as a result.

Judge Medina was compelled almost daily to warn and reprove the lawyers for the defense. The most casual observer could not have failed to see that their insolence was calculated and that they were forever intent on spreading their propaganda and trying to disrupt the administration of justice. Scores of times, as Medina sought to clarify their twisted and obscure statements, one after another would leap to his feet in order to accuse the Judge of prejudice or some other judicial misconduct.

Irving Shapiro, of government counsel, objected to the reiterated use of the term "stool pigeon" by the defense, but Judge Medina shook his head.

"I'm going to let them call people names all they want for whatever it gets them," he announced; and George Crockett, the Negro lawyer for the defense, went on with his cross-examination of William Cummings, the Negro witness, who was on the stand.

"Was there any discussion [with the FBI] about your compensation for being a stool pigeon?" Crockett asked.

"No," the witness replied.

The Judge laughed.

"Nobody said," he chuckled, " 'now, you stool pigeon, you are going to get so much'?"

Richard Gladstein, of defense counsel, was instantly on his feet objecting to the court's "levity," and within the next few minutes had six times angrily charged Judge Medina with judicial misconduct, in addition to referring several times to other actions as "improper."

John Victor Blanc, of Euclid, Ohio, another undercover contact of the FBI, followed William Cummings as a witness. Balmes Hidalgo, Jr., the eighth such informant, was next.

On Thursday, May 19, as the eighteenth week of the trial was coming to an end, United States Attorney McGohey unexpectedly rested the government's case. At once Judge Medina held that the government had presented so strong a prima facie case that he would hear only limited arguments on defense motions.

Three months had passed. The record of the case so far covered ten thousand pages, and the defense was only now about to call its first witness to the stand.

Foley Square contains half a dozen irregular island parks which are separated by streets and traffic lanes that run in several directions, and since the beginning of the trial there had hardly been a day when masses of pickets had not crowded these open places before the Court House. They marched there monotonously, around and around, carrying their placards, singing their songs, chanting their slogans. All day long they kept it up, now and again shouting in unison such comments as their leaders urged upon them. All one day they shouted "Judge Medina is a son-of-a-bitch! Judge Medina is a son-of-a-bitch!" their voices clearly audible even in the Judge's chambers on the twenty-second floor. "Adolf Hitler never died," they sang. "He's sitting there at Medina's side." "How do you spell Medina?" they asked, and promptly answered "R–A–T!" or, sometimes "K–K–K." And often, as they shuffled about the "island" directly before the Court House, they kept repeating, "If Medina's in the way, we're gonna roll right over him!"

The two primary purposes the Communists so obviously had in mind had not changed. Day after day, sometimes for hours at a time, the lawyers for the defense devoted themselves to their propaganda. As they argued their scores of motions, as they questioned witnesses, as they offered their endless objections and "interpreted" Marxist-Leninist literature, they forever had their campaign of propaganda in mind. But their other campaign—their series of operations aimed at breaking up the trial—had gone less well. It had become reasonably clear that Judge Medina, sensitive though he had occasionally shown himself to be under their ceaseless goading, was little likely to break under the strain, as Judge Eicher had done, or to fall into legal errors of any consequence. Some further pressure had to be put upon him or there would be no hope that he would give way under their campaign.

The courtroom in which the trial was being held is on the main floor of the Court House and is easy of access from the large, marble-walled entrance hall. Each morning for weeks the limited space available for the public had been filled by observers who waited in line outside the courtroom doors until they were opened. Always there were many who, because of the lack of space, could not gain admittance, and if any person left while court was in session his place was certain to be taken at once by someone else who was waiting at the door. But on the morning of June 3 the throng outside the courtroom began to gather earlier than usual. It was larger than usual, too, and by 8 o'clock, though court would not be convened until 10:30, the police assigned to the Court House entrance began to see that this gathering was made up almost exclusively of Communists and their sympathizers, many of whom they recognized from having seen them among the omnipresent pickets or at earlier sessions of the court. When the doors were opened, the courtroom was filled in a single hurried rush so that almost every person in the place, except for the officials, the reporters, and perhaps a few individuals who had gained entrance through the courtesy of some of the district judges, was a partisan of the eleven who were on trial.

John Gates, the editor of the *Daily Worker*, had been put on the stand more than a week before as the first witness for the defense, and now he was to be called again for the eighth day. At intervals during the preceding week difficulties had arisen. Gates himself had not caused much trouble until the day before, but the lawyers for the defense had been more than usually intractable, and Benjamin J. Davis, Jr., the Negro defendant who was also city councilman in New York, had been especially obstreperous.

"It's pretty hard," he had shouted at one time, "for the defendants to sit like bumps on a log while the court cuts the guts out of the defense!"

"I consider that an extremely offensive statement," Judge Medina warned.

"Well, the whole trial is offensive to me," Davis retorted, continuing to argue and object.

"If you insist on being disorderly," the Judge remarked, "I shall remand you for the remainder of the trial."

Threatened so definitely with jail, Davis sat down; and during the days that followed, the trial had gone on with little more than the usual amount of wrangling, except that Gates, also, had almost been remanded for contempt. This had been on the day before, when he had refused to answer a question.

"We have a man here," the Judge had explained, "who insists on being his own counsel. He is not learned in the law, and for his own protection I excuse the jury."

The Judge had then explained that having taken the oath as a witness, Gates could not choose which question he would or would not answer. At first, despite the explanation, Gates seemed inclined to continue to refuse, but Harry Sacher advised him to reply to the question, and when the jury had been called back he had done so. Now, as the next morning session of the court began with Gates still on the stand, the cross-examination went quietly for a time. In the course of the questioning, the witness testified that three members of the party's national veterans' committee had helped him prepare a postwar pamphlet for veterans.

"Who are they?" Mr. McGohey asked.

"These people are engaged in private industry," Gates replied. "I will not disclose their names because they will lose their jobs."

"I ask the court," Mr. McGohey began after a pause, "to instruct the witness to answer."

"Strike out the answer," Judge Medina instructed the court stenographer, and then he turned to Gates.

"Answer the question," he ordered.

Harry Sacher leaped to his feet.

"I advise him of his constitutional right to refuse," he shouted.

"I repeat my direction," said the Judge.

"On the grounds of the First and Fifth and Tenth Amendments I decline to answer," Gates replied. "I would have to bow my head in shame and I could never raise my head in decent society if I ever became a stool pigeon even under the court's direction."

"Strike out the answer," ordered the Judge.

"Would the court please tell the witness he has no such right?" asked Mr. McGohey.

"I do so advise him," said the Judge.

Gates still refused, and an argument began in which all the lawyers for the defense attempted to join. The jury was consequently excused, and Judge Medina quietly turned to the man on the witness stand.

"Now, Mr. Gates," he began, "pursuant to the authority vested in me by Title 18 of the United States Code, Section

401 . . . I now adjudge you guilty of wilful and deliberate contempt, and by reason thereof I sentence you as follows: You are to be remanded until you have purged yourself of your contempt for a period not to exceed thirty days."

The words were hardly spoken when the courtroom was filled with an angry roar. Almost as one man the whole room rose, with hardly a person remaining in his seat except Judge Medina, the counsel for the prosecution, the startled Gates, and the occupants of the press section. The defendants, their lawyers, the observers who filled the room, leaped to their feet in a pandemonium of sound. With arms waving, one or two of the defendants advanced toward the bench a step or two, almost as if threatening the Judge, and amid the angry uproar only an occasional voice, here and there, could be heard more clearly than the rest.

"It was only by the help of the good Lord," Judge Medina later told me, "that I was able to carry on that day. I really felt that Somebody was helping me. In all that excitement I felt perfectly calm. I did not raise my voice. And I know that my unguided will alone was unequal to that test. If ever a man felt the presence of Someone beside him, strengthening his will and giving him aid and comfort, I felt it on that day."

Henry Winston was shouting more loudly than most, and Judge Medina listened carefully, noting what he said, getting it down on the record.

"More than five thousand Negroes have been lynched in this country—"

"Now, Mr. Winston," the Judge said quietly.

"—and the government of the United States should be ashamed for bringing in this monstrosity."

"Mr. Winston," the Judge repeated in a voice that was almost lost in the furor, "I hereby direct that you be remanded for the remainder of the trial."

The courtroom was still filled with noise—with voices—with a scrape of chairs and the shuffle of feet. Deputy marshals who had been on duty at the Alger Hiss perjury trial which was being conducted in an upper courtroom, came hurrying down. They moved rapidly to the rail—stood tense and watchful as the defendants and their lawyers alike kept up their angry shouting.

"It sounds more like a kangaroo court than a court of the United States," shouted Gus Hall. "I've heard more law and more constitutional rights in kangaroo courts."

"Now let me see," remarked the Judge. "This is Mr. Hall?"

He paused for a moment.

"Mr. Hall," he went on quietly. "You are hereby remanded for the balance of the trial."

More argument followed, but the Judge's quiet confidence and his controlled voice began to have its effect. The shouting among the onlookers in the courtroom lessened. The visitors fell silent—listened—sat down. Only the defendants and their lawyers still remained standing. The noise was greatly less, but Eugene Dennis was still shouting, apparently bent on forcing the Judge to remand him to jail with the others.

"Mr. Dennis," the Judge remarked. "Don't you remember that I told you I was going to treat you as one of the lawyers? I have tried to stick to my determination not to do anything to counsel. They may do whatever they choose and take the consequences in due time."

He paused and then leaned forward.

"I think," he added, "that it would be much better if you all sat down."

Dennis lowered his voice and turned toward his fellow defendants, apparently telling them to sit down, and, as David Snell described it in the *New York Sun*, "they took their seats immediately, like a well-disciplined platoon."

Sacher and Gladstein asked for a stay of the order remanding the defendants. McCabe insisted that no contempt had been intended. But the Judge refused the requests—denied the motions that were offered. His order remained in effect and when, a few minutes later, a recess was ordered, Gates, Hall, and Winston were taken into custody by the marshals.

For the moment the situation had cleared, but it was not to be supposed that the defense would accept so sharp a reverse without objection. In remanding Gates, Judge Medina had carefully referred to the specific section of the United States Code that gave him the authority to act, but in remanding Winston and Hall he had made no such reference, and the lawyers for the defense were quick to note the omission.

Gate's refusal to answer a question had created a situation that was specifically covered by the section of the Code to which the Judge had referred, but the offense Winston and Hall had committed was of a different nature. Certain though the Judge was that he possessed the authority to act as he had acted, he was much less certain that he knew exactly what that authority was. It had been because of this that he had mentioned no authority in remanding these two men.

The incident occurred on Friday, and the week-end intervened before the next development materialized. But the delay also gave the defense plenty of time to think the matter over and to get out writs of habeas corpus for Hall and Winston. It was on Monday morning that these, following routine, came before Judge Vincent L. Leibell, also a federal judge of the Southern District of New York, who was sitting in "Crime 1," the defense arguing that Judge Medina had had no right to remand either Winston or Hall.

Busy as usual that morning, Medina knew none of the details of the hearing, but coming down to the courtroom after lunch, he found all the lawyers in the case—lawyers both for the prosecution and the defense—waiting to see him privately in the room set aside for the Judge adjacent to the courtroom. He noted, too, that the lawyers for the defense were all smiling as if very much pleased over something, and though he did his best to appear unconcerned, he could not help wondering what advantage they thought they had gained.

It was Harry Sacher who referred to the writs of habeas corpus, explaining that they had been taken before Judge Leibell that morning.

"Now, Judge," he continued, "Judge Leibell has submitted some questions for you to answer."

"What are they?" asked Medina.

Sacher's smile broadened.

"They are in a sealed envelope," he replied, "and you are to answer them from the bench."

Here was a difficulty. For months Medina had been struggling to carry on a fair, unbiased trial in the face of the ingenious opposition of the lawyers for the defense. From the day the trial had begun he had known that his every move was subject to attack and misrepresentation by these attorneys. He had not really been free even to call upon the other judges of the court for help. Endless questions had forever been arising, and he had been forced to solve them as best he could, knowing that his slightest error would be seized upon and magnified if possible. He was half exhausted by his months of constant effort, and could not help wondering, despite his belief to the contrary, whether this time he had actually blundered. He should have taken the opportunity offered by the week-end to check the authority he thought he had, but he had failed to do so—had tried to get a little rest—and now it almost seemed as if one of his fellow judges was playing into the hands of the lawyers of these men who were on trial. For a moment he was bitter, but he smiled as brightly as he could, knowing that it would not do to show his feelings.

"All right," he nodded, as if the problem were unimportant. "Let's have it."

He had donned his robe, and now he took the envelope. Entering the courtroom he mounted the bench, as cool and as composed, apparently, as if utterly unconcerned about the contents of that envelope.

He sat down in the leather-upholstered chair—leaned back—opened the envelope—adjusted his glasses—unfolded the note. Then he read the question aloud.

Had he punished Winston and Hall, Judge Leibell wanted to know, for contempt or for some other reason? And by what authority?

He dropped the sheet of paper onto the desk before him.

"I remanded them," he explained with only the shortest pause, "as punishment for a criminal contempt and in the exercise of my plenary power to remand a defendant during the trial, and in the exercise of any and all other powers that I may possess under the laws and the Constitution of the United States."

There. That covered it. It was general, he knew, and not specific, but it answered the question. Sacher was not smiling now. But there was something more. Judge Medina suddenly understood that Judge Leibell had been right in sending that sealed question and in asking that it be answered in public. No such question could properly have been asked privately. Even unprejudiced people might have assumed that such an inquiry, privately made, could only have been intended to cover up some doubtful or even questionable legal arrangement that could not be arrived at openly. There had been no way for Judge Leibell to share the responsibility that rested on Medina. It was his alone, and this shows the isolation under which he labored throughout the trial.

The fortieth reunion of Judge Medina's class at Princeton was held that spring, and the Judge, having been elected president of the class, was especially anxious to attend. He was unable to get away, of course, during the week, but court was never in session on Saturdays and he decided to be there for the week-end, which was the time set for the alumni "P–rade" down Prospect Street from Nassau Hall to the baseball field where the annual game with Yale was to be played.

The "P–rade," as usual, was made up of a number of bands that were interspersed among the various classes that were represented, and when the gayly costumed class of 1909 reached the field and made its way around the running track with Harold Medina at its head, everyone in the bleachers and the grandstand rose and cheered him.

Later he was to have other receptions of the kind, but this was the first—a greeting as surprising and gratifying to the Judge as it was spontaneous and enthusiastic on the part of the throng.

Not long before this event took place a tragedy quite unrelated to the trial of the Communist leaders had taken place in Maryland. James V. Forrestal, seriously ill as a result of his years of overwork as Secretary of the Navy and Secretary of Defense, had been in the Naval Hospital at Bethesda, Maryland, for an extended period. Few more able or more selfless public servants have ever served in any American cabinet, but the strain of the war years and of the years that followed had broken his health, and bitter, unreasoning critics had broken his spirit. No longer in public office, it seemed that he might have an opportunity to rebuild his shattered health, but he had waited too long and his critics were too bitter. On Sunday, May 22, 1949, when the nurse who attended him was absent from his room,

Forrestal crossed to the open window and plunged sixteen stories to his death.

This event was in no way connected with the trial over which Judge Medina was presiding, but the Communists and their sympathizers, no doubt troubled by the developments in that trial, saw in Forrestal's death a subtle and fiendish new "line" that they could utilize in their attacks on Medina.

The pickets had by now been parading before the Court House for more than four months, and in that time had changed their "line" more than once. Sometimes they had marched quietly and sometimes noisily, sometimes with few placards or with none and sometimes half-obscured by the signs they carried. Not a day had passed but what great piles of mail had reached Medina from all across the United States, and telegrams, sometimes hundreds in a single day, were forever urging some action or other on him. Clearly all this was well organized, for messages that were identical in thought, and often were similar in expression, came from all over the country—from New York, New England, the South, the Midwest, the Mountain states, and the West Coast. Telegrams came from sources just as widely spread, and sometimes these were filed at hours so carefully chosen in different time zones as actually to bring the messages to Medina's chambers almost all at once.

In the weeks that had passed since the beginning of the trial the Judge had come to understand something of the organized effort that lay behind this continuous campaign, and it had little effect on him, but now a new "line" was about to threaten him with a very definite danger.

It began with pickets who were marching before the Court House, though Judge Medina did not see it there at first. He learned of it when he saw a picture in a newspaper—a picture of pickets who were carrying placards.

"Medina will fall like Forrestal," read one. And another said "Judge Medina, get on the ball. Remember Jimmy Forrestal." He gave the matter very little thought, but now the letters, the postcards, and the telegrams changed as well.

"Medina will fall like Forrestal," read some, following the lead of the placards.

"Jump out of the window!" read others.

"Jump!" read others still.

The phone would ring, and whoever answered it would hear only the single word "Jump!" followed by a click.

Letters and telegrams sent to him at his home contained many versions of this same message, and other messages as well. Phone calls sometimes reached him there in the evening, often consisting only of that single word "Jump!" Letters were often addressed to him in red. Some contained foul messages. Some were threats. One, containing a liberally marked page from the *Daily Worker*, had a scrawled address in heavy red crayon, reading:

His Honor
Harold Medina
Federal Court House
Foley Square
c/o Gawd Amighty

During an extended period an intense campaign revolved constantly about that one word "Jump!" endlessly repeated. "Jump!" "Jump!" "Jump!"

"I know it sounds funny," he once admitted, "but of all the things they tried on me during the trial this came closest to working. As a child I used to have dreams that I was falling from some great height, and I often awakened in a kind of cold sweat. When I was sixteen my father took me to Niagara Falls, and I was afraid to go near the edge for fear I would jump over. I have always had that queer feeling. It was the chink in my armor, and this campaign of theirs really bothered me. I got so I didn't dare go near a window, and I feel it even yet."

No such campaign, carried to such lengths, could have been based on nothing. The effort that was made carried with it a strong presumption that a careful and detailed study of Judge Medina had been carried out, and that his not-uncommon weakness had come to light in the course of it. Here again was evidence of the dangerous ingenuity of those whose leaders were on trial.

Defense counsel made two attempts to have the three who had been jailed released on bail, but Judge Samuel H. Kaufman, of the United States District Court, rejected one such plea, and Judge Learned Hand of the United States Circuit Court of Appeals rejected another. Later other attempts were also made, but they, too, failed. The trial, meanwhile, continued without interruption, the three men who had been remanded being brought to court each day and returned to jail as each court session ended.

Gates, still on the stand under cross-examination, was forced into several damaging admissions: one in which he admitted that the Communists taught revolution, and another in which he admitted having lied under oath in applying for a passport. And he refused to answer another question, claiming that to do so might incriminate him.

"You mean, Mr. Gates," asked United States Attorney McGohey, "you refuse to answer my question on the grounds that an answer would incriminate you in a crime for which you could now be prosecuted?"

"I do," Gates admitted, "on the advice of my attorney."

It was only after fourteen days on the witness stand that

Gates was followed by Gilbert Green, the Communist party's Illinois chairman. He, as Gates had done, admitted that he had changed his name and though he denied that the Communists taught violence, he admitted that pressure from outside the United States influenced the decisions of the American politburo. Several times he was rebuked by Judge Medina for outbursts while his testimony was being taken, but after five days on the stand, he once more angrily burst forth with an objection when an exhibit was excluded as irrelevant.

"I thought we were going to get a chance to prove our case," he complained in what Russel Porter of *The New York Times* called "a sullen, whining tone." "That article," Green continued, "is germane to the very heart of the issue."

Judge Medina spoke so gently that his voice could hardly be heard halfway back in the courtroom.

"Mr. Green," he said, "you are hereby remanded for the balance of the trial."

Eugene Dennis promptly rose, but no one followed his example, and when he asked to be heard Judge Medina excused the jury.

"You don't seem to realize," the Judge replied when Dennis complained that the ruling was "entirely unwarranted," "that . . . it is essential to the administration of justice that proceedings be conducted in an orderly way. The amount of disorder and contemptuous behaviour I have witnessed here is beyond anything I could have thought possible in an American court. I intend there shall be no more of it."

Dennis asked for reconsideration on Green, but the Judge refused.

"The next outburst," he said, "will be followed by the same sort of ruling."

After fifteen days on the stand Green was followed by

Benjamin J. Davis, Jr., but neither his testimony nor his manner were dramatic. In the week that followed, the defense called a series of lesser witnesses, none of whom were under indictment: Fannie Hartman, a New England teacher and graduate of Smith College who was a Communist party functionary; Daniel Boone Schirmer, city secretary of the Communist party in Boston; Mrs. Frances A. Hood, six feet tall, a Bostonian, and a graduate of Radcliffe College who was descended "on both sides," so she said, from John and Priscilla Alden; Dr. Herbert J. Phillips, an ousted faculty member of the University of Washington. Their testimony seemed unimportant and even uninteresting after the furor and the shouting of the preceding two months, and it was interrupted when George L. Smith, a juror, was taken sick and had to be excused. He was replaced by one of the alternates, Mrs. Jane Schulz, a former stenographer, and the trial was resumed on July 26.

On July 27, Judge Medina, half-exhausted by the uninterrupted strain under which he was laboring, again abruptly declared a recess in order to halt Dennis in his endless objections, and the next day, pale and tired, the Judge weakly protested that "I am simply unable, physically or mentally, to go on much longer," and recessed the trial for ten minutes in order to lie down.

It was no wonder that he was approaching exhaustion. The trial had now completed its sixth month—was well into its seventh—and the ceaseless mental strain was in itself almost overwhelming. But now, too, the summer heat of New York was at its worst, the humidity intense. Never since the first few days of the trial had the Judge's back failed to trouble him. The changes he had had made in his chair had helped a little, and the stiffly stayed brace he wore had helped a little, too, but because of the torrid heat of summer, that brace was chafing badly. All about his waist, and especially at his hips, the skin was raw, sensitive, and stinging. Hardly a story about him in the papers failed to tell of his almost ceaseless rocking back and forth, and of his constant shifting of position, but none explained the reason. Normally impatient and little given to physical quiescence, he was now so constantly tormented by the chafing about his waist that he could find no comfort in any position his chair permitted him to assume. The heat and perspiration added to his discomfort, and in his efforts to reduce the chafing he packed absorbent cotton all about the edges of the brace, only to exaggerate the heat and perspiration fully as much as he reduced the chafing. Had it not been that he was now driving out each week-end to their Westhampton home, which Mrs. Medina had opened for the summer, he could hardly have had any effective opportunity at all to care for his chafed waist, but the little improvement that was apparent each week-end was offset during the days he spent in court. Except for those Saturdays and Sundays, Medina spent that summer of 1949 in New York City—the first time in his life that he had done so.

Now and again he had hinted that he was determined to find some way to expedite the trial—some way, especially, to restrain the lawyers of the defense in their endless wrangling, and now, as the trial entered the month of August, he became more determined. The preceding week he had begun to cut down the time being spent on what he called "peripheral testimony," and began to refuse to let more than one lawyer take part in the same argument.

"It has been this succession of lawyers in sequence," he remarked, "that has made this trial what it is." And his rulings, in the week that followed, were firmer.

On Monday, August 1, as if no warning had been given, the lawyers for the defense began again to bob up one after another with objections, arguments, and motions in the midst of the cross-examination by government counsel of a woman defense witness.

"I don't want any argument or interruption of the cross-examination," said the Judge, but his warning was almost instantly ignored. Two of the defense lawyers continued their interruptions at almost every question. Presently the witness declined to answer a question, and the Judge asked if she remembered the oath she had taken to tell not only the truth but the whole truth. Richard Gladstein, leaping to his feet, began a long objection.

"Sit down," ordered the Judge.

"I object to that," began Gladstein angrily, "and ask Your Honor to admonish the jury—"

"Will you sit down," demanded the Judge, "or must I call an officer to put you down? I will have no more interruptions on cross-examination. Your field day is over."

"I resent Your Honor's remarks," Gladstein insisted.

"Mr. Marshal," the Judge remarked, turning toward a deputy marshal, "will you please—"

As the marshal rose and started toward Gladstein the lawyer sat down abruptly.

"All right," said the Judge. "I see that you sat down by yourself."

But a single lesson was not enough. Two days later an even firmer hand was necessary.

A minor party functionary from Chicago, a Mrs. Geraldyne Lightfoot, was on the stand, and the Judge, endeavoring to speed the trial, stopped Abraham J. Isserman, of defense counsel, from "asking broad, general questions that lead to long speeches on irrelevant issues," and warned the attorney to "get down to issues."

"This trial is going to move now," he added.

Isserman paid little attention, and the Judge consequently took up the questioning, directing the witness to answer responsively.

"I object," shouted Gladstein, leaping to his feet, "to the court's tone and manner of badgering the witness."

"There is nothing about my tone," replied the Judge, "and you will please sit down."

"I desire to make an objection," shouted the lawyer, remaining on his feet.

The Judge turned toward a deputy marshal.

"Mr. Marshal," he began, "will you just—"

The deputy got up and Gladstein as quickly sat down, but Isserman, who had remained standing, now started to argue.

"Sit down," ordered the Judge.

Isserman did not move.

"Now, Mr. Marshal," ordered the Judge, "just escort Mr. Isserman over to his seat."

The deputy did as he was told and Isserman sat down, but the Judge had no more than asked the witness another question than the lawyer was on his feet again with another objection.

"Mr. Marshal," the Judge ordered again. "Will you show Mr. Isserman to his seat!"

This time the marshal put his hand on the lawyer's shoulder, but Isserman had hardly sat down than he rose again.

"Mr. Marshal. Get busy!" snapped the Judge, and at last Isserman remained seated.

Clearly the trial was not going as the Communists had hoped, and some new "line" was necessary if their strategy of obstruction was to be continued. And now, having determined to arrange matters so that Judge Medina would be wrong either way he moved, their attack was built about the alleged illness of Henry Winston, one of the Negro defendants.

Here, they seemed to figure, was a way of demonstrating discrimination. The man was seriousy ill, they claimed, and they demanded that he be examined by his doctor in order that it might be learned whether or not his health was being endangered by the continuation of the trial.

A dilemma obviously confronted the Judge. If he refused to grant the request he would be said to be brutally endangering the health of one of the defendants, and because that defendant was a Negro he would be charged with showing discrimination as well. On the other hand, if he granted the request, it was conceivable that the Communists might have the examination made by some doctor of their own peculiar turn of mind who, told in advance what diagnosis was needed, would swear that Winston's life—or at least his health—would be endangered if he were forced to continue as a defendant in the trial.

The problem seemed insoluble. A little thought, however, showed Medina a way out, and Winston, treated with utmost consideration, was taken to the Marine Hospital at 67 Hudson Street and given a thorough examination. The doctor took a cardiograph, too, and reported that there was nothing the matter with him.

"Boys," said the Judge, "we go ahead with the trial."

But Winston was very, very weak. He simply could not go on.

"Well," said the Judge, "we will take a fifteen minute recess."

He turned to the marshal.

"Be sure, Mr. Marshal," he suggested gently, "that Mr. Winston lies down."

And apparently he did, for Winston was wonderfully revived when the recess was over!

By the middle of August it began to be apparent that Judge Medina, to use his own expression, was "boss of the courtroom," and there was some evidence that even the Communists had begun to accept that fact. But now a veritable bombshell was exploded by the defense, and Medina was almost instantly inundated by such a flood of telegrams as had not before been equaled since the trial began.

Russell Janney, a sixty-five-year-old author and theatrical producer, was a member of the jury—had been the last juror selected—and as court opened on Wednesday, August 25, in the eighth month of the trial, he was accused by defense counsel of "an active bias against the defendants," and a motion was made for a dismissal of the case. Motions for a mistrial were made by Harry Sacher and George W. Crockett, Jr., and were based, so it was said, on an article written by the editor of the *Daily Compass*, a left-wing New York newspaper, and published the day before.

After a preliminary conference in court and a more detailed discussion in his chambers, Judge Medina adjourned court for the day and dismissed the jury.

The incident, it developed, was based on more than the article in the *Daily Compass*. Defense counsel filed an affidavit that had been prepared by a certain Miss Carol Nathanson, who identified herself as a singer-actress known professionally as Carol Nason. Also submitted were eighty-nine hand-written pages of notes Miss Nathanson had made of talks she said she had had with Mr. Janney since the beginning of the trial—notes which the editor of the *Daily Compass* had seen and on which he seems to have based his article.

Miss Nathanson had known Mr. Janney professionally for some two years and had now and again had occasion to see him about theatrical matters. Not highly successful either as a singer or an actress, she was said by friends and acquaintances to be "radical"—had been called a Communist without denying it—and, for reasons that were neither apparent nor explained, had initiated the conversations and the note-taking to which her affidavit referred, the very week the jury had been chosen.

It was on the basis of these alleged conversations that the attorneys for the defense asked for a mistrial or "at the least" the removal of Mr. Janney from the jury. They also asked Judge Medina to "discover if he has transmitted to any of the others [on the jury] his own violent bias."

United States Attorney McGohey opposed the motion "in all respects," and Judge Medina, in order to find the time to study the matter, adjourned the trial for twenty-four hours.

Never before had the organized efforts of the Communists to influence the trial been more apparent than they began to be now. The first word publicly spoken of this matter had been on the morning of Wednesday, August 24, but telegrams began to arrive almost at once. Pickets with newly prepared placards attacking Janney appeared before the Court House. Hundreds of telegrams from every corner of the United States reached Judge Medina that day, many of them having been filed before the motion to which they referred had been made, and thousands were waiting for him the following morning. "Grant motion for mistrial," "Throw out Janney the perjurer," "Conduct investigation as to perjurious conduct of Janney"—thousands of messages with no other thought.

On the morning following that on which the motion had been made, Judge Medina sternly told the five defense lawyers that he was not impressed by this obviously organized campaign of propaganda.

"This is a court of American justice," he said. "I will not be intimidated. I will not be swayed from my duty."

The courtroom was crowded, and hundreds who had attempted to gain admittance had been turned away by the time the Judge entered after a conference with the lawyers. He mounted to the bench and spoke to a silent courtroom.

"I have given this matter the most careful study and consideration," he said, "since the papers were placed in my hands yesterday. . . . The motion is denied in all respects."

He also denied a defense motion to inquire into the possible influence Janney might have had on the other jurors.

"With the filing of these papers," he went on, "I have received from all parts of the country—from Maine to California—many telegrams from various persons. This morning alone I received thousands of such communications. . . . I want the public to know about this attempt to influence justice."

The defense attorneys were quick to object, and Eugene Dennis moved that Judge Medina submit all previous motions for mistrial to some other judge, but this, too, was denied, and within half an hour of the time the Judge had reached the bench, the incident was over, the jury had been recalled, and the trial was under way once more.

There were few light moments during the long drawn months of that trial, but each morning, during the short recess the Judge regularly ordered, an amusing little program was regularly re-enacted. Leaving the courtroom and going to the Judge's room adjacent to it, Medina chose a comfortable chair and opened the morning edition of the *New York Herald Tribune*. Headlines almost always referred to the case that was before him. Not infrequently editorials did the same, and cartoons now and again touched upon the subject. But none of these caught his attention during those midmorning recesses. Instead, he opened the paper to the page on which Thornton W. Burgess' "Nature Stories" appeared, and carefully read of the adventures of Peter Rabbit and Reddy Fox, of Grandfather Frog and Jimmy Skunk, of Sammy Jay and Old Mother Nature and Buster Bear and the rest.

Not a day passed without that morning recess, and not a morning recess passed without a Thornton Burgess story. Here was real help for a tired and troubled judge—clean and simple little stories for little children, to bring relief from the constant pressure of the courtroom.

Progress was more definite after the Janney incident. Little by little, Judge Medina had evolved ways and means to control and direct affairs despite the determined ingenuity of the defense. Carl Winter, one of the defendants and chairman of the Michigan State Communist party, took the stand on the last day of August, and it began to be clear that the defense was preparing to rest. But now a new attempt was made to interrupt the trial—an attempt so ingenious that, though Judge Medina recognized the danger in advance, he could do nothing about it.

Paul Robeson, the Negro baritone and Communist sympathizer, working in cooperation with the Civil Rights Congress, an organization listed as subversive by the Department of Justice, arranged to give a pro-Communist Sunday evening benefit recital on a golf course near Peekskill, New York, some forty miles from New York City. It was widely publicized and was clearly to be in the interest of those who were on trial, though much stress was laid on it as a purely artistic exhibition. But however artistic it may have been planned to be, it was also intended as a gathering place—in the open, be it noted—for the supporters of those who were on trial and even for those defendants who were out on bail, or at least some of them. But the idea behind it, it seems clear, went much further.

For months the trial over which Judge Medina was presiding had been in the news. It had been very widely and continuously reported, and hardly a paper in the United States had failed now and again to show pictures of the defendants, their counsel, and their pickets. During these same months, too, the Judith Coplon spy trial and the Alger Hiss perjury trial, with their Communist implications, were also widely publicized, and Moscow itself had been very free with its criticisms of America and Americans—even of Judge Medina personally. It is not surprising, therefore, that many Americans were about to burst with indignation.

All this was entirely obvious to the American Communists and their supporters, and it seems to have occurred to them that if this indignation could be aroused still further—if, for instance, some group could be baited into trying to break up the Robeson recital—a situation might result which could be used by the defense to delay the trial, or at least to make it appear that the defendants were being handicapped by widespread public prejudice.

Some such reasoning as this seems clearly to have been behind the idea for the recital, and it came close to succeeding—did succeed in part.

A large gathering of veterans, antagonized until they permitted their feelings to overcome their judgment, did just what the Communists apparently hoped they would do. Paul Robeson himself, warned in plenty of time, never arrived to take part in his own recital, but when the audience began to gather on the golf course near Peekskill, about five hundred veterans appeared. They were accompanied by enough brass bands to drown out the expected recital, but they were unable to refrain from throwing things, and adequate police protection was lacking.

A riot resulted, as those who planned the recital seem to

have hoped, and before it was over, a good many people had been hurt, at least eight being taken to the hospital. One had been stabbed. Another had suffered a brain concussion. And Irving Potash, one of the defendants in the trial before Medina, was injured. How many of the defendants who were out on bail actually tried to attend the "recital" it is impossible to say. Because of the precipitate action of the veterans, traffic became tangled, and it may be that some of the defendants who wished to get to the golf course were unable to do so. At least three, however, were actually present, though only Irving Potash was hurt and he not badly. Struck in the eye by flying splinters of glass when the car in which he was riding was stoned, he had to be taken to a doctor, but he was not incapacitated. Appearing in court the next morning with his eye bandaged, he asked, through his attorney, that court be adjourned for forty-eight hours, and Judge Medina granted the request when a report arrived from the doctor who had attended Potash. That was all the "recital" accomplished, though it might easily have done far more.

"It was only by the grace of God that several of those defendants were not seriously hurt," Judge Medina remarked long after the trial was over. "It was only by accident that they weren't. And if they had been, what was I supposed to do? How could I have gone on? What would have happened to the trial? Nobody seemed to think of that, and the veterans did the very sort of thing they were baited into doing."

Another attempt to interfere with the trial had failed, but it almost seemed that the failure was in some way providential.

"I definitely think it was an outrage," said the Judge as he denied a defense motion for a mistrial. "There's no question about it." And the trial continued with Carl Winter still on the stand.

Four days later, Winter's cross-examination began, and under Mr. McGohey's questioning he refused to say whether or not a certain Alfred Wagenknecht had been present at a Communist convention that Winter himself had attended. Judge Medina called a recess, read the record, and conferred with McGohey and with George Crockett, who was Winter's lawyer. Then, returning to the bench, he said he was "convinced the question is in every way proper and material."

"Now, Mr. Winter," the Judge went on, "I direct you to answer the question: 'Was Alfred Wagenknecht at the convention?' "

Claiming that an answer would incriminate him, Winter refused.

"I advise you," said the Judge, "that you have no constitutional right to refuse to answer the question. Do you still refuse?"

"I am advised by counsel as to my legal rights," Winter replied. "I rest upon them."

Dennis leaped to his feet and asked Medina to reconsider his direction. Crockett did the same. But the Judge, turning to Winter, read the federal law which gave him the power to punish a witness in such circumstances as had arisen.

"I now adjudge you guilty of wilful and deliberate contempt," he said, "and by reason thereof I sentence you as follows: You are to be remanded until you have purged yourself of your contempt for a period not to exceed thirty days."

Court was adjourned, and the fifth defendant was led away to jail.

Winter was still returned to the stand during the days that followed. On the third day after he had been remanded, as the Judge was reading from a birth certificate which, in giving the date of the birth of Winter's daughter, also gave his address at the time, Crockett leaped to his feet and angrily protested:

"In view of Your Honor's *seemingly* unintentional reading more than—" he began, stressing the word "seemingly."

Judge Medina stopped him instantly.

"That is one of the most contemptuous things," he said, "that has occurred at this trial, and for that you will be brought to justice. You say I 'seemingly' do something and accuse me of deliberately evil motives here. That is something I cannot pass over and I shall not. I now adjudge you in contempt for that."

The Judge had long since made it clear that he did not intend to punish any of the lawyers for contempt before the end of the trial, but now, when he was asked to "vacate the adjudication of contempt," he refused.

"I think there was an obvious misunderstanding," put in Harry Sacher.

"Perhaps so," the Judge admitted. "I will take that into consideration later."

In the days that followed, a deposition by William Z. Foster was read. He admitted using so many false names that he could not remember them all, and also admitted having said that American Communists owed allegiance to the Soviet Union and the red flag. He even admitted having advocated violent revolution.

Paul Robeson followed as a witness, but had no testimony of consequence to offer. After only twenty minutes he was followed by Henry Winston, who himself had little to say. The defense was clearly about to complete its testimony, and on Friday, September 23, Harry Sacher, the "chief irritant" among the lawyers for the defense, announced so softly as hardly to be heard, "May it please the Court, the defendants rest."

"Does Mr. Sacher speak on behalf of each and every defendant, Your Honor?" asked Mr. Gordon, of government counsel.

"The defense rests," Eugene Dennis replied. "All the defendants so agree."

"The Government also rests its case, Your Honor," said Mr. Gordon, speaking in the absence of United States Attorney McGohey.

The jury was excused until October 4, after being warned again not to discuss the case with anyone, and Judge Medina turned to the lawyers for the defense and the prosecution. "Both sides," he continued, "must have in my hands at 2 P.M., Tuesday [September 27] all requests for instructions. . . . That time is absolute."

The lawyers for the defense submitted three hundred and thirteen requests for the Judge to include in his charge to the jury. The government submitted thirty-four. On September 29 Harry Sacher, during a six-hour argument on various motions that had been made, began an attack on United States Attorney McGohey.

"The early Christians used false names," he cried. "They met in secret. They taught in secret. They did so many things more than this evidence has disclosed that if Mr. McGohey were a contemporary of Jesus he would have had Jesus in the dock."

The little, black-haired defense lawyer was shouting as he gestured toward the slender, gray-haired prosecutor.

"Your Honor," cried McGohey indignantly, "I resent that!"

"I don't blame you," said the Judge.

"That is the most unconscionable thing I ever heard, Your Honor," McGohey continued. "I was born and raised in this city. It is well known that I am a member of the Catholic Church. I firmly and with all my heart believe that Jesus Christ is divine, that He is the Son of God, and to have it said in this courtroom, where I am a member of the bar, that I would persecute my God is an insult that I can't help interrupting for."

Judge Medina told Sacher to make no further references, but the lawyer resumed his argument as if he had heard nothing.

"You don't even apologize for it!" the Judge exclaimed in surprise.

"I am proceeding with my argument," replied Sacher. "I have no apologies to make."

"The depths to which you can sink—" muttered the Judge.

"I do not desire an apology," McGohey remarked. "Coming from the source it would come from, it would mean nothing."

Just before noon on Thursday, October 13, summations were concluded, and at 1:04 P.M. Judge Medina began his detailed charge to the jury.

In the months that had passed about five million words had gone into the record, but now the end had come. It only remained for the Judge to charge the jury, and for them to retire in order to reach their verdict. Time and again, as the trial had progressed, Medina had astonished prosecution, defense, and jurors alike by his ability to grasp and retain endless details of testimony and argument. They had seen him as he had jotted down his notes from time to time, but such notations as could be made during the course of the trial seemed utterly inadequate. How could mere notes serve to cover the millions of words that had been spoken—the complexities—the contradictions—the claims and arguments and motions of nine months of continuous trial?

Judge Medina had been appointed to the federal bench only a year and a half before this trial had begun. His experience on the bench was far less than that of other judges of the court he served. But he had begun his training for this very trial while still in college. At Princeton, and later at Columbia, he had kept notes on every course he had taken and had kept them so accurately and in such detail that he had been able to prepare syllabi for sale to his fellow students.

Later, when he was hardly more than a year out of law school, he had used his notes and developed them further in evolving his system of reviewing and clarifying the whole field of the law as it was covered by the difficult New York State bar examinations. In his teaching at Columbia Law School and in his law practice he had found almost constant use for such notes, and in the course of these years he had evolved so accurate and condensed a method of keeping notes that it proved adequate even to this difficult and complex trial of the Communists—the longest jury trial in the entire history of American jurisprudence.

Beginning with the first day of the trial, and continuing until now, he had kept, in his clear and delicately small script, a record of every item of consequence. Every salient fact had been noted. Every cross reference of importance had been made.

All through the trial he had found use for this material. Time and again his notes had made it possible for him to retain a grasp on the fundamentals that were at issue, despite the almost constant efforts of the defense to confuse and complicate them. Over and over again he had been able, because of his notes, to bring some "forgetful" or deliberately unclear witness back to the facts.

"Are you referring," he had not infrequently asked, "to the same person So-and-so mentioned in his testimony last Tuesday?" Or "Do you mean that you were not present at the meeting that was held on such-and-such a date?"

Now that the trial was approaching its conclusion these notes—one hundred sheets of closely written, very fine script—recorded the facts he needed to bear in mind, and served as a point of departure for the final fifteen thousand-word statement to the jury he so carefully prepared.

At 1:04 P.M., Thursday, October 13, 1949, he began his charge to the jury:*

Ladies and gentlemen of the jury,

You now approach the performance of one of the most sacred duties of citizenship, the meting out of justice. . . .

The rich and the poor, and persons of every race, creed and condition stand alike before the bar of justice; and you must consider and weigh the evidence carefully, calmly and dispassionately, without the slightest trace of sympathy or prejudice for or against any party to the proceeding. The very importance of the case makes it all the more urgent that you heed these words of caution. . . .

He clarified "the duties of the judge on the one hand and those of the jury on the other."

It is exclusively my function [he continued] clearly to set forth the rules of law which govern the case, with instructions as to their application. . . .

* For Judge Medina's complete charge to the jury, see Appendix.

On the other hand, you are the sole judges of the facts. . . . Just as you are not permitted to encroach upon my function in giving instructions on the law, so must I be careful not to encroach upon your function as the sole judges of the facts.

He read the relevant parts of the statute under which the indictment had been drawn. He read the indictment itself. For more than two hours he spoke, explaining the meaning of *reasonable doubt*, of *credibility*, of the *law*. He commented on the requests for instructions that had been submitted by counsel for the defendants and the prosecution.

Now, ladies and gentlemen of the jury [he concluded] one last word. If you find that the evidence respecting the defendants or any of them is reasonably consistent with innocence, such defendant or defendants should be acquitted. If you find that the law has not been violated, you should not hesitate for any reason to render a verdict of not guilty. But on the other hand, if you find, in accordance with these instructions, that the law has been violated as charged, you should not hesitate because of sympathy or any other reason to render a verdict of guilty.

As he completed his charge the courtroom was strangely silent. Even outside in Foley Square, where shuffling pickets had shouted their slogans for so many months, everything was quiet and only a few patrolmen strolled up and down.

The jury rose and made its way solemnly from the room as the hands of the clock approached the hour of 4.

The trial was over. Only the verdict remained to be heard—the verdict which now lay in the hands of these twelve men and women.

10

A JUDGE'S PHILOSOPHY

JUDGE MEDINA MOUNTED TO THE BENCH A LITTLE EARLIER than usual on the morning of Friday, October 14, but had no sooner opened court than he declared a recess. The jurors, unable to reach a verdict the evening before, had ultimately left to spend the night at a hotel, though they were now again in the jury room continuing their deliberations.

The Judge, too, had worked late, for he could not know when a verdict would be brought in and an important task had to be completed. As the evening passed and no word came from the jury room, he had continued at this self-appointed task, and as 10 o'clock approached completed it. Now, having opened court again, and ordered a recess, he went to his chambers on the twenty-second floor of the Court House. It was there that a note from Mrs. Thelma Dial, the jury foreman, reached him at 11:10. The jury was ready to return.

A few lawyers, newspapermen, and spectators were lounging in the courtroom, reading newspapers and talking. The defense lawyers, with eight of the defendants and groups of their relatives and friends, were standing in the corridor outside or pacing back and forth. Most of them pretended confidence but were clearly under stress. Some moved restlessly about. Some smoked constantly, lighting one cigarette from another. Some talked nervously and found it difficult to listen. None of them had had any word of developments in the jury room or had been told of the note that had been sent to Judge Medina.

The aimless activities of those in the corridor were interrupted a little after 11 o'clock by the businesslike arrival of groups of deputy marshals who had been called from other parts of the Court House. A few minutes later, United States Attorney McGohey and his staff came out of an elevator and entered the courtroom. The defense lawyers and the defendants in the corridor tossed away their cigarettes and followed. Wives, relatives, friends hurried after them. Three defendants who had been sentenced for contempt were brought in through another door by a group of marshals. Newspapermen who had been lounging in the red-upholstered chairs of the jury box hurried to the seats reserved for them. A dozen or fifteen deputy marshals entered and stood in a row behind the seats to which the defendants had now returned.

"The jury's coming," whispered someone near the door, "and here comes the judge."

"All rise!" ordered the bailiff.

In a flurry of sound everyone in the courtroom rose, and Judge Medina entered, serious and dignified in his black robe. He mounted to the bench, sat down, spread several documents out before him. The courtroom echoed softly as the standing people shuffled for a moment and then sat down.

The Judge sat erect in his leather-upholstered chair, with the American flag and the great seal of the United States behind him, vividly bright against the somber paneling. Overhead the courtroom's four great bowl-shaped chandeliers threw yellow light on the frescoed ceiling, while dim gray daylight entered through the room's tall windows.

United States Attorney McGohey leaned forward, his elbows on the table before him, his head resting on his hands. Harry Sacher sorted some papers on the counsel table. Eugene Dennis glanced aimlessly about and moved his hands nervously, despite his effort to appear calm. The shuffle and click of footsteps came from the hall and the jurors entered—made their way to the red leather chairs in the jury box—sat down. The hands of the clock stood at 11:25.

For a moment the jurors shifted self-consciously in their seats. The courtroom was almost utterly silent save for an occasional cough, a rustle of paper as some lawyer shifted his documents, or a faint sound as some reporter scribbled his notes or some observer moved.

The clerk rose and turned to face the jury.

"Madame Foreman," he began, "have you agreed upon a verdict?"

Mrs. Dial—slight, comely, neatly dressed—rose and faced the Judge, glancing nervously at a slip of paper in her hand.

"We have," she replied in a small voice.

"How say you?" asked the clerk.

Mrs. Dial hesitated, then spoke in a voice so gentle that it barely reached the press section.

"The jury," she replied, reading from the slip of paper that shook a little in her hand, "finds each of the defendants guilty."

The dark-paneled, high-ceiled room was utterly silent for a moment. Hardly a defendant moved except that Gilbert Green continued to chew his gum. Even the defense lawyers were momentarily motionless but then two of them leaned forward, one to write, one to shuffle papers. A group of reporters hurried from the room to phone their papers.

Judge Medina quietly directed the clerk to poll the jurors separately, and twelve times the same question was asked.

"You say you find the defendants Eugene Dennis, John B. Williamson, Jacob Stachel, Robert G. Thompson, Benjamin J. Davis, Jr., Henry Winston, John Gates, Irving Potash, Carl Winter, Gilbert Green, and Gus Hall guilty as charged?"

"I do," answered some. "Yes," replied others. Almost without exception they nodded as they spoke.

Hardly another sound disturbed the courtroom, and there was little movement, except as Judge Medina rocked gently back and forth. But the twelfth juror had no sooner replied than Gladstein was on his feet, asking the Judge to question "the Madame Forelady" whether the jury had considered each defendant separately in reviewing the evidence.

McGohey objected, and the Judge explained that the rules provided for no such interrogation. Gladstein sat down. The Judge turned to the jury—thanked them—said they deserved the thanks of the whole country for their "patience and careful attention." But he asked them not to discuss the case with anyone.

"Whatever you might say," he continued, "would be subject to misinterpretation, repetition, and change, and might do irreparable harm to the administration of justice."

He dismissed them, and the jurors slowly filed out as the hands of the clock reached 11:35. The Judge turned a little in his chair to watch them go, his face calm, his manner thoughtful. But as the last of them disappeared he turned back. He moved some papers aside and looked toward the lawyers for the defense. He leaned forward.

"Now I turn to some unfinished business," he said, his voice still soft, but sharper than it had been. "The following will kindly rise!"

He read the names: Harry Sacher, Eugene Dennis, Richard Gladstein, George W. Crockett, Jr., Abraham J. Isserman, Louis F. McCabe.

As their names were called they rose and stood uneasily, shifting their positions a little—moving their hands. The Judge ran his eye along the irregular row they made and began to read, glancing up occasionally:

In conformity with Rule 42 (a), Federal Rules of Criminal Procedure, I hereby certify that the series of criminal contempts set forth below were committed in the actual presence of the Court and were seen or heard by the Court during the trial of the case of United States *v.* Foster, *et al.*, C 128-87, which commenced on January 17, 1949.

By way of preliminary I may say that I would have overlooked, or at most, severely reprimanded counsel for misconduct which appeared to be the result of the heat of controversy or that zeal in the defense of a client or in one's own defense which might understandingly have caused one to overstep the bounds of strict propriety.

Before the trial had progressed very far, however, I was reluctantly forced to the conclusion that the acts and statements to which I am about to refer were the result of an agreement between these defendants (meaning you, Harry Sacher, Richard Gladstein, George W. Crockett, Jr., Louis F. McCabe, Abraham J. Isserman, and Eugene Dennis) deliberately entered into in a cold and calculating manner, to do and say things for the purpose of:

1. Causing such delay and confusion as to make it impossible to go on with the trial;

2. Provoking incidents which they intended would result in mistrial; and

3. Impairing my health so that the trial could not continue.

I find that the acts, statements and conduct of each of these defendants [the six counsel] constituted a deliberate and wilful attack upon the administration of justice, an attempt to sabotage the functioning of the Federal judicial system and misconduct of so grave a character as to make the mere imposition of a fine a futile gesture and a wholly insufficient punishment.

To maintain the dignity of the court and to preserve order in the courtroom under these circumstances, was a task of the utmost difficulty. There was, accordingly, no alternative than to give the repeated warnings which from time to time I gave, and to postpone the imposition of sentence until the close of the case. To have done otherwise would have broken up the trial and thus served the ends these defendants tried so hard to attain. . . .

During the entire trial Messrs. Sacher, Gladstein, Crockett, McCabe and Isserman, attorneys and counselors-at-law, and after March 17, 1949, Mr. Dennis, attorney *pro se*, joined in a wilful, deliberate and concerted effort to delay and obstruct the trial of United States *v.* Foster *et al.*, C 128-87, for the purpose of causing such disorder and confusion as would prevent a verdict by a jury on the issue raised by the indictment; and for the purpose of bringing the Court and the entire Federal judicial system into general discredit and disrepute, by endeavoring to divert the attention of the Court and jury from the serious charge against their clients of a conspiracy in substance to teach and advocate the overthrow of the Government of the United States by force and violence, by attacking the presiding judge and all the judges of this court, the jury system in this district, the Department of Justice of the United States, the President of the United States, the police of New York City, and the public press of New York and other cities.

To effect this plan these defendants in this proceeding contemptuously and without justification:

a. Disregarded numerous warnings of the Court concerning their wilful delaying tactics, except for ironical references thereto;

b. Suggested that various findings by the Court were made for the purpose of newspaper headlines;

c. Insinuated that there was connivance between the Court and the United States Attorney;

d. Insisted on objecting one after another to rulings of the Court, despite a ruling on the first day of the trial, repeated several times thereafter, that all objections and exceptions would inure to the benefit of each of their clients unless disclaimed;

e. Persisted in making long, repetitious, and unsubstantial arguments, objections, and protests, working in shifts, accompanied by shouting, sneering, and snickering;

f. Urged one another on to badger the Court;

g. Repeatedly made charges against the Court of bias, prejudice, corruption and partiality;

h. Made a succession of disrespectful, insolent, and sarcastic comments to the Court;

i. Disregarded repeatedly and flagrantly the orders of the Court not to argue without permission and to desist from further argument or comment;

j. Disregarded rulings on the admissibility of evidence so as to endeavor to place before the jury by leading questions the subject matter excluded;

k. Persisted in asking questions on excluded subject matters, knowing that objections would be sustained, to endeavor to create a false picture of bias and partiality on the part of the Court;

l. Accused the Court of racial prejudice without any foundation; and

m. Generally conducted themselves in a most provocative manner in an endeavor to call forth some intemperate or undignified response from the Court which could then be relied upon as a demonstration of the Court's unfitness to preside over the trial.

Then followed thirty-nine detailed further specifications of contemptuous conduct by the various lawyers with quotations of their very words and reference to the page numbers of the transcript. The document contained sixty pages of closely typewritten matter and is to be found in the law reports "sub.nom. United States *v.* Sacher *et al.*, 9 F.R.D. 394."

This was the statement on which Judge Medina had concluded his work only the evening before, checking each fact with the notes he had made throughout the trial and with the stenographer's minutes, and hoping to have it ready for this moment.

"I will now proceed to judgment," he went on, and listed the lawyers again, one by one, with the contempts charged against them and their punishment. Harry Sacher—six months; Richard Gladstein—six months; George W. Crockett, Jr.,—four months; Louis F. McCabe—thirty days; Abraham J. Isserman—four months; Eugene Dennis—six months.

Isserman was the first to speak, and excitedly insisted that the finding "was unwarranted by anything that took place during the trial." Sacher followed, shouting his comments and finally referring to "the price of liberty."

"It is not the price of liberty," the Judge replied calmly. "It is the price of misbehavior and disorder."

Gladstein, Crockett, McCabe, and Dennis followed, Dennis speaking in a harsh, threatening tone, Crockett softly and most effectively of all.

"Let this be notice to you," the Judge replied, "and all who may be tempted to follow your example, that there is power in the laws and Constitution of the United States to maintain the dignity of the Courts and the administration of justice therein."

A motion to permit the defendants to be freed on bail was denied, pending the imposition of sentences on Friday, October 21, and court was adjourned at 12:35 P.M. The trial had occupied nine months and four days, and one week later the eleven, standing before Judge Medina, were sentenced—ten to the limit under the existing law: five years in prison and a fine of ten thousand dollars each. Because of his war record and his Distinguished Service Cross, Robert Thompson, the thirty-four-year-old New York State Chairman of the Communist party, was sentenced to three years and a ten-thousand-dollar fine.

"The prisoners remained silent," reported Russell Porter in *The New York Times*, "and sat down when the Judge had finished. Defense counsel then argued at length that the prisoners be admitted to bail."

"These defendants," Judge Medina replied, "were not convicted merely for their political beliefs or for belonging to the Communist party. I made it plain in my charge that the jury could not convict for anything like that, but they had to find there was specific intent to overthrow the Government by force and violence.

"It seems to me absurd on its face to say, as you do, that there must be a clear and present danger of immediate overthrow to justify prosecution. By any such test, the Government would be overthrown before it could protect itself and the very important right of freedom of speech would be gone with all the other freedoms."

The prisoners were led from the courtroom, and as pickets in Foley Square shouted "We want bail! We want bail!" were taken to the Federal House of Detention. Whatever future action might be taken would be before the United States Court of Appeals or the Supreme Court of the United States. The District Court had spoken.

All through the preceding summer and early fall the Judge had spent each week-end at his Westhampton home, and he went there now. Clearly a vacation was in order and he planned to take one, but there were a few odds and ends to clear up in his chambers in the Court House. Once that work was done he and Mrs. Medina would board a plane and within three or four hours would be in Bermuda, far from courtrooms, Communists, and Foley Square.

That was the plan, but it went astray.

Returning to his chambers the following Monday Judge Medina found more to do than he had planned. The odds and ends were just about what he had expected, but in addition he found such an accumulation of mail as had never arrived in any similar period of time during the trial. The Communist-organized campaign of letters and telegrams that had waxed and waned throughout the trial had suddenly been suspended "as though someone had turned off the spigot," said the Judge. But if one spigot had been turned off, another and a greater one had been turned on. In the first three days after the trial had finally ended, thirty thousand letters of a very different nature arrived, and during the weeks that followed they continued to come by thousands.

They came from friends, from acquaintances, from strangers. They came from the great, the near-great, and the unknown. Political figures, movie stars, clergymen, and authors wrote him, but most came from lesser people—from those in smaller posts, from clerks in department stores, from housewives, from mechanics and taxi drivers, from shopkeepers and other small businessmen—"from the little people," as the Judge explained, "who really make up America."

Letters came from every state and territory. They came from Canada and England, from France and Portugal, from Spain, Brazil, and Mexico.

During the preceding months Judge Medina had grown accustomed to the bitterly partisan letters condemning him —demanding special treatment for the defendants—cursing

—execrating—fulminating. But that had stopped. The letters that were coming now were utterly different.

"None of them," the Judge commented at the time, "are 'send-the-bums-to-jail' stuff. The astounding thing is that they nearly all stress fair play, the American tradition, and the proper administration of justice."

It was impossible for him to read them all. Even with three stenographers, it was impossible to keep up with them as they came flooding in. Nevertheless, they had to be read and many of them had to be answered. Hundreds contained invitations to address bar associations and other groups. Others contained resolutions and offers of medals and plaques from American Legion posts, city councils, and elsewhere. The town board of Medina, North Dakota, where the name had always been pronounced *muh-dye'-na*, wrote to say that the pronunciation had officially been changed to *muh-dee'-na* in honor of the Judge. Strangers phoned from the Middle West, the South, and from other portions of the country, and for more than a month the vacation that had been planned had to be held in abeyance. The Judge had foreseen many of the developments in the trial, but this was utterly unexpected. "It has been a tremendous experience," he told a group of reporters at the time.

On November 30, five weeks after the trial had ended, Judge and Mrs. Medina left for Bermuda, though thousands of those letters still remained unanswered. Many had not even been read, for they were still coming in, though in smaller numbers now. But the vacation was overdue, and Miss Elizabeth Gorman, the Judge's secretary, could attend to many of them while he was away, especially as she had been given assistants to help her with the task. Ultimately the Judge read every single one of them. He did it systematically for, as Mrs. Medina once told me, "Harold's middle name is System."

The Judge and his wife spent Christmas in Bermuda, flying back to New York on New Year's Day, 1950. The next two days he spent in his chambers, dictating almost constantly, but left for California with Mrs. Medina on January 4. They visited Pasadena and San Diego. They spent three weeks at Rancho Santa Fe, where the Judge divided his time between golf and the study of Horace. They went to San Ysidro Ranch at Montecito, near Santa Barbara, and then to San Francisco.

Even before the Communist trial had ended, the Judge had been asked by Mrs. Natalie Wales Paine, head of an organization known as "Common Cause, Inc.," to attend a dinner in his honor to be held in March. The invitation followed some preliminary overtures by Colonel Charles E. Greenough, who had been a student in Judge Medina's classes at Columbia Law School. The Judge knew little of the group, thought that the trial would be all but forgotten by March, 1950, and regarded the occasion as nothing more than just another testimonial dinner. Then, with the end of the trial occupying his attention, followed by his trips to Bermuda and California, he quite forgot about the dinner until a friend approached him at the Valley Golf Club near Montecito.

"Look here, Harold," the friend remarked, holding out a letter he had received. The Judge read what he was shown—a letter asking for a generous contribution for the Common Cause dinner, and explaining that the affair was to be widely publicized as an attack on communism and the Communists.

It was apparent from this that money was to be raised and that the affair was to be vastly different from what it had seemed to Judge Medina when he had accepted the invitation.

He had been so preoccupied that he had not seen the implications, and until this moment the matter had slipped his mind. But now he saw the impropriety of letting his name be used in any such connection, and understood that it was imperative that he sever his name from the affair. The Communist case was pending in the Court of Appeals, and he simply could not permit himself to appear at such a gathering as was planned. But the question was how to get out of it.

At the moment he was shown the letter, Judge Medina was reading one of Horace's *Odes*—the Thirty-fourth Ode of Book One, which is often described as the one *Against the Epicurians*—and had read its final portion:

. . . *Valet ima summis*

Mutare et insignem attenuat deus,
Obscura promens; hinc apicem rapax
Fortuna cum stridore acuto
*Sustulit, hic posuisse gaudet.**

Horace, in other words, was pointing out how a person can be up one day and down the next, and Harold Medina was quick to see how that might apply to him.

"I was being patted on the back," he once told me in referring to this incident, "but one mistake and I could fall on my face."

It was unfortunate that he had made the mistake of accept-

* Lord Lytton's translation in verse, while of course not literal, gives the meaning quite accurately:

. . . A god reigns,

Potent the high with low to interchange,
Bid bright orbs wane, and those obscure come forth;
Shrill-sounding, Fortune swoops—
Here snatches, there exultant drops a crown.

ing the invitation, but in any event he had to withdraw that acceptance. It was not an easy thing to do, for he had given his word and no "diplomatic" excuse was possible. What to do was not immediately clear, but in characteristic fashion he met the issue frankly, and sent a telegram which read as follow:

Mrs. Natalie Wales Paine,
Common Cause, Inc.,
Plaza Hotel,
New York City.

After much reflection I have reached the conclusion that the dinner in my honor which you have worked so hard and so successfully to organize must be called off. Circumstances now are such that inevitably I and perhaps the Federal Judiciary of which I am a part would appear to be taking sides in a matter tried before me and now pending on appeal, despite the fact that I was scrupulously impartial throughout the recent trial. No matter what was said or not said by me and others at the dinner I would be put in a false position and the dignity and reputation of the court would suffer. All this should have been clear to me before and I deeply regret that I feel compelled to make this decision after you have taken so much trouble and treated me so graciously. But when one has made a mistake and finds it out there is only one straightforward thing to do and that is to acknowledge the mistake and do what one can to rectify it. You may imagine how hard it has been to bring myself to send this telegram as I fully appreciate the distress it will cause you and your associates but once I realized even at this late hour how this dinner might be misconstrued and that there was a possibility of impairing public confidence in the courts my course was clear.

Harold R. Medina

But the dinner was not called off. Instead, the Judge's telegram was released to the newspapers, the dinner was held as scheduled, and Judge Medina was praised *in absentia.* But from that time on he was more than ever conscious that he should consistently refuse to discuss the trial publicly or even to discuss what lay behind it. Now and then he mentioned it, but he refused to enlarge upon it, and there were other subjects he refused to discuss.

There were those who wanted him to run for governor of New York, but he rejected the idea.

He was suggested as Baseball Commissioner, but he refused to permit his name to be used.

He was offered a contract that would have paid him fifty thousand dollars for a series of addresses, but he would not consider it.

He refused to appear on television or the radio, and it soon became clear that here was a man who was not thinking of money or of personal aggrandizement. He said—and he obviously meant—that he was dedicated to the bench for life, that all he wanted was to improve the administration of justice. In a world in which men often seem selfish and grasping, here was one who gave no such impression, and the people liked him for it.

Wherever he went he was received with the utmost enthusiasm. Throngs gathered whenever he appeared. Small gatherings grew into large ones, even into immense ones, if it was announced in advance that he was to be present, and he was often recognized even when he thought himself most alone. Walking one day in San Francisco, he was recognized by a workman on a cable car that was slowly making its way up hill. For a moment the man merely stared, but then jumped off the slowly moving car, and with his lunchbox in his hand, ran across to the sidewalk, took hold of Judge Medina's arm and looked into his face. He said nothing—not a word. He merely squeezed the judge's arm once and then turned and ran back to the slowly climbing cable car. He leaped upon the step, glanced back once more, and was gone. No other greeting has ever touched the Judge so deeply.

Returning to New York late in February, Medina began once more on the mountain of letters that still awaited him. Then, early in March, he was assigned to "Crime 1" in his regular turn. He was back again in the routine of the District Court.

He was now less often in the news than he had been, but his popularity remained high. People greeted him eagerly wherever he went. Strangers approached him to shake his hand and thank him for what he had done. Walking alone one day on 43d Street he saw a taxi stop abruptly. It was carrying several passengers but none of them made any move to alight. Instead, it was the driver who got out, leaving his motor running. He hurried to the judge, holding out his hand.

"Will you shake hands with me, Judge?" the fellow asked.

"Why certainly," replied Medina. "I'm glad to."

"Thanks," said the driver. "Thanks, Judge. You sure did a job!" And he hurried back to his cab and drove off toward Sixth Avenue.

But others than taxi drivers were eager to give him their approval. For one thing, the flood of mail that reached him in the months that immediately followed the end of the Communist trial brought letters from eighteen colleges and universities, offering honorary degrees to be awarded during the June commencement exercises.

Here was an insuperable problem. Each of these degrees had to be accepted personally, and there was so great a conflict of dates that the Judge was forced, much against his will, to decline a round dozen of these important honors, and even then he accepted four honorary degrees in five days, and a fifth one a week later.

On June 7, New York Medical College honored him as "the first non-medically trained citizen in its ninety years of history to receive *pro causa honoris et pro merito* the honorary degree of Doctor of Humane Letters."

On June 8, Columbia University awarded him its honorary degree of Doctor of Laws. In its citation, reference was made not only to his loyalty, his "tireless interest in the larger problems of his profession," his effectiveness "in our School of Law," and his "outstanding career," but also to the importance of his work "in the preparation of young men for their entrance into the legal profession." Here, nearly thirty years after his associates on the faculty at Columbia had disapproved of his bar examination course as *infra dig*, Columbia University itself was awarding him its highest honor, in part because of that very activity.

On June 9, Lafayette College awarded him its honorary degree as Doctor of Humane Letters, saying in its citation that "America is stronger because of your character and personality."

On June 11, Dartmouth honored him "as one eminently worthy of her Doctorate of Laws."

On June 18, Williams College gave him its honorary degree of Doctor of Laws, citing him as "A great teacher of the law, wise, patient and understanding, who in the classroom and on the bench has by precept and by example maintained the standards of his high calling."

Shortly after his appointment to the bench in 1947, Judge Medina had been awarded an honorary Doctorate of Laws by St. John's University in Brooklyn, which stands only a few blocks from the public school he had attended as a boy. But now, other institutions wished to honor him. Bates

College, in Lewiston, Maine, gave him its honorary Doctorate of Laws on November 4, 1950. Northeastern University, in Boston, awarded him its honorary Doctorate of Laws on June 24, 1951, as the University of Denver did on August 22. But it would be hard to imagine that any of these honors pleased him more than did the degree of Doctor of Laws *honoris causa* awarded him by Princeton on June 12, 1951.

"In one of the most turbulent of trials," read the Princeton citation, "in the face of vehement provocation, he maintained the rules of jurisprudence with patient resolve, dignity and justice in accordance with the traditions of free men." Truly, the "unpopular" sophomore of 1906 had traveled far.

Nor were these degrees more than a fraction of the honors that came to him in the two years following the Communist trial. Before me as I write are ten typewritten pages which list the scores of awards, citations, and other special honors that have been given him by bar associations, city councils, religious societies, service clubs, labor unions, veterans' associations, fraternal orders, patriotic societies and others; and his library at Westhampton contains so many scrolls, plaques, gold medals, and other awards as to hide a good many of the books that occupy the shelves and even actually to displace some of them.

On May 1, 1950, counsel for the Communist leaders filed briefs with the United States Court of Appeals. Challenging the constitutionality of the Smith Act, under which the eleven had been convicted, their main 403-page brief set forth sixteen principal questions on appeal, and a ninety-two-page supplementary brief questioned the constitutionality of the federal jury system. Judge Medina was bitterly attacked for "judicial misconduct" and was charged with "sustained manifestation of hostility" toward the defendants.

His action on the juror, Russell Janney, was attacked, and he was said to have put "prosecutional questions" to defense witnesses. Even his charge to the jury, which had been so widely praised, was held to be improper.

The three-day argument began on June 21, Harry Sacher and Abraham J. Isserman contending that the government had failed to show any "clear and present danger" of violent overthrow and that the Communists' freedom of speech should not have been abridged. But on August 1, the Court of Appeals unanimously affirmed the conviction, upholding the constitutionality of the Smith Act and praising Judge Medina's handling of the trial.

The court which heard this appeal, and which now upheld the action of the District Court, was composed of Chief Judge Learned Hand, who presided, and Judges Thomas W. Swan and Harrie B. Chase. Judge Hand wrote the opinion, a twenty-thousand-word document, and Judge Swan concurred, while Judge Chase wrote a two thousand-word concurring opinion of his own.

Judge Hand, who is widely accepted as one of the outstanding judges of twentieth-century America, has always been especially clear and forceful in his written opinions, as he was in this instance. He found "abundant" evidence to sustain the conviction, and upheld Judge Medina in the ruling which held that upon the facts of the case as found by the jury the defendants were not entitled to the protection of the First Amendment, which guarantees freedom of speech.

"Nobody doubts," Judge Hand's opinion made clear, "that when the leader of a mob already ripe for riot gives the word to start, his utterance is not protected by the Amendment."

He also upheld Judge Medina's management of the trial.

"We know of no country," he wrote, "where they [the defendants] would have been allowed any approach to the license accorded them; and none, except Great Britain, where they would have had so fair a hearing."

In so far as the opinion referred specifically to the charges brought by the lawyers for the convicted Communists against Judge Medina's direction of the trial, the following extract is most pointed, even, apparently, in Judge Hand's own belief. He personally read this portion aloud when, in discussing with me another phase of Judge Medina's career, this subject arose:

> The trial was punctuated over and over again with motions for mistrial, often for patently frivolous reasons; by innuendo, and at times openly, the Judge was charged with unfairness and "judicial misconduct"—often in most insulting language. Those occasions on which the defendants rely to show his intemperate hostility, so far as the record preserves what happened, are completely unconvincing. At times, it is true, he rebuked the attorneys; at times he used language short of requisite judicial gravity; at times he warned them that if they persisted in conducting themselves as they had been doing, he would punish them when the trial was over. (An entirely proper action, for to commit them pending the trial would have broken it up, and to be silent might well have misled them.) These cautions they answered most unwarrantably, as threats to prevent the discharge of their duties. Throughout, the Judge kept repeating to the jury that they were not to take what he said to the attorneys against their clients; and, although we do not of course mean that that would have been enough to excuse him had he in fact weighted the scales against them, none of the instances adduced give support for saying that he did; or that he denied them adequate opportunity to present their case. What he did do, was to attempt to keep the trial within measurable

bounds; and in that he failed, because, and only because, the attorneys were obviously unwilling to accord him that cooperation which was his due, so far as it did not curtail their clients' rights. The length of the trial is itself almost an answer to that; the defense's case occupied nearly twice as much time as the prosecution's. Justice can be as readily destroyed by the flaccidity of the judge as by his tyranny; impartial trials need a firm hand as much as a constant determination to give each one his due. The record discloses a judge, sorely tried for many months of turmoil, constantly provoked by useless bickering, exposed to offensive slights and insults, harried with interminable repetition, who, if at times he did not conduct himself with the imperturbability of a Rhadamanthus, showed considerably greater self-control and forbearance than it is given to most judges to possess. So much for the charge of hectoring counsel and unduly limiting them in the presentation of their defense. As for any disposition in any other ways to lean towards the side of the prosecution, we cannot find it in the record; if it existed it must have been in tone or bearing which print does not preserve; for . . . his charges and his rulings were, if anything, too favorable to the defense.*

The public had long since acclaimed Medina for his handling of the trial, but in this opinion one of America's greatest and most experienced jurists did the same. And in further demonstration of Judge Medina's fundamental rightness, the United States Supreme Court, on June 4, 1951, also upheld the conviction in a 6-to-2 decision, Justices Black and Douglas dissenting.

The lawyers for the Communist leaders, too, appealed their sentences for contempt, but this action of Judge Medina's was also upheld by the Court of Appeals, and, on March 10, 1952, by the Supreme Court itself in a 5-to-3 decision. Justices

* United States *v.* Dennis, 183 F. 2d 201, pp. 225-226.

Black and Douglas again dissented, this time joined by Justice Frankfurter.

In September, 1950, Judge Medina was elected vice chairman of the American Bar Association's section of judicial administration, and a year later was made chairman. This section, which is made up of judges and other officials interested in improving the administration of justice, plays an important part in the evolution of our judicial methods, and is especially interested in "the improvement of the administration of justice through the selection of qualified judges and adherence to effective standards of judicial administration and administrative procedure." It implements the Bar Association's program, operating through committees that are set up in each state. It works toward certain minimum standards of judicial administration and plays an important part in gradually improving such administration throughout the country. The section has a Committee on Cooperation with Laymen, a Committee on Improvement of Traffic Courts, a Committee on Improvement of Justice of the Peace Courts, and many others.

This is work of supreme importance, and Judge Medina, as is typical of him, has not only thrown himself energetically into it but has also done his utmost to further and to broaden the work of the section's various committees. Basically the idea rests upon the thought that the people look up to their judges for leadership in such matters and rely upon them for improvements in the field of judicial administration —a thought that deeply appeals to Medina and encourages him to approach the work with his customary enthusiasm.

"There is only one kind of justice," he insists, "and that is 100-per cent justice!"

It has no doubt been with this thought in mind that he

has so energetically attacked the problems his Section of the American Bar Association has before it, but his influence is felt elsewhere as well.

Only a few months after he was made vice chairman of this section he was asked to address the annual dinner of the Church Club, an Episcopalian organization in New York. The dinner was to be held at the Waldorf-Astoria Hotel on February 5, 1951, and Medina accepted, but for a time was doubtful of the wisdom of speaking on the subject that most appealed to him. The very name of the club he was to address suggested that his subject should have some religious or moral connotation, but he recognized that his words would need to be chosen with some care lest he give the impression that they were insincere.

The more he thought about the matter the more he was inclined to speak on "The Judge and His God," and finally he decided to do so. Certainly the subject would be appropriate. It only remained for him to handle it appropriately.

While there is much in the Bible about judges [he began when he was introduced] I do not recall any occasion on which a judge has been called upon to discuss the impact of religion upon the performance of the judicial function. Perhaps this is because this is an intimate matter, thoughts about which one is likely to keep to one's self. In any event, I have chosen as my subject here tonight 'The Judge and His God.' If the subject has not been discussed before, it is high time that someone did so, for I rather suspect that my own experiences, which I am about to relate to you, are typical of most other American judges and doubtless others, too.

As you will see, my address is divided into two parts. The first has to do with the subject of humility, and the second with the subject of prayer.

I suppose I am a more or less typical American. From boyhood

I have had an implicit and unquestioning faith, which I got when I attended the classes in the Episcopal Church at Ossining, New York, in preparation for my confirmation when I was a boy at Preparatory School. Like most other people I know, I wanted to be a better Christian but, as I look back over the years, I find that I did comparatively little to put this wishful thinking into effect.

As a law student and as a lawyer, I fought hard for what I thought was right, and I had a deep and almost passionate interest in the rules of law and the history of their development. They were the tools of my trade and I worked hard with them.

It was not long after I became a judge that I began to feel a new sense of responsibility. It is something very difficult to explain. It was not simply that I wanted to be right and that I took my duties seriously. There came a feeling that everything I did, even the decision of nice questions of interpretation of mere rules of procedure, was in some way becoming a part of a huge fabric which on the whole was part and parcel of the moral law governing mankind and which must of necessity be of divine origin.

As I passed upon the credibility of witnesses and as I wrote my opinions and formulated my judgments, I gradually came to realize that I was weaving my small part of this huge fabric; and I knew that I would not perform my task aright unless I was constantly mindful of the fact that all these matters, large and small, would be mere futility unless I tried to make each one fit into its proper place in the moral law which governed all.

Right here is the part that is difficult to explain. I was still reasoning as a lawyer. The fundamental principles of law were the same. I was still manipulating the techniques of my profession as before. But there was some subtle force, the impact of which was new to me, which was spiritual in quality. It was as though Someone were always watching me and telling me to make very sure that my rulings and my decisions were fundamentally right and just.

You know we judges are the servants of the People, as are all government officials in our particular type of democracy. But I think it will not be difficult for you to see from the things I have been telling you about that it didn't take me very long to perceive that we judges are the servants of Someone else too. And I often think of that part of the Twenty-second Chapter of the Gospel according to St. Luke, which follows immediately after those verses which are so important a part of our communion service. I refer to the following:

> 24 And there was also a strife among them, which of them should be accounted the greatest.
>
> 25 And he said unto them, The kings of the Gentiles exercise lordship over them; and they that exercise authority upon them are called benefactors.
>
> 26 But ye shall not be so: but he that is greatest among you, let him be as the younger; and he that is chief, as he that doth serve.
>
> 27 For whether is greater, he that sitteth at meat, or he that serveth? is not he that sitteth at meat? but I am among you as he that serveth.

Years ago I often heard Chief Judge Benjamin N. Cardozo, before he became an associate justice of the Supreme Court of the United States and while he was still chief judge of our New York State Court of Appeals, speak about humility. He was, indeed, a humble man. One could not fail to observe that. But the full impact of what he had to say about humility was not felt by me until I was myself a judge, and found myself struggling with forces too great and too complicated for me to fathom. I saw in a new light the difficulties which beset one in the search for truth and justice. This was particularly true when I suddenly found myself in the vortex of the trial of the Communists in the midst of the play of great forces upon which, for all I know, the destiny of the human race may hang. Later it suddenly dawned upon me that some queer turn in the wheel of fate had singled me out, for the moment, to feel the impact of America's love of justice. And the result was what must be inevitable under the circumstances, that I found myself to be a small, indeed a very small and insignificant particle in the scheme of things. It has been an extraordinary experience. So much for the first part of what I have to say.

Fortunately for me, I was taught to pray from so early a time that I cannot remember going to bed at night without saying my prayers. And only once in all these years have I failed to do so. I remember that occasion very vividly. It was my first night in boarding school, when I was fourteen years old. And in all the excitement of my room at school and my new roommate, and in the general excitement, I forgot to say my prayers.

Well, in the course of time I became a judge. I need not tell you that the toughest part of the judge's work is sentencing the people who are convicted or who plead guilty to the various offenses. I had always wondered what I should do if at the time of sentence some prisoner was impudent to me. It seems so clear that in the stress of such an occasion the judge should not mete out a greater punishment for some feeling of personal pique.

One day this happened to me. Most of you probably do not know about it but the fact is that, with these millions of government checks that go out through the mail from day to day, many are placed in these mail boxes on the ground floor of walk-up apartment houses and tenements, and they furnish a constant temptation to people in distress or people of naturally predatory instincts. Most of the time they get caught and, as it is a federal offense, they come before the judges of my court.

On this particular occasion a woman who, it was plainly to be seen, would soon become a mother, came before me, and I struggled away with the probation report and with questions and so on, to see what I should do. She suddenly burst out and gave me a tongue-lashing that was a work of art. After reflecting for a moment or two, I made up my mind that it would not be right to sentence her that day, and so, over her resounding protests, I put the matter off for a week.

The following Sunday I was sitting in my pew at Saint James Church when the Rector, at a certain point in the services, said that he would pause for a moment or two so that every member of the congregation could make a silent prayer in connection with whatever matter was troubling them. I do not remember that having been done before, but I suppose it has. Anyway, I prayed for that woman just as hard and as fervently as I knew how; and, a day or two later she was back there in court standing before me. I told her about what I had been going through; I told her that I had prayed for her in church, just as I have been telling you. I shall not make a long story of it. But the outcome was that I gave her a suspended sentence, and I do not think there is very much chance that she will be in my court or any other court again.

I do not see why a judge should be ashamed to say that he prays for divine guidance and for strength to do his duty. Indeed, there came a time not so long after the incident I have just described, when I did the most sincere and the most fervent praying that I ever did in my life.

As I mentioned in passing, at the beginning of this address, I suddenly found myself in the midst of that trial of the Communists. It took me a long time to realize what they were trying to do to me. But as I got weaker and weaker, and found the burden difficult to bear, I sought strength from the one source that never fails.

Let me be specific. There came a time when, doubtless due to previous planning, one of the defendants was on the stand and he refused to answer a question, pleading a supposed constitutional privilege which obviously had no application. I gave him time to consult with his counsel about it; I held the matter in abeyance overnight to make sure that I was making no misapplication of the law, and then the next day, Friday, June 3d, of the year 1949, I sentenced him to prison for thirty days, unless he should sooner purge himself of contempt by answering the question. Pandemonium broke loose. The other ten defendants and their lawyers, and many of the spectators, rose to their feet; there was a great shouting and hullabaloo, and several of the defendants started toward the bench.

In all that excitement, I felt just as calm as I do now when I speak to you; I did not raise my voice over the tone which you hear me use now; and I singled out several of those men, identified the language they were using, got it on the record, and sentenced each of them to imprisonment for the balance of the trial.

And I tell you, as I stand here, that my unguided will alone and such self-control as I possess, were unequal to this test. If ever a man felt the presence of Someone beside him, strengthening his will and giving him aid and comfort, it was I on that day.

And so it was later and toward the end of August, when I finally left the courtroom one day and went to lie down, thinking that perhaps I should never go back. But, after ten or fifteen minutes, I was refreshed and I did go back; and I gained from that moment on to the end.

Perhaps someone will think it wrong for me to tell you these things. But I could not come to this gathering prepared to discuss the ordinary platitudes, or to hold forth on philosophy or international affairs, about which I know nothing. It seemed better, particularly in these trying, difficult times, when each of us is worried, and each of us is troubled over this great country of ours that we love so well, to sound a note of comfort.

After all is said and done, it is not we who pull the strings; we are not the masters, but the servants of our Master's will; and it is well that we should know it to be so.

He had hesitated to give this address for fear that it might be thought insincere, but he need not have worried. Its effects were astonishing. It was printed and reprinted a dozen times, under the title he gave it and under other titles. It appeared in religious publications, in *The Reader's Digest*, and elsewhere. It appeared in its original form and it appeared variously edited and abridged, but invariably it made a wide appeal. Letters came to the Judge from all across the country, one of which was from a man condemned to go to the electric chair, asking Medina to pray for him the night he was to die. People approached him almost wherever he appeared and thanked him for what he had said. After an address he gave before a group of judges in the state of Washington an elderly gentleman approached him and shook his hand.

"That speech of yours about a judge and his God," he said. "I had kind of slipped away from those beliefs, but your speech brought me back. I want to thank you."

On June 1, 1951, Judge Learned Hand, of the United States Court of Appeals for the Second Circuit, retired after forty-two years on the federal bench. In the history of the United States few judges have ever served more effectively or have attained greater eminence in the eyes of their associates. But it was no sooner known that this outstanding judge was about to end his long period of service than a spontaneous demand arose for the appointment of Judge Medina to succeed him.

Judge Hand had himself served for fifteen years as a district judge before being elevated to the Court of Appeals in 1924, but now Judge Medina was about to be appointed to the higher court after only four years as a district judge. In 1947, when he had first been suggested for the bench, there was so much political opposition that his appointment appeared anything but certain. For this higher judicial position, however, no opposition arose. The very day Judge Hand's resignation was announced the Association of the Bar of the City of New York suggested Medina for appointment. It was even said that Judge Hand's written opinion affirming the conviction of the Communist leaders and praising Medina's handling of the trial had in itself been enough to assure Medina's appointment, and there were some who were inclined to believe that Judge Hand himself had actually urged it. But when I asked the retired judge whether or not this was true he assured me that it was not. Not long before the appointment was made he had a conversation with Peyton Ford, then deputy attorney general, and when Ford mentioned Medina's name in connection with the vacancy, Judge Hand recalls saying, in substance, that he was the man for the place, but aside from that recalls taking no action that influenced the appointment one way or the other.

Medina, however, was in no great need of additional support. In view of his enormous popularity, it was perfectly clear that the appointment would be "good politics," and it would seem that no other name was seriously considered. Certainly President Truman made the appointment promptly, word of it reaching Medina while he was at Princeton to receive his alma mater's Doctorate of Laws *honoris causa*. The Senate gave its approval almost at once, and District Judge Harold R. Medina became a United States circuit judge when he took the oath as a judge of the Court of Appeals of the Second Circuit on June 28, 1951.

A few days later, as he was about to get into his car to drive downtown to the Court House, a couple of carpenters who were working on a new structure nearby came hurrying up to him.

"Good work, Judge," said one of them as they both patted him on the back. "We're glad you got a raise."

It was universally recognized that he had been elevated to the higher court because of the work he had done during the Communist trial, just as United States Attorney McGohey had been appointed to the district bench for the same reason. But few realized that Judge Medina, despite this new appointment, would not be able actually to serve on the Court of Appeals for a considerable time.

Early in 1948, before the grand jury had even indicted the Communist leaders, he had been assigned to handle all motions and other matters preliminary to trial in the enormously complicated case of United States *v.* Henry S. Morgan *et al.* In this suit the government was charging seventeen of the nation's leading investment banking firms with having conspired to restrain trade and monopolize an important segment of the field of investment banking, and Judge Medina was not only to attend to all the preliminaries but also to preside when the case came up for trial. Three preliminary hearings connected with the case came before him in 1948; much of the vast task of answering interrogatories and authenticating thousands of documents and stipulating the accuracy of basic data concerning the details of an endless series of security issues had been completed, or was well on its way to completion, under Judge Medina's guidance before the trial of the Communist leaders commenced. But the Communist trial then delayed this complicated suit, and in the spring of 1950 there were further proceedings and a series of what the Judge called "pow-wows" in an endeavor to clarify the issues as well as could be done, and clear the decks for the trial, which actually began on November 28, 1950. As I write, it is still in progress and seems likely to continue until late in 1952—a trial that will undoubtedly prove to be much longer, and in many ways more complicated, than the Communist trial itself. In this trial, however, Judge Medina is sitting without a jury, and despite the complexities and technicalities of the matter—despite the fact, too, that more than thirty lawyers are engaged in the case—the problems that confront him are less menacing than those which confronted him during the nine-month trial of 1949. But until this task has been completed Judge Medina will be unable to assume his position on the Court of Appeals, and must continue to sit in the District Court until this case is over and his opinion deciding it has been filed.

As I write, there is no way accurately to estimate the time he will be forced to spend on the case he is hearing, and the task is a difficult one. Nevertheless, he has more freedom than when the Communists were before him. He is able to see his friends, though less often than formerly. He finds a little time to devote to perfecting his game of billiards (a pastime that has begun to displace golf). He is able to attend the theater and the opera occasionally and to spend the week-ends at his Westhampton home. He is able, too, to accept some of the many invitations he is forever receiving to address bar associations and other groups before which, more and more, he has come to express various phases of his philosophy—a philosophy which seems, primarily, to stem from his deep belief in America and his faith in personal morality.

"It seems to me," he said in an address before the Columbia University Alumni Federation, "that what this troubled world of ours most needs, now and always, is individual integrity. . . . Integrity is nothing in the mass. It is necessarily and by definition a personal, individual thing. We must each do our bit as separate, identifiable, particular persons. But if great numbers [of us] . . . put such teaching into effect in our own lives, there need be no fear for the future."

Whatever else Harold Medina may or may not be, there can be no doubt that he is peculiarly and forcefully individual, and in what he said in his address before the Church Club, as much as anywhere, is to be found his mature philosophy. His sincerity is evident in every word of it, and if, now and again, he fails to live up to the best that is in him, I believe that it is merely because of the vitality and healthy humanity of the man.

He is inclined to marvel at the widespread good will he has aroused, and more than once has spoken to me of his fear of "taking a nose dive."

"But I believe," he once remarked, "that people think of me as being fairly representative—that they see that I'm trying to do the things that millions of other Americans are trying to do."

Perhaps that is true, in part at least, for as he himself has said, "There is no trouble with the heart of America. All our people need is leadership."

And in Harold Medina's moral values many feel that they have found it.

Appendix

CHARGE OF THE COURT

MEDINA, District Judge.

Ladies and Gentlemen of the Jury:

YOU NOW APPROACH THE PERFORMANCE OF ONE OF THE MOST SACRED duties of citizenship, the meting out of justice. Just after you were sworn in as jurors I took occasion to make a few remarks which I shall now repeat in somewhat different form, as the thoughts I then expressed are peculiarly applicable to the period of your deliberations in order to reach a just and true verdict. I then told you to be patient and said that there are few qualities in life so important. I said that if you once get yourself in the frame of mind where you know that you have a task ahead and it has to be done carefully and it has to be done just right and you know that it will be wrong to let little things disturb you, then there comes a certain calm and peace of mind which are of the essence in the administration of justice. When you get yourself in that frame of mind, you find not only that the task ahead becomes much easier, but in addition that the quality of your work in the administration of justice is of the quality that it should be. Justice does not flourish amidst emotional excitement and stress.

The rich and the poor, and persons of every race, creed and condition stand alike before the bar of justice; and you must consider and weigh the evidence carefully, calmly and dispassionately, without the slightest trace of sympathy or prejudice for or against any party to the proceeding. The very importance of the case makes it all the more urgent that you heed these words of caution. In this connection you will bear in mind at all times that these eleven men are charged here as eleven individuals, the guilt of innocence of each of which must be passed on by you separately, pursuant to and in accordance with the instructions which I am about to give you.

Never in all my long experience as a lawyer and in my brief experience as a judge have I seen a jury exhibit so much patience and pay such careful attention at all times to the testimony of the witnesses and the reading of exhibits despite the prolonged duration of this trial. Let me express my sincere appreciation of the way in which you have performed your functions. You deserve special commendation and you are entitled to the gratitude of all citizens of the community for the sacrifice you have made and for the services you are rendering in the faithful performance of a public duty. And so I beg of you to continue on in the same spirit until the end.

The jury is composed of twelve men and women. While undoubtedly their verdict should represent the opinion of each individual juror, it by no means follows that opinions may not be changed by conference in the jury room. The very object of the jury system is to secure unanimity by a comparison of views and by arguments among the jurors themselves, provided this can be done reasonably and consistently with the conscientious convictions of the several jurors. Each juror should listen, with a disposition to be convinced, to the opinions and arguments of the others. It is not intended that a juror should go to the jury room with a fixed determination that the verdict shall represent his opinion of the case at that moment. Nor is it intended that he should close his ears to the arguments of other jurors who are equally honest and intelligent with himself.

The first thing I wish to make plain to you is the way in which our American system of jurisprudence defines the duties of the judge on the one hand and those of the jury on the other. It is exclusively my function clearly to set forth the rules of law which govern the case, with instructions as to their application. On these legal matters you must take the law as I give it to you; you are not at liberty to do otherwise. Thus I shall read the indictment and the statute applicable to the case and I shall construe the statute in those respects in which I think it requires construction and interpretation. I shall explain the function of the indictment, the presumption of innocence, the burden resting upon the government of proving its case to your satisfaction beyond a reasonable doubt and I shall give you the rules governing the trial of conspiracy cases, the rules to guide you in determining the credibility of witnesses and so on. My function is exclusively to instruct you on the law; and you must not permit any notions of your own or any matters referred to by counsel to obscure the fact that you must apply the law as I give it to you.

On the other hand, you are the sole judges of the facts and I shall refer to this circumstance again to impress it upon you. Just as you are not permitted to encroach upon my function in giving instructions on the law, so must I be careful not to encroach upon your function as the sole judges of the facts.

The relevant parts of the statute under the terms of which the indictment was drawn are as follows:

"Sec. 2. (a) It shall be unlawful for any person—

"(1) to knowingly or wilfully advocate, . . . or teach the duty, (or) necessity, . . . of overthrowing or destroying any government in the United States by force or violence, . . . ;

. . .

"(3) to organize . . . any society, group or assembly of persons who teach, (or) advocate, . . . the overthrow or destruction of any government in the United States by force or violence; . . . .

"(b) For the purposes of this section, the term 'government in the United States' means the Government of the United States, the government of any State, Territory, or possession of the United States, the government of the District of Columbia, or the government of any political subdivision of any of them." 18 U.S.C.A. § 10 [Now § 2385].

"Sec. 3. It shall be unlawful for any person . . . to conspire to commit, any of the acts prohibited by the provisions of this title." 18 U.S.C.A. § 11 [Now §§ 2385, 2387].

The indictment reads as follows:

The Grand Jury charges:

1. That from on or about April 1, 1945, and continuously thereafter up to and including the date of the filing of this indictment, in the Southern District of New York, and elsewhere, William Z. Foster, Eugene Dennis, also known as Francis X. Waldron, Jr., John B. Williamson, Jacob Stachel, Robert G. Thompson, Benjamin J. Davis, Jr., Henry Winston, John Gates, also known as Israel Regenstreif, Irving Potash, Gilbert Green, Carl Winter, and Gus Hall, also known as Arno Gust Halberg, the defendants herein, unlawfully, wilfully, and knowingly, did conspire with each other, and with divers other persons to the Grand Jurors unknown, to organize as the Communist Party of the United States of America a society, group, and assembly of persons who teach and advocate the overthrow and destruction of the Government of the United States by force and violence, and knowingly and wilfully to advocate and teach the duty and necessity of overthrowing and destroying the Government of the United States by force and violence, which said acts are prohibited by Section 2 of the Act of June 28, 1940, Section 10, Title 18, United States Code Annotated [Now § 2385)], commonly known as the Smith Act.

2. It was part of said conspiracy that said defendants would convene, in the Southern District of New York, a meeting of the National Board of the Communist Political Association on or about June 2, 1945, to adopt a draft resolution for the purpose of bringing about the dissolution of the Communist Political Association, and for the purpose of organizing as the Communist Party of the United States of America a society, group, and assembly of persons dedicated to the Marxist-Leninist prin-

ciples of the overthrow and destruction of the Government of the United States by force and violence.

3. It was further a part of said conspiracy that said defendants would thereafter convene, in the Southern District of New York, a meeting of the National Committee of the Communist Political Association on or about June 18, 1945, to amend and adopt said draft resolution.

4. It was further a part of said conspiracy that said defendants would thereafter cause to be convened, in the Southern District of New York, a special National Convention of the Communist Political Association on or about July 26, 1945, for the purpose of considering and acting upon said resolution as amended.

5. It was further a part of said conspiracy that said defendants would induce the delegates to said National Convention to dissolve the Communist Political Association.

6. It was further a part of said conspiracy that said defendants would bring about the organization of the Communist Party of the United States of America as a society, group, and assembly of persons to teach and advocate the overthrow and destruction of the Government of the United States by force and violence, and would cause said Convention to adopt a Constitution basing said Party upon the principles of Marxism-Leninism.

7. It was further a part of said conspiracy that said defendants would bring about the election of officers and the election of a National Committee of said Party, and would become members of said Party, and be elected as officers and as members of said National Committee and the National Board of said Committee, and in such capacities said defendants would assume leadership of said Party and responsibility for its policies and activities, and would meet from time to time to formulate, supervise, and carry out the policies and activities of said Party.

8. It was further a part of said conspiracy that said defendants would cause to be organized Clubs, and District and State units of said Party, and would recruit and encourage the recruitment of members of said Party.

9. It was further a part of said conspiracy that said defendants would publish and circulate, and cause to be published and circulated, books, articles, magazines, and newspapers advocating the principles of Marxism-Leninism.

10. It was further a part of said conspiracy that said defendants would conduct, and cause to be conducted, schools and classes for the study of the principles of Marxism-Leninism, in which would be taught and advocated the duty and necessity of overthrowing and destroying the Government of the United States by force and violence.

In violation of Sections 3 and 5 of the Act of June 28, 1940, Sections 11 and 13, Title 18 United States Code Annotated [Now §§ 2385, 2387], commonly known as the Smith Act. To this indictment each of the defendants has pleaded not guilty thus placing in issue each and every one of the material allegations contained in the indictment.

As an indictment is a rather technical document, there are one or two points which require a little explanation. You will observe that it is the first paragraph which alleges the conspiracy. While it refers to a conspiring to organize as the Communist Party a society, group and assembly of persons who teach and advocate the overthrow and destruction of the Government of the United States by force and violence and also a conspiring to advocate and teach the duty and necessity of overthrowing and destroying the Government of the United States by force and violence, I charge you that but a single conspiracy is alleged. You will doubtless remember from Mr. McGohey's opening address that the prosecution has undertaken to prove that the defendants conspired to organize the Communist Party as a society, group and assembly of persons who teach and advocate the overthrow and destruction of the Government by force and violence as a mere preliminary to the second phase of this same conspiracy which has to do with the teaching and advocacy of the duty and necessity of overthrowing and destroying the Government by force and violence. Probably the prosecution could have urged me to construe the indictment as charging a single conspiracy with two separate objects or as charging two separate conspiracies, but it has not done so and the construction just given is adopted because plainly in the interest of defendants and not conceivably prejudicial to them. As there is a single conspiracy alleged, this will also simplify your labors.

Let me repeat that the crime charged is a conspiracy. The crime charged is not that these defendants personally advocated or taught the duty or necessity of overthrowing and destroying the Government of the United States by force and violence; nor is the charge that the Communist Party as such advocates or teaches such violent overthrow and destruction. The charge is that these defendants conspired with each other, and with others unknown to the Grand Jury, knowingly and wilfully to advocate and teach the duty or necessity of such overthrow and destruction and, in this connection, to organize the Communist Party as a society, group, or assembly of persons who teach or advocate such overthrow and destruction.

You may have noticed, however, that the statute which I read to you makes it unlawful to advocate or teach the duty or necessity of overthrowing *or* destroying the Government by force and violence and also makes it unlawful to organize any society, group, or assembly of persons who teach or advocate the overthrow *or* destruction of the Government by force and violence. It is in the disjunctive by reason of the use of the word "or." In accordance with the rules of pleading the prosecution has in the indictment charged both, by using the conjunctive "and" in the phrase "overthrow and destruction"; but it is sufficient if the evidence adduced convinces you by the required degree of proof that defendants, or any of them, conspired as alleged, to teach and advocate either the overthrow *or* the destruction of the Government of the United States by force and violence, in accordance with these instructions. Thus it may be said that the objects of the alleged conspiracy were the organizing as the Communist Party of a society, group, and assembly of persons who teach and advocate the overthrow or destruction of the Government by force and violence and the advocacy and teaching of the duty and necessity of overthrowing or destroying the Government by force and violence.

Now let us turn to the remaining nine paragraphs of the indictment. The conspiracy is alleged in paragraph 1. Each of the remaining nine paragraphs allege that it was "part of said conspiracy" that defendants would do various things, such as: inducing the delegates of a special National Convention of the Communist Political Association to dissolve the Communist Political Association; causing to be organized Clubs, and District and State units of the Communist Party and recruiting and encouraging the recruitment of members of that Party; and the publication and circulation of books, articles, magazines and newspapers advocating the principles of Marxism-Leninism; and so on. These paragraphs merely allege the means by which it is claimed the defendants agreed that the conspiracy was to be made effective. And so I shall charge you later that it is not necessary for the prosecution to prove that all these means were actually used or put in operation, provided that it be established to your satisfaction by the required degree of proof that one or more of these means described in the last nine paragraphs of the indictment were agreed upon to be used to effect the conspiracy, in accordance with these instructions.

This indictment that I have read to you is merely a method by which the prosecution calls into a court of justice individuals who, it is claimed, have violated the law. It is not evidence of the guilt of the defendants nor does it detract in any degree from the presumption of innocence with which the law surrounds them until their guilt is proven. This presumption of innocence remains with them throughout the trial of the case and applies to the consideration of each of the essential ingredients going to make up the crime charged unless and until you, the jury, are satisfied beyond a reasonable doubt, from the evidence adduced by the prosecution, on whom is the burden of proof, of the guilt of the defendants as charged.

And a reasonable doubt means a doubt founded upon reason. It does not mean a fanciful doubt, or a whimsical or capricious doubt, for anything relating to human affairs and depending upon human testimony is open to some possible or imaginary doubt. When all of the evidence in the case, carefully analyzed, compared and weighed by you, produces in your minds a settled conviction or belief of a defendant's guilt, such a conviction as you would be willing to act upon matters of the highest importance relating to your own affairs, when it leaves your minds in the condition that you feel an abiding conviction amounting to a moral certainty of the truth of the charge, then, and in that event you would be free from a reasonable doubt. Absolute or mathematical certainty is not required but there must be such certainty as satisfies your reason and judgment, and such that you feel conscientiously bound to act upon it.

A conspiracy may be defined as a combination of two or more persons, by concerted action, to accomplish a criminal or unlawful purpose, or some purpose not in itself unlawful or criminal, by criminal or unlawful means. The gist of the offense is the unlawful combination or agreement to violate the law. As Justice Holmes said many years ago: "A conspiracy is a partnership in criminal purposes."

However, it is not necessary in order to constitute a conspiracy that two or more persons should meet together and enter into an explicit or formal agreement for an unlawful scheme, or that they should directly, by words or in writing, state what the unlawful scheme was to be, and the details of the plan or means by which the unlawful scheme was to be made effective.

It is sufficient if two or more persons, in any manner, or through any contrivance, impliedly or tacitly, come to a mutual understanding to accomplish a common and unlawful design, knowing its object. In other words, where an unlawful end is sought to be effected and two or more persons, actuated by the common purpose of accomplishing that end, knowingly work together in any way in furtherance of the unlawful scheme, every one of said persons becomes a member of the conspiracy, although his part therein be a subordinate one, or be executed at a remote distance from the other conspirators. All the conspirators need not have originally conceived the conspiracy, or participated in its conception. Those who come in later, with knowledge of the aims and purposes of the conspiracy, and cooperate in the common effort to attain the unlawful results become parties thereto. A conspiracy is not ended as long as the evidence shows an intention to continue it. Each alleged conspirator who was the agent of the others at some time during the life of the conspiracy remains an agent during all of its existence, except that a conspirator has the right to withdraw from the execution of the conspiracy, but it requires affirmative and effective action thus to withdraw and terminate his liability in the conspiracy. It is a principle of law that a condition once shown to exist continues until a different situation is shown.

Persons may be guilty of being parties to a conspiracy though the objects of the conspiracy were never accomplished. On the other hand, proof concerning the accomplishment of the objects of a conspiracy is the most persuasive evidence of the existence of the conspiracy itself. The agreement is generally a matter of inference deduced from acts of the persons accused done in pursuance of an apparent criminal purpose.

You are further instructed that where several persons are proved to have combined together for the same illegal purpose, any act or declaration made by one of them during the pendency of the illegal enterprise, and in furtherance of the common objects, is not only evidence against himself but is evidence against the other conspirators, who, when the combination is proved, are as much responsible for such declarations and acts as if made and committed by themselves, because each is deemed to assent to or command what is done by any other in furtherance of the common objects.

It is not incumbent upon the prosecution to prove that all of the means set out in the indictment were, in fact, agreed upon to carry out the conspiracy, or that all of them were actually used or put into operation. It is sufficient if it be established to your satisfaction, and beyond a reasonable doubt, that one or more of the means described in the indictment was agreed upon to be used to effect the conspiracy.

With these general principles as a guide you will approach the important question of whether the prosecution has proved beyond a reasonable doubt the existence of the conspiracy alleged in the indictment, and if such a conspiracy did exist, whether the defendants or any of them were parties to it and whether such defendants entered it with knowledge of its nature and purposes. It will be well for you to take up and consider separately the evidence as it relates to each defendant on trial.

You must first determine from all the evidence in the case, relating to the period of time defined in the indictment, whether or not a conspiracy existed. If you decide that a conspiracy did exist, you must next determine, as to each defendant, whether or not he was a member of the conspiracy. In considering whether or not a particular defendant was a member of the conspiracy, you must do so without regard to and independently of the statements and declarations of others. In other words, you must determine the membership of a particular defendant from the evidence concerning his own actions, his own conduct, his own declarations, or his own statements, and his own connection with the actions and conduct of others. However, once you have determined that a defendant was a member of the conspiracy, using this test, you may then consider as if made by him the statements and declarations of other co-conspirators, made in furtherance of the conspiracy and during the existence thereof as alleged.

There has been testimony in the case of acts and declarations by persons, for example, instructors and party functionaries, who are not named in the indictment as defendants. However, the indictment does refer to co-conspirators unknown to the Grand Jury. If you find that the conspiracy charged in the indictment existed and that any of these persons acted on behalf of the defendants and in furtherance of the conspiracy, then those persons are co-conspirators and their acts and declarations are binding on whatever defendants you find to have been members of the conspiracy.

I may explain this in a different way. First, you will recall that as to every material fact the prosecution has the burden of proving such fact to your satisfaction beyond a reasonable doubt. Let us assume then, for the purposes of argument only, and merely by way of hypothetical illustration, that after deliberating together you are convinced beyond a reasonable doubt that a conspiracy existed and that the defendants or some of them were parties to it and you come to the question of whether or not you should consider as binding upon such defendants the testimony of one of the prosecution witnesses to the effect that Mr. or Miss So-and-So, claimed to have been one of the instructors in one of the Communist Party schools, had said thus and so about the dictatorship of the proletariat and how it would be brought about by Communists in the United States of America. Before you could consider this evidence against the defendants or any of them you would have to be convinced beyond a reasonable doubt that the instructor in question was a member of the conspiracy, with knowledge of its aims and purposes, and that the teaching in question was during the period of the indictment and in furtherance of the aims and purposes of the conspiracy. For, as I have explained a moment or two ago, if you are convinced beyond a reasonable doubt that there was a conspiracy to organize a society, group and assembly of persons who teach and advocate the overthrow or destruction of the Government of the United States by force and violence and to advocate and teach the duty and necessity of overthrowing or destroying the Government of the United States by force and violence, and if you are convinced beyond a reasonable doubt that one or more of the defendants knowingly were parties to such conspiracy, you may consider the acts and statements of co-conspirators, engaged in the same enterprise, and done or said in furtherance of the conspiracy and in the time specified in the indictment, just as though such statements and acts were said and done by the defendant or defendants who were found by you to be members of the conspiracy. Accordingly, before considering as binding on said defendants such testimony as I have above described, it would be necessary for you also to be convinced beyond a reasonable doubt that the instructor in question was in fact a co-conspirator, with knowledge of the aims and purposes of the conspiracy, and that the teaching he or she was said to have done was within the period of the indictment and knowingly in furtherance of the aims and purposes of the conspiracy. In this connection you will recall what I have already told you that all the conspirators need not have originally conceived the conspiracy or participated in its conception. Everyone coming into a conspiracy, with knowledge of its aims and purposes, is as much a co-conspirator as though in it from the beginning, in the absence of some affirmative action to effect a withdrawal from the conspiracy.

Now do not go off on a tangent and get confused about these instructors or party functionaries or anyone else, not named in the indictment, whom you may find to be a co-conspirator. You are not called upon to name any of these persons in your verdict or to pass upon their guilt or innocence in any way. No charge against them of violating the criminal laws of the United States is before you for determination. The sole question before you is whether these defendants, named in the indictment which I have read to you, are guilty of the charge laid against them. Your only task is to determine whether they or any of them are guilty as charged. If the evidence points to the guilt of any person or persons not named in the indictment and not on trial before you, you are in no sense to consider such evidence except insofar as it bears upon the question of the guilt or innocence of the defendants or any of them, in accordance with these instructions.

In conspiracy cases there is necessarily considerable latitude of admissible evidence, so that some of the testimony may be applicable to one but not to the others of the defendants on trial. During the course of the trial certain evidence was received concerning acts, declarations and teachings of various of the defendants during the period prior to April 1, 1945, the initial date of the conspiracy alleged in the indictment. As I have told you, you must be satisfied beyond a reasonable doubt that the defendants wilfully conspired, during the period April 1, 1945 to July 20, 1948, to accomplish the two objectives which are charged in the indictment and which I have previously mentioned. The evidence which has been received relating to the period prior to the conspiracy should be considered by you only in determining the intent of the defendants concerned and in determining whether they contemplated that the overthrow or destruction of the Government by force and violence would be taught during the period from April 1, 1945 to July 20, 1948. You may not consider such evidence in determining the intent of any other defendant to commit the offense charged, or for any other purpose.

Government's Exhibit No. 3, the "Program of the Communist International," was originally received against the defendant Stachel only. Thereafter, evidence was admitted that this Program was the subject of teaching in a Party School and was quoted from or referred to in one or two of the outlines distributed after April 1, 1945. If you are satisfied by the required degree of proof that the Program was so used after April 1, 1945, you may consider it not only as bearing upon the intent of the defendant Stachel but also on the issue of the existence of the conspiracy as alleged.

For two or more persons to conspire, confederate or combine together to commit or cause to be committed a breach of the criminal law of the United States is an offense of grave character which involves not only a plotting to subvert the law, but also the preparation of the conspirators for further criminal practices. It is almost always characterized by secrecy, rendering detection difficult and requiring much time for its discovery. Because of this the statute has made a conspiracy to commit a crime a distinct offense from the crime itself. From the point of view of the law there is danger to the public when two or more people conspire to do something that is unlawful because by virtue of the aggregation of numbers the intent assumes a more formidable disadvantageous aspect to the public.

For your guidance and assistance, I shall now briefly discuss the contentions of the prosecution and those of the defendants relative to the proofs adduced by each and instruct you on the rules of law which will govern your deliberations in passing upon the credibility of the witnesses who have testified on behalf of one side or the other.

Before I do this I wish to emphasize again that you are the sole judges of the facts. In a case such as this, with hundreds of exhibits and many thousands of pages of testimony it is impossible for me to attempt any complete and satisfactory summary. Therefore, I solemnly tell you that the brief statement which I shall make concerning the contentions of the parties is merely by way of passing remark to help refresh your recollection and get you started on your deliberations. It is solely your function to determine not only what testimony was given and by whom, but also to determine the relative importance or lack of importance of the vast number of details with which the case is replete. The circumstance that I mention some of these and omit others must not be taken as an indication that I have any opinion to the effect that one phase of the case is of more importance than another. It is for you alone to determine what evidence you will believe and what weight you will give it, in accordance with these instructions.

But I can help to eliminate certain matters which are not in issue. Books are not on trial here nor are you concerned with the philosophical validity of any mere theories. It is not your function to pass upon the relative merits of communism or capitalism or any other issue. You are concerned with the intent of these defendants and what these defendants, and any other persons with whom you may find they conspired in accordance with the rules already stated, did and said. The books, pamphlets and so on come into the case only to the extent that you may be satisfied beyond a reasonable doubt that these books and pamphlets were used by the defendants, and those conspiring with them, if there be any such, as instruments, apparatus or paraphernalia for the propagation of teaching and advocacy of the overthrow or destruction of the Government by force and violence.

Nor will you be called upon to decide any of the miscellaneous matters injected into the case by counsel for the defendants and received by me on the theory that they could not satisfactorily show that the defendants at no time organized or conspired to organize as the Communist Party of the United States of America a society, group and assembly of persons who teach and advocate the overthrow or destruction of the Government by force and violence and taught or advocated, or conspired to teach or advocate, the overthrow or destruction of the Government by force and violence, without showing, to a reasonable extent, what they claim that they did teach and advocate. I have taken great pains during the trial to keep the real issues clearly before you, lest confusion and injustice to one side or the other might result. And so I charge you now that questions or issues relative to the grievances of young people, trade unions, farmers, working people in general, veterans, or housewives, or Jim Crow, lynching and the like, discrimination based upon race, creed or color and so on are not before you for determination. You must be scrupulously careful to see to it that the testimony on these subjects does not attract your minds away from the real issues as clearly defined in these instructions, or stir up emotions and sympathies which may make it difficult for you to consider the real issues and the evidence carefully, calmly and dispassionately, without the slightest trace of sympathy or prejudice for or against any party to the proceeding, as I have already charged you to do. The same is true about the utterances of defendants, as contained in the proofs, on the subjects of the wisdom of the Marshall Plan, the withdrawal of American troops from China, the war in Spain and similar subjects.

It is perfectly lawful and proper for the defendants or anyone else to advocate reforms and changes in the laws, which seem to them to be salutary and necessary. No one has suggested that the defendants transgressed any laws by advocating such reforms and changes. No syllable of the indictment refers to any such matters. Furthermore, should you find from the evidence that the defendants organized or helped to organize and assumed or were given leadership in the Communist Party as a legitimate political party solely with the view of electing candidates to political office by lawful and peaceful means and advocating reforms and changes in the laws or the adoption of policies by the Government favorable to their contentions in the matters just referred to, you must render a verdict of not guilty. And, even if you do not so find from the evidence, you cannot bring in a verdict of guilty against any defendant unless the prosecution has satisfied you of his guilt beyond a reasonable doubt, in accordance with these instructions.

Put the other way around and more succinctly, I charge you that if you are satisfied beyond a reasonable doubt that the defendants, or any of them, wilfully conspired to organize a society, group, and assembly of persons who teach and advocate the overthrow or destruction of the Government of the United States by force and violence, and to advocate and teach the duty and necessity of overthrowing or destroying the Government of the United States by force and violence, in accordance with these instructions, it is immaterial that they may also have contemplated the teaching and advocacy of other matters, such as rent control, civil rights legislation, or any other subject.

I need not remind you that the case bristles with issues of veracity. In instances too numerous to specify the testimony of witnesses called by the prosecution is flatly contradicted by the testimony of witnesses called by the defendants. It is your function and yours alone to decide where the truth lies, remembering always that the prosecution has the burden of proof and this burden, as I have already told you, is that of satisfying you beyond a reasonable doubt as to each essential ingredient of the crime charged.

The prosecution claims that the defendants conspired together and with others to organize as the Communist Party of the United States of America a society, group and assembly of persons who teach and advocate the overthrow or destruction of the Government of the United States by force and violence and to teach and advocate the duty and necessity of overthrowing or destroying the Government of the United States by force and violence; that defendants as part and parcel of the conspiracy sought to mask their purposes by pretending that they were fighting always and solely for democracy and the interests and welfare of the workers and to bring about salutary reforms and even socialism as a goal to be reached in the nebulous future, all by straightforward, peaceful and strictly lawful means, whereas in truth and in fact they resorted to many clandestine and fraudulent devices in teaching those subject to their influence secretly to prepare for the coming of some crisis, such as a deep depression or a war with the Soviet Union, to spring into action when the word of command was given, to paralyze power houses, the transportation system and the vast industrial machine at the heart of our economic system and in the resultant chaos and confusion to bring about, by violent and unlawful means, the overthrow or destruction of the Government and the establishment of the dictatorship of the proletariat. To this end, according to the contentions of the prosecution, under circumstances involving some communication from Dimitri E. Manuilsky, a delegate of the Ukrainian S. S. R. to the United Nations Conference at San Francisco, and an article by Jacques Duclos, a leading French Communist, the Communist Political Association was dissolved, Browder's policy of the peaceful collaboration of the classes, or revisionism, was repudiated and the Communist Party was reconstituted, and an elaborate and far-reaching network of schools and classes established for the propagation of the Marxist-Leninist principles of the overthrow or destruction of the Government by force and violence. The prosecution further contends that Aesopian language, only understood by Communists thoroughly indoctrinated in the use of such verbiage, was used in their Constitution of 1945 and elsewhere, and that defendants also habitually used in their writings and teaching a species of double-talk which they used to convey one meaning to themselves and their followers, but which would be otherwise understood by the uninitiate and the public at large; that a rigid system of party discipline was rigorously enforced, hedged about with the appearance of prolonged democratic discussion, amendments of resolutions and so on, to becloud the fact that this discipline was enforced from above and with the active cooperation of the defendants themselves; that deliberate lying and false swearing were condoned and even encouraged, when the needs of the Communist Party so required; that the use of false names, the destruction of membership books or cards and various other secret and devious devices were resorted to; that plans were deeply laid to place energetic and militant members of the Communist Party in key positions in various industries indispensable to the functioning of the American economy, to be ready for action at a given signal; and that such action was to consist of strikes, sabotage and violence of one sort or another appropriate to the consummation of the desired end, that is to say the smashing of the machine of state, the destruction of the army and the police force and the overthrow of the Government and what Communists call "bourgeois democracy."

The prosecution further claims that the process of indoctrination at these various schools and classes was sought to be accomplished by the defendants by: (1) a persistent and unremitting playing upon the grievances of various minority groups such as young people, veterans, Negroes, housewives, Jews and those suffering from economic handicaps of one sort or another —rubbing salt into these wounds and doing their best to arouse and inflame antagonisms between various segments of the population; (2) by insistence that the Communist Party alone is qualified to assume and to retain leadership of the revolutionary movement for the smashing of the capitalist state machine, and the ushering in of the dictatorship of the proletariat, and that accordingly Communists must at all times maintain what they call their Vanguard Role and the elimination at all times of others who claim to be seeking by various means to attain the same or similar ends; (3) by constant study and discussion of the steps by which the Communists came to power in the Soviet Union, including the details of the revolution of October, 1917, in Russia, the strategy and tactics followed, including the wearing by the workers of uniforms of the Russian soldiers and sailors, the street fighting and so on; (4) by constantly stressing their claim that capitalism during the period of time specified in the indictment was on its last legs, or moribund, that the dictatorship of the proletariat was inevitable, that the workers should hate the capitalist system and their employers, and the army and the police as mere instruments of Wall Street monopolists and exploiters, who are said to hold the Government of the United States in their clutches; (5) by picturing the Government of the United States as imperialistic and tending toward fascism and the Soviet Union as the protector of the rights of minorities, the only true and complete democracy and as dedicated to peace; (6) by inculcating the doctrine that a war with Russia would be an imperialistic and an unjust war, in which event it is said to be the duty of those subscribing to defendants' principles to turn the imperialistic war into a civil war and fight against their own government, meaning the Government of the United States.

It is the further claim of the prosecution that defendants, during the period specified in the indictment, did and said what they did, and what it is claimed that the evidence, testimonial and documentary, shows that they did, with the specific intent and purpose of overthrowing or destroying the Government of the United States by force and violence, and doing so at the earliest time that circumstances would permit.

On the other hand, the defendants' version in this case is as different as white from black. The two versions of the facts are utterly irreconcilable. Thus defendants deny that they or any of them ever conspired among themselves or with anyone else to organize as the Communist Party of the United States of

America a society group and assembly of persons who teach and advocate the overthrow or destruction of the Government of the United States by force and violence or to advocate and teach the duty and necessity of overthrowing or destroying the Government of the United States by force and violence; they deny that there was at any time anything furtive or deceptive about any of their acts or writings and they assert, on the contrary, that their very principles as Communists forbid them to conceal their aims and purposes from the people and that they have taught openly and for a long time the peaceful principles of Marxism-Leninism as they understand them to everyone they could induce to listen to them or to read their writings.

The defendants characterize as "unmitigated bunk," and as a vicious libel, the charges levelled against them and to some extent summarized by me in the foregoing instructions. They claim that the whole prosecution is based on a "frame-up," supported by the testimony of Government agents whom defendants describe as stool pigeons. It is charged that these agents and certain of the F.B.I. men who also testified against defendants and others, such as the witness Budenz, wilfully perjured themselves and that their testimony is a tissue of lies made up out of whole cloth.

They assert that at least Dennis and Green backed up Foster in his opposition to the dissolution of the Communist Party and the formation of the Communist Political Association in 1944 and that the elimination of the Communist Political Association and the reconstitution of the Communist Party of the United States of America in 1945 were in no respect due to any orders from abroad or elsewhere but, on the contrary, were the result of spontaneous and growing criticism of Browder's policies, springing from the ranks of the Party, as a result of general dissatisfaction with revisionist and opportunist views, which it was widely thought would wreck the Party and perhaps, if continued, render wholly unattainable the ultimate goal of socialism. They point to Foster's letter of January 20, 1944, and the views which he pressed upon the members of the National Committee, and Foster's position of leadership in the Party, as demonstrating that the Duclos article merely helped to bring things to a head. They further assert that, while the Communist Political Association was still in existence, and long before its dissolution, the course of events had begun to demonstrate that Browder was wrong; that capital revealed itself less cooperative than Browder had anticipated, that the unity of the wartime allies had weakened and the United States and Great Britain had begun to show signs of adopting an imperialistic and unjustifiable anti-Soviet attitude; that, accordingly, when the Duclos article appeared, members of the Communist Political Association were receptive to its criticisms, since these criticisms accorded with their own developing experience; and that thereupon as a result of a reappraisal of party policies arrived at in a frank and democratic manner, it was decided in open convention that the policies of the Communist Political Association during the 1944–45 period were a revision of Marxism, and the Communist Party was reconstituted; that the Communist Party was then set up with its various subdivisions, and the defendants were elected, at the times indicated by the evidence, to positions of leadership in it; and that they took part in disseminating party literature and supervising its dissemination, teaching and advocating party principles, and in setting up and supervising schools and classes for the teaching and advocating of party principles.

Now do you think this is a good time for a little recess?

"The Jurors: Yes.

"The Court: We will take a ten-minute recess." (Short recess.)

"The Court: The defendants assert that they regard the establishment of socialism in this country as necessary if the people are to live in peace and prosperity; that all their activities are directed toward the ultimate establishment of socialism, and take two major forms which interact with and influence each other; the political and the educational.

Their political activities, they contend, stem from their belief that the people of the country can attain socialism in a legal and democratic way, in spite of the opposition of the capitalists, but that socialism can never be achieved, no peace or freedom at all is possible, if the manifestations of reaction and fascism which the defendants discern continue unchecked, and the power of the trusts and monopolies continues to increase. Therefore the immediate problem, according to the defendants, is to overcome the warmongers and the powers of reaction. This the defendants say they have attempted to accomplish by organizing or attempting to organize the broadest kind of national coalition of anti-fascist and democratic forces, with strong emphasis placed upon the independent role and initiative of the working class and especially the progressive labor movement and Communists. This coalition, according to the defendants, is a political coalition consisting of the workers, the Negro people, small farmers, the city middle class, small shopkeepers, small income professionals, intellectuals and even those of the capitalist class who desire to fight against war and fascism and in favor of peace, freedom and security.

They assert that the purpose of this broad coalition is to elect a Democratic and People's Front Government, such as was elected in Poland, Czechoslovakia, Hungary and Rumania, and that this would only come about if and when a majority of the people wanted it and were ready to struggle for it. Thus they say that their political activities are directed toward inducing the electorate to bring such a People's Front Government to power by peaceful democratic means on the basis of a program of democratic demands; and that when such a People's Front Government is in power and is able to curb the warmongers, monopolists and other forces of reaction, the people will then desire to move toward socialism, and, by peaceful democratic means, will do so.

Hand in hand with the political activities of the defendants go their educational activities, for they assert that the people will be unable to appreciate their political program unless they understand the principles which actuate it and see how the application of these principles will solve the problems that beset them. As Mr. William Z. Foster testified in his deposition, which was read to you:

"The Communist Party proceeds upon the practical assumption that the question of socialism in the United States is now in the educational stage; that is, that it is a question of teaching the masses the necessities for socialism or the inevitability of socialism and the means for bringing about socialism."

The defendants contend that they engage in these political and educational activities in order to benefit the masses of the American people, and to preserve and extend American democracy. They contend that their activities on behalf of the poor and oppressed, as well as in support of liberal legislation, and their opposition to all discriminatory and reactionary policies, show that they have no such intent as is necessary to support the charge in the indictment.

The defendants deny that the principles of Marxism-Leninism, as taught by them, have anything to do with the overthrow or destruction of the Government of the United States by force and violence. These principles as taught by them, they assert, form a unified whole, and are a true social science.

According to some of the testimony introduced on behalf of defendants, there was taught the principle of the class struggle. This principle is said to be that the workers and farmers and other segments of the population are engaged in a constant struggle with the capitalists, since the capitalists seek to exploit them, and they naturally resist. There also was taught the principle of the increasing crisis of capitalism, which is said to be that capitalism all over the world, by its very nature sinks into deeper and deeper crisis, with ever-widening circles of economic distress; that the capitalists, seeking to preserve their tottering dominion, intensify the class struggle and increase their exploitation of the mass of the people.

The defendants contend that socialism is the only solution to the crises of capitalism, and assert they engage in the political and educational activities which I have already mentioned, looking first toward the establishment of a broad democratic coalition to restrain the abuses of the reactionary capitalist class which has been goaded to desperation by the deepening crises of capitalism, and then toward the eventual establishment of socialism.

The defendants assert that they do not believe in and do not teach the use of force and violence to gain their ends. They contend that the capitalist class uses force and violence to prevent the transition to socialism, and that they justified the use of force and violence only as a method of preventing an attempted forcible overthrow of a succeeding government which had obtained control in a peaceful manner, or as a method of last resort to enforce the majority will if, at some indefinite future time, because of peculiar circumstances, constitutional or peaceful channels were no longer open. But as long as the peaceful electoral paths are open, the defendants assert that they can meet the reactionary class at the polls and defeat them peacefully.

It is manifestly not possible for me to give any complete summary of what was taught in the various Communist Party schools, according to the witnesses called by defendants. But I shall try to refer to some of these teachings which, according to my recollection, these witnesses seemed particularly to emphasize. Thus they say that the Marxist-Leninist principles taught in these schools are adaptable in various ways to a variety of historical conditions, that they cannot be applied dogmatically. Lenin showed, the defendants contend, that the capitalist system has developed in an uneven manner in various countries, that the contradictions and crises of capitalism, and imperialism, the final stage of capitalism, have all manifested themselves differently in different countries throughout the course of the late 19th and early 20th Centuries, and that therefore the transition to socialism has occurred and will occur in different ways, based upon the unique situations at a given time and place.

Thus the defendants warn against a mechanical transference of the experience of the Russian October Revolution of 1917 to the situation now prevalent in this country. The fact that socialism came to Russia in the form of soviets following a violent revolution does not mean the same will happen here. The notion that the October Revolution of 1917 in Russia can be used as a "blueprint" for any changes in the American political or social system, the defendants assert, is in flat contradiction of their teachings to the contrary.

With respect to the slogan "turn the Imperialist War into a Civil War," the testimony on behalf of defendants is to the effect that the reference to this slogan was by way of an explanation of its use in specific historical contexts and that the use of such slogan was not for the purpose of teaching or advocating the duty or necessity of converting a prospective imperialist war between the United States and the Soviet Union into a civil war.

One of their teachings which they say is axiomatic is that the constant interaction between theory and practice is itself a principle of Marxism-Leninism as propounded in their elementary as well as advanced and leadership schools. Thus it is possible for their day-to-day political and educational approach to vary, depending on the particular problems that have to be faced. Hence they say that prior to 1935 the issue was socialism against capitalism, although, as I understand it, every witness for the defense who was questioned on the subject vigorously asserted that at no time, prior or subsequent to 1935, did they teach that the Government of the United States or any government was to be overthrown or destroyed by force and violence in order to usher in socialism. They further say, according to Mr. Foster, that the People's Front policy about which I spoke a few moments ago, began to take shape at the 7th World Congress of the Comintern in Moscow in 1935, and that the development of this new policy had the effect of rendering obsolete many of the books about which Mr. Foster and others were questioned by the prosecution.

In this connection defendants refer to Article XIV, Section 1, of the 1945 Constitution of the Communist Party, which provides:

"The Communist Party is not responsible for any political

document, policy, book, article or any other expression of political opinion except such as are issued by authority of this and subsequent conventions and its regularly constituted leadership."

And so Mr. Winter, one of the defendants here on trial, testified that in his address to the 1945 Convention, he said:

"It was not a program for socialism. It was a program for the strengthening of the forces of democracy in our country to save our country from the menace of fascism and thus to lay the foundation for the majority of the American people winning government power through the free exercise of their choice."

Finally, as negativing the claim that defendants conspired to organize a society, group, and assembly of persons who teach and advocate the overthrow or destruction of the Government of the United States by force and violence and to advocate and teach the duty and necessity of overthrowing or destroying the Government of the United States by force and violence, defendants point to Article IX, Section 2, of the 1945 Constitution of the Communist Party, which reads as follows: "Adherence to or participation in the activities of any clique, circle, faction or party which conspires or acts to subvert, undermine, weaken or overthrow any or all institutions of American democracy, whereby the majority of the American people can maintain their right to determine their destinies in any degree, shall be punished by immediate expulsion."

From this brief recital of the contentions advanced on behalf of the defendants you can see how completely irreconcilable are the versions of the facts presented by the prosecution on the one hand and the defendants on the other. And so this seems to be an appropriate time for me to amplify somewhat my statement, at the outset of these instructions, that you are the sole and exclusive judges of the facts.

No matter how careful a judge may be to avoid it, there is always the possibility that the jury or some particular juror may get an impression that the judge has some opinion with reference to the guilt or innocence of the defendants, or that he thinks that some particular phase of the case is more important than another, or that some particular witness is more credible than another or that a certain inference of fact should or should not be made and so on. If you have formed any such impression you must put it out of your mind and utterly disregard it. Nothing I have said during the trial nor in these instructions was intended to give any such impression; nor were any remarks or questions addressed to any of the witnesses or to counsel so intended. On the contrary, I have been scrupulously careful to avoid any comment which might even remotely suggest that I considered the subjects of the weight of testimony, the credibility of witnesses, the inferences to be drawn or the relative importance of one segment of the evidence as against another, or the determination of the guilt or innocence of the defendants, as coming within the orbit of my functions as the presiding judge in this trial. Despite the power which a federal judge has to comment on the evidence, provided he unequivocally leaves the determination of the facts to the jury, I have refrained from any such comments in these instructions and during the trial, lest, by reason of the extreme length of the trial and the large number of witnesses and exhibits, my comments might be misunderstood. And so I tell you again, you are the sole and exclusive judges of the facts of this case; you, and you alone, will pass upon the credibility of all the witnesses, including the credibility of those defendants who testified, all in accordance with instructions on that subject which I shall give you later. Despite anything said by me or by counsel, your recollection of the testimony must prevail whenever your recollection differs from what I have said or what counsel for either side have said in argument or otherwise; it is for you to determine what the proofs adduced by both sides disclose, regardless of anything said by me in the brief and necessarily incomplete summaries which I have given you of the contentions of the parties; and it is for you and you alone to weigh the proofs, draw such inferences of fact therefrom as you determine should be drawn and to decide each and every one of the issues of fact in the case.

By the same token and by virtue of principles of law equally fundamental to American jurisprudence, you must decide these facts solely upon the basis of the exhibits received in evidence and the testimony given from the witness chair. Arguments of counsel are entitled to respectful consideration, but arguments and statements of fact by the lawyers for either side are not evidence. This includes arguments by the defendant Dennis, who was his own lawyer throughout the trial. Nothing said by him from the beginning of the trial down to this very moment constitutes evidence of any fact or circumstance involved in the case. For the same reason, you must utterly disregard and put out of your minds all testimony stricken by me, and all evidence offered and rejected.

I have already told you not to read anything about the case in the newspapers or listen to the radio about it, and now, in what may seem an excess of caution, I tell you that you must not consider, in your determination of the guilt or innocence of these defendants in accordance with these instructions, anything you may ever have read or heard other than the exhibits and testimony received and given in this courtroom. And when I say "anything" I mean it in the fullest sense of the word. This includes anything you may have read about this case or any other case. Newspapers, radio, movies, television, what people generally may think, and what you yourselves may ever have thought, about communists or communism or the Soviet Union, all this is out. What views the public or public officials of every name, nature and description may or may not entertain on these subjects have absolutely nothing to do with the case. Do not permit any extraneous matters affecting race or religion or color or anything else affect you one iota. You must concentrate on the evidence to the complete exclusion of everything else. For this reason you are also to make quite sure that you are not in any manner affected by the nature of the charge made against these defendants. You are to consider the evidence bearing on this charge of conspiring to organize a society, group, and assembly of persons who teach and advocate the overthrow or destruction of the Government of the United States by force and violence and to advocate and teach the duty and necessity of overthrowing or destroying the Government of the United States by force and violence, just as you would consider the evidence bearing on any other charge of committing a crime against the laws of the United States; and the government here must be considered in no different light than any other litigant who pleads for justice; and counsel for the government must be considered in no different light than counsel for the defendants or for any other litigant. What the case requires, and what every case in this or any other American court requires, is calm, cool, deliberate consideration of the evidence. Then, when in accordance with these instructions, you find the true facts and apply the law, return a just and true verdict, no matter whom it hurts. The law does not permit jurors to be governed by conjecture, passion or prejudice, public opinion or public feeling.

The fact that any defendant, who has a right so to do, has not seen fit to testify in this case cannot be considered by you as any evidence against him or against any of the other defendants, or as a basis for any presumption or inference unfavorable to him or to them. You must not permit such fact to weigh in the slightest degree against any defendant, nor should it enter into your discussions or deliberations. The prosecution must prove defendants guilty by the required degree of proof as explained in these instructions. They are not required under our law to establish their innocence.

And so we come to one of the crucial questions in the case. By what yardstick and in accordance with what rules of law are you to judge the credibility of the witnesses, including that of the defendants who offered themselves as witnesses.

This judging of testimony is very like what goes on in real life. People may tell you things which may or may not influence some important decisions on your part. You consider whether the people you deal with had the capacity and the opportunity to observe or be familiar with and to remember the things they tell you about. You consider any possible interest they may have, and any bias or prejudice. You consider a person's demeanor, to use a coloquial expression, you "size him up" when he tells you anything; you decide whether he strikes you as fair and candid or not. Then you consider the inherent believability of what he says, whether it accords with your own knowledge or experience. It is the same thing with witnesses. You ask yourself if they know what they are talking about. You watch them on the stand as they testify and note their demeanor. You decide how their testimony strikes you.

Take the matter of interest, for example. You may feel that some of the witnesses, whether for the prosecution or the defense, have an interest in the outcome of the case. Where a witness has a strong personal interest in the result of the trial the temptation may be strong to color, pervert, or withhold the facts. Or with all the honesty in the world a witness who has an interest in the case may unconsciously shade his testimony. On the other hand, such a witness may be telling the exact truth, despite his interest in the outcome. You must consider all the attendant circumstances in deciding whether and to what extent interest has affected the witness.

The greater a person's interest is in the case, the stronger is the temptation to false testimony, and the interest of the defendants who took the stand is of a character possessed by no other witness. Manifestly they have a vital interest in the outcome of the case. This interest is one of the matters which you may consider along with all the other attendant circumstances in determining the credence you will give to their testimony. Here again you may find that a defendant is telling the exact truth despite his obvious interest in the outcome.

What I have said concerning the interest of any witness applies with equal force to the matter of bias and prejudice. Where you find that any witness, whether called by the defense or by the prosecution, has any bias or prejudice for or against any of the parties, or for or against Communists or Communism, you will consider whether and to what extent such bias and prejudice has affected his testimony. Here again you must consider such bias and prejudice, where you find that it exists, in connection with all the attendant circumstances.

You will accordingly observe that, before reaching any conclusion as to whether or not you will believe the testimony of any particular witness, or as to whether you will believe part of the testimony of a particular witness and reject the rest, it is of the essence that you give consideration to all the circumstances bearing on the question of the credibility of the particular witness, as I have just indicated. For this reason you must be careful not to act in an arbitrary manner. Thus you are not at liberty arbitrarily to say that simply because a witness happens to be an F.B.I. agent, an informer, a present or former member of the Communist Party or a Communist official of functionary or a defendant or other witness falling into one category or another, or because a witness is called by the prosecution or by the defendants, he or she is therefore more than usually credible or less than usually credible. Credibility cannot be determined by any such rule of thumb.

While you are not at liberty to reject the testimony of a witness arbitrarily, there are occasions when you may be justified in rejecting it in toto. The law has a rule with a Latin name, "falsus in uno, falsus in omnibus," which applies to these occasions. It is: if you find that a witness wilfully falsely testified to a material fact, you are privileged to reject all his testimony, or if you elect to do so you could believe part of it and accept that part of it which appealed to your reason, or which was corroborated by other credible evidence and reject the rest. It is the application of what we do every day, that when a person tells you a lie about an important matter you may say, "Well, I will never believe him again," or you may say, "some of the things he told me I will accept because they jibe with everything else in my experience, or because they are corroboratd by what I am told by someone whom I believe, but where that is not so I won't accept his testimony." So here if you find a witness cannot be trusted to observe his oath in one particular, you may say that you cannot believe or trust him in any other particular.

In this connection, I charge you that a material fact includes a fact bearing on the credibility of the witness, as well as those bearing directly on the issues in this case. Facts going to the credibility of a witness who has given material evidence are facts within this rule, and if you find that any witness has wilfully falsified with respect to any fact going to his credibility, you may disregard his entire testimony in accordance with the falsus in uno, falsus in omnibus rule with respect to which I have just given you instructions.

Some of the witnesses refused to answer certain questions. You may consider these refusals in connection with the credibility of these witnesses and the weight you will give to their testimony. Witnesses—and by witnesses I again mean always to include the defendants who offer themselves as witnesses—are required to answer relevant and material questions unless the court sustains some claim of constitutional privilege and rules that the witness need not answer. Defendants need not take the stand at all, as I have told you. But if they elect to testify in their own defense, they must answer questions like any other witness. So wherever a witness thus refuses to answer questions put to him, you may take that refusal into consideration along with all the other attendant circumstances, unless the court has ruled that his refusal to answer is legally justified.

This brings me to another and a very important phase of this case. Among the most vital and precious liberties which we Americans enjoy by virtue of our Constitution are freedom of speech and freedom of the press. We must be careful to preserve these rights unimpaired in all their vigor.

Thus it is that these defendants had the right to advocate by peaceful and lawful means any and all changes in the laws and in the Constitution; they had the right to criticize the President of the United States and the Congress; they had the right to assert that World War II, prior to the invasion of Russia by Germany, was an unjust war, an imperialist war and that upon such invasion it became a just war worthy of all material and moral support; and they had the right publicly to express these views orally and in writing. They had the right thus to assert that the government was at all times exploiting the poor and worthy workers for the benefit of the trusts and monopolies. They had a right thus to assert that what they call the democracy of Russia is superior in all respects to American democracy. They had a right thus to assert that the Marshall Plan was a mistake, that billions of dollars should be loaned to Russia and that legislation adversely affecting Communists should not be passed. Whether you or I or anyone else likes or dislikes such or similar and analogous views or agrees or disagrees with them is wholly immaterial and not entitled to the slightest consideration in deciding this case. Unless a minority had a right to express and to advocate its views, the democratic process as we understand it here in America would cease to exist and those in power might remain there indefinitely and make impossible any substantial changes in our social and economic system or in the texture of our fundamental law.

I charge you that if the defendants did no more than pursue peaceful studies and discussions or teaching and advocacy in the realm of ideas, you must acquit them.

For example, it is not unlawful to conduct in an American college or university a course explaining the philosophical theories set forth in the books which have been placed in evidence by the prosecution such as the Communist Manifesto, Foundations of Leninism and so on. Of course these books are to be found in Public Libraries and in the libraries of American Universities. Indeed, many of our most outstanding and sincere educators have expressed the view that these theories should be widely studied and thoughtfully considered, so that all may thoroughly appreciate their significance and the inevitable effects of putting such theories into practice. Do not be led astray by talk about thought control, or putting books on trial. No such issues are before you here.

But no one could suppose nor is it the law that any person has an absolute and unbridled right to say or to write and to publish whatever he chooses under any and all circumstances. If he did have such a right and if such were the law the words

"WE THE PEOPLE of the United States, in Order to form a more perfect Union, establish Justice, *insure domestic Tranquility*, provide for the common defence, *promote the general Welfare*, and secure the Blessings of Liberty to ourselves and our posterity, do ordain and establish this Constitution of the United States of America."

as contained in the Preamble to the Constitution would be no more than empty phrases. Doubtless you observed that I placed emphasis on the "insure domestic Tranquility" and "promote the general Welfare" clauses of the Preamble. Words may be the instruments by which crimes are committed, as in many familiar situations; and it has always been recognized that the protection of other interests of socicty may justify reasonable restrictions upon speech in furtherance of the general welfare.

And so I come to the construction and interpretation of the statute. You will have noticed that, to infringe this law, a defendant must not only have conspired to organize as the Communist Party of the United States of America a society, group and assembly of persons who teach and advocate the overthrow or destruction of the Government by force and violence, and to advocate and teach the duty and necessity of overthrowing or destroying the Government by force and violence. The statute makes such conduct unlawful only when persons have so conspired "wilfully" or "knowingly"; and the indictment so charges these defendants.

Thus the question of intent also enters into the offense charged. If you find that the defendants, or any of them, participated in the conspiracy charged in the indictment, one of the questions for you to consider and determine is whether they acted wilfully. This is a question of their intent. You must be satisfied from the evidence beyond a reasonable doubt that the defendants had an intent to cause the overthrow or destruction of the Government of the United States by force and violence, and that it was with this intent and for the purpose of furthering that objective that they conspired both (1) to organize the Communist Party of the United States as a group or society who teach and advocate the overthrow or destruction of the Government of the United States by force and violence and (2) to teach and advocate the duty and necessity of overthrowing or destroying the Government of the United States by force and violence. And you must further find that it was the intent of the defendants to achieve this goal of the overthrow or destruction of the Government of the United States by force and violence as speedily as circumstances would permit it to be achieved.

In further construction and interpretation of the statute I charge you that it is not the abstract doctrine of overthrowing or destroying organized government by unlawful means which is denounced by this law, but the teaching and advocacy of action for the accomplishment of that purpose, by language reasonably and ordinarily calculated to incite persons to such action. Accordingly, you cannot find the defendants or any of them guilty of the crime charged unless you are satisfied beyond a reasonable doubt that they conspired to organize a society, group and assembly of persons who teach and advocate the overthrow or destruction of the Government of the United States by force and violence and to advocate and teach the duty and necessity of overthrowing or destroying the Government of the United States by force and violence, with the intent that such teaching and advocacy be of a rule or principle of action and by language reasonably and ordinarily calculated to incite persons to such action, all with the intent to cause the overthrow or destruction of the Government of the United States by force and violence as speedily as circumstances would permit.

No such intent could be inferred from the open and above-board teaching of a course on the principles and implications of Communism in an American college or university, where everything is open to the scrutiny of parents and trustees and anyone who may be interested to see what is going on. That is why it is so important for you to weigh with scrupulous care the testimony concerning secret schools, false names, devious ways, general falsification and so on, all alleged to be in the setting of a huge and well disciplined organization, spreading to practically every State of the Union and all the principal cities, and industries.

It is obviously impossible to ascertain or prove directly what were the operations of the minds of the defendants. You cannot look into a person's mind and see what his intentions are or were. But a careful and intelligent consideration of the facts and circumstances shown by the evidence in any given case enables us to infer with a reasonable degree of accuracy what another's intentions were in doing or not doing certain things. With a knowledge of definite acts we may draw definite logical conclusions. We are in our affairs continually called upon to decide from actions of others what their intentions or purposes are. And experience has taught us that frequently actions speak more clearly than spoken or written words. You must therefore rely in part on circumstantial evidence in determining the guilt or innocence of any of these defendants.

Circumstantial evidence may be received and is entitled to such consideration as you may find it deserves depending upon the inferences you think it necessary and reasonable to draw from such evidence. No greater degree of certainty is required when the evidence is circumstantial than when it is direct, for in either case the jury must be convinced beyond a reasonable doubt of the guilt of the defendants. Circumstantial evidence consists of facts proved from which the jury may infer by process of reasoning other facts sought to be established as true.

Different inferences, however, may be drawn from the facts and circumstances in the case, whether proved by direct or circumstantial evidence. The prosecution asks you to draw one set of inferences while the defendants ask you to draw another. It is for you to decide and for you alone, which inferences you will draw. If all the circumstances taken together are consistent with any reasonable hypothesis which includes the innocence of the defendants, or any of them, the prosecution has not proved their guilt beyond a reasonable doubt, and you must acquit them. On the other hand, if you find that all of the circumstances established by the evidence in this case, taken together, satisfy you beyond a reasonable doubt of the guilt of the defendants, in accordance with these instructions, it is your duty to find the defendants guilty.

Thus, if you find that the evidence has established to your satisfaction beyond a reasonable doubt that any defendant has violated the statute as thus construed by me, you will find such defendant guilty. Otherwise you will acquit him by a verdict of not guilty. Under these instructions you may find all the defendants guilty or all of them not guilty or you may find one or more of them guilty and the others not guilty.

If you are satisfied that the evidence establishes beyond a reasonable doubt that the defendants, or any of them, are guilty of a violation of the statute, as I have interpreted it to you, I find as matter of law that there is sufficient danger of a substantive evil that the Congress has a right to prevent to justify the application of the statute under the First Amendment of the Constitution.

This is matter of law about which you have no concern. It is a finding on a matter of law which I deem essential to support my ruling that the case should be submitted to you to pass upon the guilt or innocence of the defendants. It is the duty of counsel for both sides to present by way of objections, motions, and similar procedural devices, matters of law affecting the case for my consideration and determination. All such matters of law and their presentation by counsel, including motions of every name, nature and description, challenges, questions relating to the admissibility of evidence and things of that sort must be entirely disregarded by you. These are matters of procedure with which you have no concern. Neither the presentation of such matters by counsel for either side, nor any argument made in support or in opposition to any of them, have any bearing upon your deliberations. Put all such matters out of your minds. They should not influence you in any way in arriving at your verdict.

This brings me to certain of the requests for instructions, submitted by counsel for the defendants and by the prosecution which I have ruled to be proper. I charge them as follows:

Submitted on behalf of defendants:

Request No. 38. I charge you that you cannot find any defendant in this case guilty of the crime charged against him merely from the fact, if you find it to be a fact, that he associated with any other defendant or defendants whom you may find guilty of the offense charged.

Request No. 39. I charge you that under our system of law, guilt is purely personal and that you may not find any of the defendants guilty merely by reason of the fact that he is a member of the Communist Party of the United States of America, no matter what you find were the principles and doctrines which were taught or advocated by that Party during the period defined in the indictment.

Request No. 75. Circumstantial evidence is not direct proof of a fact. It is that evidence which tends to prove a disputed fact by proof of other facts which have a legitimate tendency to lead the mind to infer that the fact sought to be established is true.

Request No. 76. I charge you that you may not presume the existence of a fact and then infer from such presumed fact the existence of any other fact or circumstance; nor may you infer from any presumed fact or facts that the defendants, or any one of them, are guilty of the offense alleged in the indictment.

Request No. 84. I charge you that it is not enough for the prosecution to show the existence of an agreement and the membership therein of any particular defendant. This alone would not prove that such defendant participated in the agreement "knowingly and wilfully." With respect to each defendant, the prosecution has the further burden of proving beyond a reasonable doubt that such defendant participated in such agreement wilfully; that is, the prosecution must prove that such defendant entertained the specific intention to teach or advocate the duty or necessity of overthrowing or destroying the government of the United States by force of violence and to organize as the Communist Party a group of persons who teach or advocate the overthrow or destruction of the Government of the United States by force of violence and that in either case that he intended to teach or advocate such doctrine with the specific intention and for the evil purpose of bringing about the overthrow or destruction of the Government of the United States by force or violence, and not that he intended some result other than that.

If you are not convinced beyond a reasonable doubt that such defendant acted "wilfully," your verdict must be not guilty.

Request No. 98. There has been testimony in this case by prosecution witnesses of acts and statements of persons other than defendants which were alleged to have taken place prior to the period defined in the indictment. I charge that you may not consider any such statement or act as evidence against any defendant unless any such statement was made or any such act was done by the direction or authority or with the approval of such defendant. And even if you find such statement was made or act was done by the direction or authority or with the approval of any defendant you must consider such evidence only in your determination of whether or not such defendant had the specific intent to engage in the conspiracy charged in the indictment at the time alleged in the indictment.

Request No. 99. There has been testimony in this case by prosecution witnesses concerning acts or statements purported to have been done or made by certain defendants prior to the period defined in the indictment. I charge that you may consider such testimony only against the particular defendant or defendants alleged to have made such statement or engaged in such act and then only to the extent that it tends to establish the specific criminal intent of the particular defendant to commit the offense charged in the indictment in the period from on or about April 1945 to July 20, 1948. You may not consider such testimony in determining the intent of any other defendant to commit the offense charged, unless you find such statement was made or act was done by the direction or authority or with the approval of any such defendants.

Request No. 107. I charge you that if you are convinced that any defendant or defendants taught or advocated any statement, principle or program prior to the period defined in the indictment which was abandoned by any such defendant prior to the period defined in the indictment and not adopted thereafter you may not consider such statement, principle or program in the determination of whether or not any such defendant had the specific intent to engage in the conspiracy set forth in the indictment.

Request No. 135. I charge you that even if you find from the evidence that there was such a conspiracy, as charged in the indictment, nevertheless any statements made by a defendant as to the purposes, policies or aims of the Communist Party and any other acts or declarations of a defendant may not be imputed to any of the other defendants unless done or made in furtherance of such conspiracy and while such conspiracy was in existence.

Request No. 237. The indictment alleges that it was part of the conspiracy that "defendants would publish and circulate, and cause to be published and circulated, books, articles, magazines, and newspapers advocating the principles of Marxism-Leninism." I charge you that the words "books and articles" as thus used in the indictment include pamphlets.

Request No. 273. I charge you that the word "revolution" in its broadest significance is generally used to designate a sweeping change; as applied to political change, it denotes a change in a method or system of government, or of the power which controls the government. It is frequently, though not always, accomplished by, or accompanied by violent acts, but it needs not be violent in its methods. It does not necessarily denote force or violence.

Request No. 275. I charge you that the statute under which the defendants were indicted does not prohibit the teaching or advocacy of peaceful change in our social, economic or political institutions, no matter how fundamental or far-reaching or drastic such proposals may be.

Submitted by the prosecution:

Request No. 18. There are several kinds of conspiracies made illegal by federal statutes. Some of these statutes require the allegation and proof of the commission of an overt act by one or more of the conspirators before a crime is complete. However, the statute under which this indictment was returned does not require the allegation or proof of the commission of an overt act.

Request No. 31. You are instructed that the question of possible punishment of the defendants or any of them, in the event of conviction is no concern of the jury, and should not in any sense enter into or influence your deliberations. The duty of imposing sentence rests exclusively upon the court. The function of the jury is to weigh the evidence in the case and determine the guilt or innocence of the defendants solely upon the basis of such evidence. Under your oaths as jurors, you cannot allow a consideration of the punishment which may be inflicted upon the defendants, if they are convicted, to influence your verdict in any way.

Request No. 34. During the course of the trial there have been various references to the Opinion of the Supreme Court in the case of Schneiderman v. United States, 320 U.S. 118,63 S.Ct. 1333,87 L.Ed. 1796. That case was not a prosecution under the statute involved here and the Supreme Court did not determine any issue which is before you for determination.

Now, ladies and gentlemen of the jury, one last word. If you find that the evidence respecting the defendants or any of them is reasonably consistent with innocence, such defendant or defendants should be acquitted. If you find that the law has not been violated, you should not hesitate for any reason to render a verdict of not guilty. But, on the other hand, if you find, in accordance with these instructions, that the law has been violated as charged, you should not hesitate because of sympathy or any other reason to render a verdict of guilty.

INDEX

INDEX